Silver "Thieves," Tin Barons, and Conquistadors

ARCHAEOLOGY OF INDIGENOUS-COLONIAL INTERACTIONS IN
THE AMERICAS

Series Editors
Liam Frink
Aubrey Cannon
Barbara Voss
Steven A. Wernke
Patricia A. McAnany

Silver "Thieves," Tin Barons, and Conquistadors

Small-Scale Mineral Production in Southern Bolivia

Mary Van Buren

THE UNIVERSITY OF ARIZONA PRESS
TUCSON

The University of Arizona Press
www.uapress.arizona.edu

We respectfully acknowledge the University of Arizona is on the land and territories of Indigenous peoples. Today, Arizona is home to twenty-two federally recognized tribes, with Tucson being home to the O'odham and the Yaqui. Committed to diversity and inclusion, the University strives to build sustainable relationships with sovereign Native Nations and Indigenous communities through education offerings, partnerships, and community service.

© 2024 by The Arizona Board of Regents
All rights reserved. Published 2024

ISBN-13: 978-0-8165-5333-4 (hardcover)
ISBN-13: 978-0-8165-5334-1 (ebook)

Cover design by Leigh McDonald
Cover photograph by Mary Van Buren. 2016 Conectando el pasado con el presente: la antropología histórica de la producción de metal de pequeña escala en Porco, Bolivia. *Boletín de Arqueología PUCP* 20:63–82.
Typeset by Sara Thaxton in 10.5/13 Garamond 3 LT Std

Publication of this book was made possible in part by support from the Department of Anthropology and Geography at Colorado State University.

Library of Congress Cataloging-in-Publication Data
Names: Van Buren, Mary, author.
Title: Silver "thieves," tin barons, and conquistadors : small-scale mineral production in southern Bolivia / Mary Van Buren.
Other titles: Archaeology of indigenous-colonial interactions in the Americas.
Description: Tucson : University of Arizona Press, 2024. | Series: Archaeology of indigenous-colonial interactions in the Americas | Includes bibliographical references and index.
Identifiers: LCCN 2023037918 (print) | LCCN 2023037919 (ebook) | ISBN 9780816553334 (hardcover) | ISBN 9780816553341 (ebook)
Subjects: LCSH: Small-scale mining—Bolivia—Quijarro—History. | Small-scale mining—Social aspects—Bolivia—Quijarro. | Quijarro (Bolivia)—Social conditions.
Classification: LCC HD9506.B63 V36 2024 (print) | LCC HD9506.B63 (ebook) | DDC 338.20984/14—dc23/eng/20240203
LC record available at https://lccn.loc.gov/2023037918
LC ebook record available at https://lccn.loc.gov/2023037919

Printed in the United States of America
♾ This paper meets the requirements of ANSI/NISO Z39.48-1992 (Permanence of Paper).

This book is dedicated to
the late Carlos Cuiza, who opened a door
and
Dimitris Stevis, who accompanied me through it.

Contents

List of Illustrations	ix
Acknowledgments	xi
Introduction. Small-Scale Metal Production and Long-Term History: Lessons from Porco, Bolivia	3
1. Small-Scale Metal Production at the Turn of the Twenty-First Century	26
2. Small-Scale Metal Production in the Age of Industrialization (1825–1964)	56
3. Silver Extraction Under the Colonial Regime (1573–1825)	87
4. Spanish Conquistadors and Indigenous Control of Mineral Production (1539–1572)	126
5. Inka Silver Mining and Its Antecedents in the Southern Andes	151
6. A Return to the Present: *Kajcheo* in Global Perspective	180
Conclusion	201
References Cited	211
Index	239

Illustrations

Figures

1. Apu Porco and Huayna Porco — 27
2. Village of Porco in 1997 — 30
3. The cross named Tata Apu — 37
4. Recently constructed headquarters of Cooperativa Huayna Porco — 41
5. Carlos Cuiza repairing a huayrachina — 47
6. Cupellation hearth (small reverberatory furnace) — 49
7. Trapiche adjacent to the San Juan River — 60
8. Sun dial in plaza of Porco — 64
9. The Agua de Castilla mill completed in 1915 — 68
10. Excavated cupellation hearth located near the confluence of San Juan and Cebada Cancha Rivers — 78
11. Photograph of man with huayrachinas near Porco — 79
12. Recently erected statue in Porco of a miner breaking his chains — 82
13. Facility for dressing alluvial tin ore — 84
14. Sector A of Sora Sora — 99
15. Ferro Ingenio — 102
16. Structure 3 at Site 35 — 110
17. Structure 7 at Site 35 — 111
18. Reverberatory "dragon" furnace in Structure 10 at Uruquilla — 118
19. Reverberatory furnaces excavated at Uruquilla — 120
20. Sixteenth-century drawing of Porco showing the village and initial division of the mines — 129
21. Sixteenth-century watercolor of Natives smelting ore in huayrachinas — 135
22. Ceramic huayrachina and crucible fragments from Site 80, Porco — 138
23. Southeastern sector of Ferro Ingenio — 139
24. Ceramics from Ferro Ingenio — 140
25. Uruquilla (Porco Viejo) looking east — 141
26. The site of Huayrachinas — 144

27. Provincial Inka jar fragments from Site 80; provincial
    Inka bowl fragments from Huayrachinas   146
28. Carangas bowl fragment and Chillpe bowl fragment
    from Cruz Pampa   146

Maps
1. Location of Porco   4
2. Location of Porco and nearby landscape features   28
3. Location of mines mentioned in text   63
4. Location of homesteads and cupellation hearths identified
    during survey   71
5. Location of key places mentioned in text   94
6. Location of sites mentioned in text   97
7. Location of sites mentioned in text   137
8. Location of sites mentioned in text   153
9. Qaraqara-Charka federation   159

Acknowledgments

THE RESEARCH FOR THIS BOOK began two decades ago, and over that lengthy period I have received support from many different people to whom I am very grateful. I would like to thank my collaborators, David Goldstein, Jeff Eighmy, Ana María Presta, Lizette Muñoz, Maya Benavides del Carpio, Sofía Alcón, and especially Susan deFrance for their expertise and collegiality. I would also like to include in this list the late Catherine Julien, who visited us in Porco and shared a copy of her preliminary work on Inka labor organization. Ludwing Cayo was the co-director of the project and he, along with Delfor Ulloa, provided crucial logistical support and helped supervise fieldwork. Together they also documented the artisanal production of charcoal that Carlos Cuiza conducted at his homestead.

Saul Arista, Erin Baxter, Ivan Berrios, Oskar Burger, Jason Bush, Sergio Fidel, Carla Flores, Dan Martinez, Sheiry Vargas, and Rosa Villanueva played key roles in overseeing excavations and survey, while Veronica Arias, Claire Cohen, Christy Eylar, Sara Hoerlein, Barbara Mills, Holly Stinchfield, and Brendan Weaver contributed much of the data that appear in this book. I am grateful to all of them for enduring challenging field conditions with grace and humor. Brendan began his participation in the project as a student and over time has become a valued colleague. He generously created the maps that are included in this book and allowed me to reproduce a number of his photographs, providing informative and welcome breaks in the text.

Of course, none of this research could have taken place without a great team of workers who excavated, conducted surveys, and washed and labeled artifacts among other tasks. I would like to thank Dionicio Ecos, Jhanet Ecos, Juan Equise, Julia Equise, Amalia Gutierrez, Lidia Gutierrez, Zandra Gutierrez, Eleuterio Porco, Luperia Portillo, Nancy Javier, Olivia Javier, Wilfredo Javier, Malena Quispe, Maribel Quispe, Ramiro Rojas, Mabel Vaca, and Julian Viscarra for their hard work, tolerance, and insights into life in Porco. Pelagia Torrez and Marta Gutierrez prepared wonderful meals and kindly accommodated the unusual tastes of outsiders. Barbara Gutierrez allowed us to store the artifact collection in her *sala* for many years, and René Gutierrez helped us find a permanent home for it in the newly constructed Porco Museum. Bautista Ecos and Eloy Mamani have begun the important work of preserving Porco's history and culture. Carlos Flores and Sandra Quispe began working with me as teenagers when I was conducting excavations in Tarapaya and were the first crew members to participate in the project at Porco. They showed up for work one day because Sandra overheard a woman talking on the phone about some foreigners needing help to "pick stones from the river" and ended up becoming skilled excavators and dear friends.

Edwin Quispe started his work with the project as a driver. Being insatiably curious, however, he was soon accompanying us into the field. He played a key role in translating Carlos Cuiza's Quechua into Spanish, and our questions into something that Carlos could make sense of. Edwin and his wife, Elsa Villafuerte, have always made us feel at home in Potosí, as have Carlos and Sara Serrano. Finally, Julio Calla and his daughter, Pamela, welcomed us to Bolivia and provided us with a home base in La Paz during the early years of my research. I will always remember with great fondness our family lunches with them.

This book would not have been possible without the assistance of Carlos Cuiza who allowed us to observe him smelt ore, refine silver, and make charcoal all while answering innumerable questions. This information not only provided insight into the archaeological record, but, just as importantly, alerted us to the politics of small-scale production. With his passing, this technology appears to have become extinct, and I am grateful that he permitted us to see it in operation.

In the United States, I would like to thank Bill Bartholomew, who shares my love of Bolivia, and the members of my writing group, Sarah Payne and Kristina Quynn. They were always supportive, patient, and kind. Three anonymous reviewers provided thoughtful, detailed comments that improved the book in many ways. I thank you for your time and effort, but acknowledge, of course, that any remaining errors, omissions, or misjudgments are mine alone.

On the home front, my love and gratitude to Maria and Michael for accompanying me to Porco so that I wouldn't have to be apart from them for long. And finally, I want to acknowledge my partner, Dimitris Stevis, who provided unconditional support at each stage of this process. Since there is too much to say, I will only say thanks—I love you.

Funding for this research was provided by the National Endowment for the Humanities (RZ-20934-02), National Science Foundation (BCS-0235954), National Geographic Society, H. John Heinz III Charitable Trust, Curtiss T. and Mary G. Brennan Foundation, Colorado State University, and Trinity University. The writing of this book was supported by a National Endowment for the Humanities Fellowship (FEL-267930-20). Permission for the fieldwork was provided at the national level by the Unidad Nacional de Arqueología and its subsequent incarnations. Locally, permission was granted by the Honorable Alcalde de Porco, Honorable Consejo Municipal de Porco, and the Autoridades Originarias de Porco to whom I am grateful.

Silver "Thieves," Tin Barons, and Conquistadors

Introduction

Small-Scale Metal Production and Long-Term History

LESSONS FROM PORCO, BOLIVIA

THE SPANISH CONQUEST OF PERU was motivated by the quest for precious metals, a search that resulted in the discovery of massive silver deposits in the southern Andes. Silver produced in this region financed the Spanish empire, transformed Indigenous communities, and impacted the economies of nations as far away as China. The enormous flow of specie into the world economy is usually attributed to the Spanish imposition of a forced labor system on the Native population as well as the introduction of European technology for processing silver ores. While accurate, this narrative is incomplete. It omits the role played by thousands of independent miners, often working illegally, who at different points in history generated up to 30 percent of the silver produced in the region. The long-term history of these workers, the technology they used, and their relationship to successive large-scale mining operations in southern Bolivia, are the focus of this book.

The Spaniards invaded Peru in 1532, and in 1539 the Pizarros took control of Porco, one of the most important silver mines in the Inka Empire. Located in the Bolivian tin and silver belt, an arid highland region studded with high peaks, Porco was the first Andean silver mine exploited by the Spaniards. Its reputation as a source of precious metal was eclipsed, however, in 1545 when an indigenous metallurgist working in the village discovered the largest silver deposit on earth just 35 km to the northeast. The economic potential of this deposit, the Cerro Rico of Potosí, resulted in a population boom, and the center became one of the largest cities of the world and the axis around which the colonial economy turned (Assadourian 1980; Cross 1983). Many miners, Spanish and Indigenous, abandoned Porco

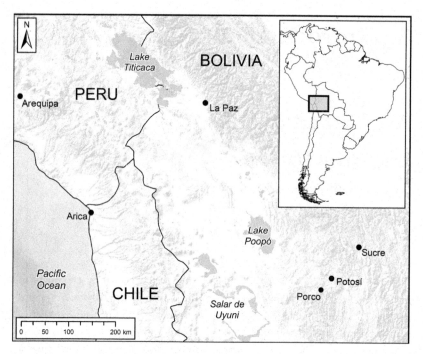

MAP 1 Location of Porco. Map by Brendan Weaver.

to seek their fortunes in Potosí, but the earlier center continued to produce ores of various types under the auspices of conquistadors, tin barons, and a Bolivian president.

Porco was initially chosen as a study site because of its long mining history as well as the relatively intact archaeological record in the area surrounding the modern village, unlike Potosí. Proyecto Arqueológico Porco-Potosí (PAPP) was established in 1995 with the intent of examining the ways in which the organization of silver production changed with the imposition of first Inka and then Spanish rule. While unusual at the time for its focus on what Wernke (2007) later called a "transconquest" approach, the research design was conventional in its emphasis on changes in the organization of production over a relatively short span of time. Two factors, however, led to a reorientation of this initial focus. First was the unexpected discovery that a type of Indigenous smelter, or huayrachina, was still in use near Porco. Huayrachinas were the primary technology employed to smelt silver during the first few decades of Spanish rule in Potosí, but in the 1570s were replaced by amalgamation, a chemical process that relied on the use of large stamp mills. Huayrachinas were rarely mentioned in historical documents after that date,

INTRODUCTION 5

and the last published description occurred in the late nineteenth century (Peele 1893). The continued use of huayrachinas in the shadow of the largest industrial zinc mine in Bolivia raised the question of why this small-scale technology had persisted into the twenty-first century.

The second and more profound factor was the experience of working in a Bolivian mining town. One cannot live in the Andes or study its past without developing an acute awareness of the ways in which its history and current position in the world economy shape the region's institutions and daily life. In Bolivia, the colonial legacy is stark. Widespread poverty, of course, is the most apparent result of colonialism and its aftermath, but the cultural divide between urban and rural, volatile internal politics, racist treatment of the Indigenous population, and economic dependence on the export of raw commodities are also the consequences of European domination, as they are in many other regions of the world. On the other hand, the legacy of Bolivia's pre-Hispanic cultures is equally inescapable, particularly in the highlands. Even in Porco, a mining center that has been exploited by outsiders for centuries, kin groups, called *ayllus*, exist, most people speak Quechua as well as Spanish, and ritual offerings are performed on important occasions. However, an examination of the intersection of colonial legacies and Native culture is obviously not sufficient for understanding current Bolivian realities since historical processes have continued to unfold since the conquest.

One aspect of life in Porco that was particularly salient in the early 2000s and raised questions about the trajectory of mining in Bolivia was the continual conflict between miners and the state as well as with the international company that controlled the local mines. Between 2004 and 2005, over 650 social conflicts occurred in Bolivia (Evia 2008). These included strikes, protests, and, most importantly, blockades of the few roads that connect Bolivian cities, paralyzing transportation and choking commerce. These actions were mounted by a variety of workers who used this highly effective tactic to force the state to attend to their demands. In the case of mining towns, these protestors were not unionized laborers working for large operations, but cooperative miners who lease less productive deposits from multinational or state companies and work them with small-scale technology for what usually amounts to subsistence-level incomes. The contemporary conflicts over mineral resources and the political ramifications of such struggles cast the archaeological record in a new light, one that illuminated the existence of multiple scales of production that existed at Porco in different forms since the sixteenth century. The nature of small-scale production, its relationship to state and corporate mining, and the ways in which these relationships changed over time became the primary issues shaping the research and led to

6   INTRODUCTION

an examination of the long-term history of silver production at Porco from pre-Hispanic to current times.

Doing Historical Anthropology Backward

This book seeks to make a contribution to historical anthropology (Lightfoot 1995, 2005; Orser 2001; Panich 2020), which combines archaeology, ethnohistory, and cultural anthropology to produce long-term histories that illuminate contemporary conditions as well as the past. Historical anthropology challenges the division of scholarly investigation into discrete periods defined by subdisciplinary boundaries rather than historical processes and emphasizes the holistic nature of anthropology.

Multidisciplinary historical anthropology has enormous potential in the Andes, a region where Indigenous culture is vibrant and the legacy of colonialism remains palpable. Ethnography, pre-Hispanic archaeology, and ethnohistory have all flourished in the region. The synergy among the three disciplines was especially productive in the 1970s when the work of John Murra (1964, 1967, 1972, 1975, 1978), Maria Rostworowski de Diez Canseco (1977, 1978, 1983), Franklin Pease (1973, 1976, 1978), and other ethnohistorians inspired archaeologists as well as cultural anthropologists. Unfortunately, rather than viewing the material record as one means of examining the specific histories of Native groups from pre-Hispanic times to the present, archaeologists instead used colonial documents as a lens through which to view the more distant past (Van Buren 2016). This entailed a kind of historical "leapfrogging" (Cooper 2005, 17) by which evidence for cultural phenomena that were documented in colonial and ethnographic records was sought in the archaeological remains left by pre-Inkaic cultures, rather than by tracing the specific historical trajectories of such practices through time. The search for "*lo andino*" was predicated on the assumption, structural in nature, that aspects of Andean culture are durable over time and through space despite the vagaries of history and geography. This approach was an attempt both to validate Andean culture and to move beyond an Inka-centric understanding of pre-Hispanic societies and in those regards was highly successful. An unintended consequence, however, was a deflection of interest away from the historicity of Andean societies and the complex ways they had changed and persisted over time (Jamieson 2005; Starn 1991; Van Buren 1996). As Stahl (1994) has argued in the case of the Banda, this use of the direct historical approach underestimates the profound changes that occurred as a result of European—and earlier—entanglements (see also Chase 2018).

INTRODUCTION 7

In the Andes, the dialogue among the subfields of anthropology did not serve as an impetus to the formation of historical archaeology in the Andes, a development that has occurred only recently. As a result, the trajectory of Andean history was broken into segments according to disciplinary specialty, obfuscating both continuity and changes in the Indigenous past. During the last decade, however, colonial-era archaeology has exploded in the Andes, particularly in Peru (Álvarez Calderón 2016; Boza Cuadros 2022; Corcoran-Tadd et al. 2021; deFrance 2021; Hu 2022; Norman 2021; Saita and Rosas Lauro 2017; Ramón 2016; Rice 2013; Traslaviña et al. 2016; VanValkenburgh 2021; Weaver 2021; Wernke 2013), and a number of scholars are pushing beyond the colonial period to investigate more recent times as well (Chirinos Ogata and Saucedo Segami 2021; Chuhue et al. 2012).

One method for the historical analysis of contemporary social conditions is doing history backward. Historical archaeologists have long acknowledged the political implications of their research, and many have advocated for a critical approach (Leone et al. 1987; Pinsky and Wylie 1989; Saitta 2007) that is intended to peel back ideological camouflage and historical silences to reveal the construction and current operation of capitalism and the many sorts of oppressive relations that it generates. Recently Wurst and Mrozowski (2014) have suggested another tactic for making archaeological research socially relevant. They advocate the method outlined in Bertell Ollman's (2003) book, *Dance of the Dialectic*, in which he argues that to understand both contemporary conditions and future possibilities, scholars need to begin with the present and work backward to identify the social relations that engendered them, and then return to the present in order to consider possibilities for the future. This method is predicated on Marx's dialectical approach to internal relations in which different aspects of social phenomena are conceptualized in terms of their mutually constitutive interactions. These interactions change over time, a process that is also constitutive of subsequent social forms. Ollman (2003, 116) provides the example of Marx's analysis of the emergence and operation of capital and labor, but a wide range of social phenomena can be examined in the same way, such as relations between individuals and society, humans and the environment, different genders, "races," and, of course, classes.

The investigation of complex, interrelated phenomena that are constantly in flux poses formidable analytical challenges that can be overcome, according to Ollman, by employing a series of "abstractions." His definition of this term is simply "a piece that has been pulled apart from or taken out of the whole and is temporarily perceived as standing apart" (Ollman 2003, 60)—and standing still. This entails creating temporal, geographic, and other boundaries that delineate phenomena so that they can be more easily analyzed. A slightly different way to conceptualize abstraction is as a mental process that breaks complicated phenomena into manageable units of different types.

Ollman (2003, 74–75) identifies three overlapping aspects of the process of abstraction. The first is the delimitation of the geographical and temporal extension of the phenomena under study. The second is the determination of the level of generality at which social entities are examined and characterized. This entails shifts among lower and higher levels, with the culturally and historically unique details abstracted out at higher levels of generalization. The third process is the establishment of a vantage point, a place from which to view relations among parts and their relation to the larger "system." As is the case with levels of generality, the vantage point can be shifted in order to examine the same phenomenon from different perspectives. The use of abstractions, of course, creates the risk of reification, the treatment of time periods, social processes, and other phenomena as "real things," which is exactly what a dialectical approach is intended to circumvent. By making explicit decisions about what kinds of abstractions to employ and how to define them, however, the creation of naturalized, assumed categories can be avoided. This risk is also mitigated by framing the analysis in terms of multiple scales and moving among them as necessary.

Doing history backward might strike some scholars as logically parallel to the search for "lo andino," and has, in fact, been criticized on the grounds that it constitutes a genealogical approach that ignores the specific contexts in which ideas and practices developed (Cooper 2005, 18–19), a search for origins that equates present-day phenomena with formally similar occurrences in the past. Critics have also claimed that the explanations generated by this approach are teleological in that they make the present appear as an inevitable outcome of past conditions. As Wurst and Mrozowski (2014) point out, however, these problems do not arise when the focus is on internal relations rather than reified entities and researchers pay close attention to changing historical conditions. The goal is to both identify factors that shape social practices at a given point in time and consider antecedent conditions that generated them. For Ollman, the ultimate objective is to reveal the way capitalism works. The goal of this book is to use some of the methods outlined by Ollman to investigate a question that is anthropological in nature, and thus almost the inverse—to understand how people who engaged in a specific industry negotiated their place in an expanding world economy and, in the process, created their own history. This history is unique to Bolivia, but, at a more general level, parallel to the trajectories of agricultural populations in other regions who have engaged in artisanal and small-scale mining under similar political and economic conditions.

The Historical Analysis of Mineral Production at Porco

The investigation of how mineral production has changed over time in Porco and the ways in which current practices embody aspects of this history require the use of a variety of abstractions. Since the focus of this study is on the political economy of mineral production, and specifically the relationship between small and large-scale enterprises, the temporal and geographic parameters are largely shaped by the incorporation of Porco into overarching political entities. The Inkas were the first to exert this sort of power in the region, and their reign lasted from the fifteenth century until the Spanish conquest of Peru in 1532. Seven years later the Spaniards gained direct control over the Porco mines and exploited them using primarily Native methods of ore extraction and processing; the 1570s mark another break, not because of a change in political regime, but because of a reconfiguration of labor and technology that resulted from the reforms instituted by Viceroy Toledo. In 1825 Bolivia gained independence from Spain. During the ensuing Republican period the nation-state of Bolivia was run by successive governments operating primarily in a liberal and, more recently, a neoliberal environment. Technically this period ended around 1930, but the predominant commitment to capitalism has remained roughly constant up to the present. However, important shifts in political and, to some extent, economic relations did occur after the Bolivian Revolution of 1952 and, to a lesser degree, in 2006 with the election of President Evo Morales. This periodization of the history of Porco is based on changes in the political economy that coincided, for the most part, with dramatic political ruptures. However, conditions in Porco did not always precisely mirror processes at the imperial or national level nor did those processes start and stop at specific historical events like cars at a traffic light (Swenson and Roddick 2018). In fact, when residents of Porco talk about the past, they often conflate Colonial and Republican times, referring to individuals of European descent during both periods simply as "Spaniards"; the similarity in unjust labor demands, not the overarching state, is what is most relevant to them. In addition, as Wolf (1982) and many others have clearly demonstrated, the Spanish Empire, the Bolivian state, and even the Inka Empire were not clearly bounded, homogeneous entities that operated independently of conditions outside their territorial borders but were internally varied and penetrated by forces originating in other places. These periods and political regimes are thus not static things, but useful abstractions based on salient aspects of historical processes.

Porco, and specifically the organization of small-scale mineral production over the centuries, is at the center of this study and constitutes the vantage point from which much of the analysis takes place. The name "Porco" has been used to denote different geographical phenomena: Apu Porco, the sacred mountain that dominates the landscape; the mines within Apu Porco as well as in the adjacent mountain, Huayna Porco; the village at the foot of these mountains; the colonial *corregimiento*, or political unit, named Porco; and the modern municipal district of Porco as well as the eponymous canton in which it is located. The term *Colque Porco* has also been used, especially in Spanish colonial times. *Colque* is the Hispanicized version of the Quechua and Aymara word *qullqui*, which means silver, or money, and is often associated with mountains. It should probably be noted here that despite the similarity between the words Porco and *puerco*, which means "pig" in Spanish, the name is unrelated to swine. When used in this book, the name "Porco" refers to the mines or nearby village, a place with a unique history but one that parallels, in many respects, that of nearby Potosí as well as other mining centers in the highlands of what is now southern Bolivia.

Two additional terms are key to the analysis of mineral production in Porco at different levels of abstraction: *kajcheo* and artisanal and small-scale mining, or ASM. The first has Indigenous roots and has been used in what is now south-central Bolivia from early colonial times until the twentieth century. It refers to a variety of ways in which small-scale mineral extraction was organized, and particularly the relationship between mineowners and the people who did the actual mining. The second term, *ASM*, has emerged over the last two decades to describe small-scale mining in poor countries. As these terms relate to two levels of generalization that will be broached in this book—practices that are culturally and historically specific to Porco and the surrounding region and the occurrence of similar phenomena in many regions of the world—they will be discussed in more detail below.

Kajcheo

The Quechua terms *kajcha* (also spelled *k'aqcha*, *k'accha*, *qagcha*, etc.) and the Hispanicized *kajcheo* (*k'aqcheo*, *k'accheo*) are critical to a historical analysis of mining in south-central Bolivia as they are culturally specific concepts related to small-scale mineral production. Grammatically, the first refers to a person and the second to an activity performed by that person. The term *kajcha* first appears in historical sources dating from the seventeenth century, but it may have arisen a century earlier when the Cerro Rico of Potosí was first exploited by Spaniards (Tándeter 1993, 6). The entry in Stubbe's compendium of colonial mining vocabulary states that *cagchas* were independent miners in Potosí

INTRODUCTION 11

who worked in the mines from Saturday night until Monday morning with the obligation of giving half of the mineral to the owner (Stubbe 1945, 38), a definition echoed by Cole (1985, 14), who notes that *kapcha* was the right of a forced laborer to work the mine for his own benefit over the weekend. Blacut (1968, 137) defined *ckajcha* as a "*barretero solitario en interior mina*" which refers to a pickman who works alone, or independently, within the mine, and *ckaccheo* as "*labor sin control; productor de mineral en trabajos difíciles y abandonados*" or unregulated work, production in difficult or abandoned works. Referring to more recent arrangements, Alonso (1995, 129) defines *kacchas* as miners who work in a group, paying a third of their production to the owner and retaining two-thirds for themselves. He goes on to add that they work without a system, removing ore from anywhere and obtaining low profits.

These definitions, as well as examples provided by ethnographers and historians (Absi 2014; Barragán 2015; Godoy 1990; Platt 2000; Rodríguez Ostria 1989; Tándeter 1981a; Zulawski 1987), indicate that in the most general sense kajcheo is the direct appropriation of ore from mines that are owned by others. The word encompasses a variety of practices that were shaped by specific historical and local contexts (Absi 2014), with the richness of the deposit, market price of minerals, and availability of labor being the most salient. As Barragán's (2015) analysis of eighteenth-century records from the Banco de San Carlos in Potosí demonstrates, the income earned by kajchas was as varied as the nature of the labor relations in which they engaged. Often, the terms on which extraction occurred were based on explicit agreements, oral contracts that were negotiated by owners and miners. However, Cole's assertion that the term *kapcha* refers to the right of a laborer to mine for his own benefit points to another aspect of kajcheo, or ore-sharing, that has been prevalent throughout the region's history: the direct appropriation or "theft" of high-quality ore by employed miners working their regular shifts or at nights and on weekends. At some points in time, particularly when labor was scarce, this was accepted by mineowners, who, like the miners, viewed it as a means to supplement wages, but at others it was regarded as theft, a practice that required surveillance in order to mitigate losses incurred both by the appropriation of the best ore and the destruction caused by indiscriminate extraction (Zulawski 1987).

The Quechua word *kaj* means a sharp sound, and the term *kajcha* may have emerged as a description of the activities associated with independent miners removing ore. Abercrombie (1996), though, identified a very early use of the term by Guaman Poma de Ayala, who, in 1613, referred to a common Indian who had been designated as a *kuraka*, or local leader, by Spaniards ignorant of his low rank as "don Juan Q'aqcha mundo al revés"—sir Juan

Q'aqcha, world upside down. He argued that the term was related to category-transgressing individuals who represented a threat to the social order.

Tándeter (1993) described the ambivalence with which kajchas were regarded historically. Mineowners and officials sometimes considered the appropriation of ore as a legitimate supplement to their wages, while others regarded them as thieves who threatened the economic order, marginal, menacing, but also, perhaps, valiant (Betancourt 2007). The etymology of the word kajcha may reflect belligerence in response to official intervention in their activities. An eighteenth century source cited by Tándeter (1993, 86) stated that the term meant "crack of the sling" in Quechua and referred to the kajchas' attacks on authorities who attempted to prevent them from invading mines with stones launched by slings. The historian Gunnar Mendoza offered another hypothesis—that the term originated with the Quechua word for "energetic, animated, feared" or the Aymara word for thunderbolt (Tándeter 1993, 87). All these possibilities suggest potential violence, the evocation of which has been associated with Bolivian miners into the twenty-first century. A number of eighteenth-century observers, however, also acknowledged the legitimacy of what others understood as theft.

In the Andes, the notion that miners have a right to a portion of the ore derives from two sources. First, the Indigenous relationship between agriculturalists and the land they farm is rooted in the maintenance of reciprocity between people and the earth, and this sensibility was extended to encompass the relationship between miners and mines. Just as respect and proper ritual treatment of the divinity associated with the earth results in good harvests and healthy herds, the offerings made by miners to the spiritual entities that produce the ore are rewarded by the appearance of rich veins. This relationship will be explored in the subsequent two chapters, but for the purpose of this discussion, it is the fact that mining is regarded as part of a broader moral economy that is important. Miners have a right to ore because they are the ones who sustain the reciprocal relationship between humans and the spiritual entities who are the ultimate producers of mineral wealth.

The second source of this attitude is that miners believe that the physical sacrifices they make while working underground entitle them to a part of the ore they extract. This sensibility is based on their assessment of the exploitation that characterizes labor relations in the mining industry; men who risk their lives every day extracting and processing ore receive a pittance for their work compared to the administrators and owners who enjoy a high standard of living without an equivalent sacrifice. This perspective, which is generated by the gross inequalities apparent in colonial and capitalist enterprises, is common among miners throughout the world, many of whom engage in ore theft;

INTRODUCTION 13

in English, the practice is called "high-grading." Interestingly, another term, *juku* or *juco*, is used in Bolivia today to describe an ore thief. This word literally means "owl" in Aymara, evoking the nocturnal depredations of the men who steal ore at night. The term was used in place of the word *kajcha* in the province of López as early as the seventeenth century (Gil Montero and Téreygeol 2021) but appears to have become common in the Potosí area only as the term *kajcha* was subsumed by cooperative mining in the latter half of the twentieth century. While intersecting with the meaning of the word *kajcha*, the term *juku* now connotes theft without the associated sense of a moral right to the ore. Jukus often come from outside the community and take mining equipment and previously extracted ore, in addition to mineral that they remove from the mines themselves. Like the kajchas before them, their activities have a significant impact on the economy; they steal approximately 25 percent of the available mineral in Porco (*El Potosí* 2017), and theft has become so rampant that some mining centers, such as Huanuni in the neighboring department of Oruro, have demanded military protection (*La Razón* 2018). Over the last half-century, the varied arrangements by which independent miners gained access to ore have been encompassed by mining cooperatives, which are legal entities recognized by the state. Cooperative mining is viewed by academics, nongovernmental organizations, and government officials as a type of artisanal and small-scale production, a term that will be discussed below.

Artisanal and Small-Scale Mineral Production

While kajcheo is specific to the Andes, it and the mining cooperatives that emerged during the twentieth century can be understood in terms of a global phenomenon that has been glossed as artisanal and small-scale mineral production. ASM is common in poor countries where jobs are scarce. It employs many more people than does large-scale mining and is critical to the survival of hundreds of thousands of households; for example, worldwide, 15 million people are engaged in the artisanal and small-scale production of just gold (Sippl and Selin 2012). In Bolivia mining cooperatives employed 88 percent of the total mining workforce in 2013 and accounted for 30 percent of mineral exports by value (Marston and Perreault 2017). This sector thus plays an important economic role on national and global scales and has increasingly attracted the attention of policymakers, nongovernmental agencies, and environmentalists who are concerned with the social and economic implications of such activities as well as their environmental consequences (e.g., Hentschel et al. 2002; Hilson 2003; Lahiri-Dutt 2018a). Conflict between small- and large-scale producers is also common, as poor miners struggle to gain access to high-quality mineral sources. An examination of ASM and how it has changed over time thus provides insight into the complex and shifting linkages between local practices and the broader political economy in which they occur.

Like kajcheo, there is no single accepted definition of artisanal and small-scale mining, although it is usually conceptualized as a continuum with regard to scale and level of mechanization. In some contexts, like the Ghanaian case described in chapter 6, the same deposits are worked by people using hand tools as well as groups who have purchased some heavy machinery with painstakingly accrued capital. The latter could be considered medium-scale producers, a distinction that is erased by the division into large- and small-scale mining. However, many of these "medium-scale" operations exhibit some of the same characteristics as ASM, described below.

In its report on mining worldwide, the International Institute for Environment and Development (IIED 2002, xxii) defines ASM as mineral exploitation or processing by "people working with simple tools and equipment, usually in the informal sector, outside the legal and regulatory framework." The focus is on the low level of capital required to engage in mineral production of this type and the fact that ASM is often considered illegal. The report goes on to state that workers engaged in ASM usually exploit marginal deposits and tend to be poor and rural. They work under harsh conditions, and the environmental impacts of their activities are often severe, the latter problem being of particular concern to researchers and policy makers (McMahon et al. 1999; Swenson et al. 2011). The definition used by the IIED is meant to describe contemporary mineral producers, like the Bolivian mining cooperatives, who operate within the context of global capitalism, but it can be extended, with some qualifications, to earlier situations in which states and empires attempted to monopolize the most productive mines, a tactic that was, for instance, employed by the Inkas. In the pre-Hispanic Andes neither capitalist relations nor regular market exchange existed, so the way in which metal production was organized differed significantly from the present day. Under the Inkas metals, ores, mines, and the processes associated with production were imbued with religious significance, and the finished products were used in ritual contexts as well as being an important component of exchange between state and local elites that was integral to the creation and maintenance of political relationships. The Inkas claimed ownership of all mines and monopolized the richest ones, permitting subject groups to exploit less productive deposits (Berthelot 1986). These smaller pre-Hispanic mines share characteristics with ASM in that they were worked with simpler technology, were relatively marginal with regard to productivity, and were exploited by less powerful groups who were either authorized to do so by more powerful entities or who clandestinely engaged in illegal mining.

The definition of ASM used in this book builds on that provided by the IIED but includes some additional factors. First, and most importantly, ASM usually occurs in relation to larger-scale mining, and this relationship often involves conflict over mineral resources. Second, exclusion from mineral deposits can be created by economic exigencies, not just legal means. In fact, the fluctuation between legally conducted ASM and its prohibition when mineral prices are high is a salient characteristic of artisanal mining in the Andes over the last 500 years. Third, ASM is not necessarily embedded in a capitalist system, but can also occur in societies shaped by different economic relations. In other words, ASM can vary in terms of scale, mechanization, and whether it is an illicit activity, but it is most often constituted in relationship to larger mining enterprises run by states or companies. This definition includes mining in non-capitalist societies, but also distinguishes ASM from pre-Hispanic forms of mineral exploitation that did not occur in societies marked by notable differences in wealth and power. Kajcheo is thus a locally specific form of ASM that occurred under the Spanish colonial and Republican regimes in Bolivia. Framing ASM in this way is an abstraction that facilitates analysis at a more general level but has the potential for obscuring the wide variety of ways in which small producers in Bolivia organized mineral production. The latter challenge will be approached by delineating the specifics of the Porco case to the extent possible and considering how it relates to the broader political economy rather than using it as the basis for extrapolation.

The definition of ASM outlined here provides the key for addressing the issues at the center of this study because it requires an investigation of local practices in relation to broader relations of production that shifted over time. For instance, the question of why small-scale, Indigenous metal production continued for hundreds of years after more efficient processes were introduced from other regions of the world can only be addressed by examining the distinct historical conditions under which it was used. Defining ASM as a practice that occurs in relation to larger mining enterprises facilitates the examination of the persistence of Native technologies without attributing them to perduring traditions that are seen as essential to Andean identity. Using the term *ASM* is not meant to imply that small-scale mining under the Inkas or Spaniards was identical to mineral production today, but, instead, that contemporary ASM has historical roots in and was thus shaped by earlier conditions. While important continuities do exist and practices often persisted even through significant historical watersheds such as the Spanish conquest, a focus on the relationship between ASM and large-scale mineral extraction requires recognition of how the organization of production and thus the social context in which a technology was embedded has changed over time.

Labor and Technology

After the first few decades following the conquest, during which a plunder economy (Spalding 1984, 109) prevailed, the primary objective of the Crown and colonists alike became the effective deployment of labor in order to generate revenue through means other than outright theft. Much has been written about the *mita*, a system of forced labor that the Spaniards modeled loosely on Inka practice and which they imposed on Indigenous communities throughout the south-central Andes. The majority of these workers were sent to the mines and mills of Potosí as well as smaller mining centers such as Porco, and the physical and social impact on them as well as the economic consequences in their natal villages were devastating. Although wage laborers became an important component of the workforce by the seventeenth century (Bakewell 1984a, 121–23), in Bolivia the mita was not permanently abolished until 1832, seven years after independence, and the development of an industrial proletariat in the mining centers occurred very slowly. This process and the history of small-scale mineral extraction, in particular, were intimately tied to the ways in which peasants combined agricultural work and mining to sustain themselves economically as well as socially. By the mid-twentieth century, however, mining unions were powerful enough to play a critical role in the Bolivian Revolution. From a substantive point of view, then, the examination of labor is key to understanding the trajectory of the political economy in Bolivia. There are also, however, compelling theoretical and methodological reasons for focusing on labor.

Labor is a fundamental characteristic of human life that distinguishes us from other animals and connects us to other people (Marx and Engels 1947, 7). This latter aspect of labor, the fact that it is constituted by complex social relations that include workers, owners, managers, families, and representatives of the state, makes it an especially productive analytical concept. Rather than parsing out the nature of specific identities and then reconstituting them on the basis of "intersectionality," labor itself is shaped by multiple kinds of social positions such as ethnicity, race, gender, and class (Silliman 2006). As Silliman (2006) and Voss (2008) argue, an examination of labor is also crucial for archaeologists seeking to understand colonial societies in which the economic exploitation of Indigenous workers was the goal of colonizers and the

INTRODUCTION 17

daily reality of the colonized. Labor is also a site of struggle, a realm in which coercion, resistance, avoidance, violence, and creative appropriation played out with varied results (Shackel 2009; Silliman 2006).

The organization of labor, which includes access to mineral resources and markets, the relationship between workers and employers, belief systems, and technology, is what shapes the constitution of large- and small-scale mining. The fact that Porco is an industrial site where work in the mine was—and still is—the only reason why people reside there makes a focus on labor that much more appropriate. Its small size and the monofocal nature of the economy render the class differences in Porco especially visible (Hardesty 1998). Mine administrators work in an office building perched far above the village that is protected by guards, while some engineers and other professionals reside in a small, gated compound named Yuncaviri. Others, along with the company administrators, many of the teachers, and the health professionals who staff the local medical post commute daily to Porco from Potosí. Almost all these people have university educations and live urban lifestyles, although many, especially the teachers, are not particularly well off. The miners and their families, however, reside in the village below the mines where their daily lives are shaped by the rhythm of work underground, caring for children, and, often, engaging in agro-pastoral activities. The distinction between company and cooperative workers is more subtle, in part because it can be fluid; some men attempt to shift from company to independent mining or vice versa depending on the relative balance of income and job stability, which is shaped by the price of ore. Differences between the two groups do exist, though, in wealth, access to medical care and education, participation in institutions such as mothers' clubs, and other characteristics. Differences in access to resources—from mineral deposits to company support—generate tension and sometimes outright conflict among these classes (Amengual 2018).

Silliman (2006) and Voss (2008) also make a convincing argument for the methodological utility of the concept of labor, particularly with regard to conceptualizing the different scales at which social relations operated within empires. For instance, productive activities in which households engaged can be linked to larger-scale phenomena such as labor requirements imposed by regional elites, imperial policies intended to regulate labor and the revenues it generated, and international markets that absorbed the commodities that were produced. A focus on labor, then, facilitates the examination of social relations at different levels of generality, from the local to the transcontinental.

Over the last few decades, a consensus has emerged among archaeologists regarding the need to examine the development and use of technology in specific social contexts (Dobres 2000; Hosler 1994; Knapp et al. 1998;

Lemonnier 1986; Pfaffenberger 1992), a view that has been embraced by scholars investigating Native Andean technology (Costin 2016; Hayashida 1999; Lechtman 1988; Shimada and Craig 2013; Shimada and Wagner 2007; Zori 2016). These perspectives represent a decisive break with previous research that was narrowly focused on objects and predicated on the assumption that each technological challenge could be solved by a single most efficient response dictated solely by the physical parameters of the materials and processes involved. More recent holistic approaches have shed light on diverse issues such as the nature of technological choice, the social organization and gendered nature of production, and the relationship between technological processes and cultural values. These are, of course, aspects of labor, the process by which humans deploy knowledge and energy to create material life from nature.

In the case of Porco, a focus on labor is especially important for understanding the relationship between large- and small-scale mining and metallurgy, and particularly the technology associated with the latter. Much of the ASM of hard-rock deposits depends on infrastructure created by highly capitalized enterprises with the resources to construct underground workings. Mines excavated by these companies, ore faces within them, and ore dumps outside them are leased to or in some other way, directly appropriated by small-scale miners or *pallliris* (ore-pickers) who are thus dependent on the activities of large-scale enterprises for access to minerals. Although shaped by the specific historical context, the technologies deployed at these different scales are usually distinct. Large-scale enterprises tend to invest in costly, often imported, technology that requires skilled workers to maintain and operate. In contrast, individuals engaged in ASM use inexpensive technology that is readily available or produced from local materials that they can operate and maintain themselves (Priester et al. 1993). This is especially evident in the case of Indigenous metallurgy. Historically, the technology associated with the production of silver emerged in the context of agrarian households, and the knowledge and materials required to create and use it were available to individual families until the early twenty-first century. In the Andes this technology was used almost exclusively by Native households, and thus could be understood as an expression or indicator of ethnic identity. However, while small-scale silver production of this sort certainly was shaped by and shaped Indigenous culture, its continued deployment into recent times is also related to poverty. As Van Bueren (2004) has argued for the small mills used to process silver ore in the western United States, it is a "poor man's" technology employed by families who occupy a marginalized position within the world economy.

INTRODUCTION 19

This book, then, examines the long-term history of Porco from the perspective of the changing organization of labor and the technologies in which it was embedded. The goal is to illuminate the dialectical relationship between small- and large-scale production in order to understand how Indigenous households engaged with large-scale enterprises—that were, in turn, shaped by global economic forces. In the case of Bolivia, this trajectory resulted in the emergence of cooperative mining that plays a key role in the country's political economy but continues to be in conflict with state and private companies. Bolivia's history is unique, but many aspects of ASM in that nation are parallel to small-scale mining in other countries. These points of convergence reveal similarities in the operation of colonial and capitalist regimes despite the specific cultural and historical circumstances of the societies that are subsumed by them.

Organization of the Book

Since the goal of this book is to examine the history of small-scale mining in Porco to shed some light on current conditions, it begins with the present, works backward, and then concludes with a consideration of contemporary relationships among small-scale miners, large mining companies, and the state in different parts of the world. Each of the first five chapters is anchored in the archaeological data on mineral processing facilities that were employed during a specific period of Porco's history and that are contextualized using information derived from documentary, ethnographic, and other archaeological sources. These periods are framed by important shifts in the way in which production was organized that correspond to broader changes in the regional political economy. The structure of the book is intended to facilitate the analysis of historical conditions at particular points in time; in order to avoid eliding what is known about distinct historical periods, an attempt is made to present only information derived from the period under consideration. As Stahl (1993, 246) notes in her discussion of the use of analogies by archaeologists "we must confront the possibility that by conflating sources from widely separated temporal contexts and potentially collapsing variability into homogenized holistic models we build in an assumption of persistence. The collapsing of time and the emphasis on homogeneity deflects attention from variability in time and space, and as a result may inhibit our ability to address change." Presenting history backward is a tactic meant to avoid combining sources from different periods and presenting descriptions of generalized "Andean" phenomena. It does, however, occasionally result in the sporadic treatment of issues—such as gender or ritual—for which limited information exists for specific historical contexts.

Chapter 1 provides an overview of zinc-lead-tin production in Porco during the first decade of the twenty-first century when PAPP was conducting research there. During the first years of the decade the Porco mines were controlled by the Compañía Minera del Sur (COMSUR), which was owned by Gonzalo Sánchez de Lozada, a two-time president of Bolivia who sold the company's assets to Glencore after he fled the country in 2003 in the face of massive street protests. The chapter describes some of the ways in which the existence of dual scales of production by company and cooperative miners have shaped life in the village. It then focuses on one member of the community who used small-scale technology to smelt and refine silver near his rural home. In 2001 our team was introduced to Carlos Cuiza, an elderly former miner who produced small quantities of silver a few times a year using huayrachinas and a cupellation furnace. This chapter describes the smelts that Cuiza allowed us to observe and addresses the question of why traditional techniques had persisted four hundred years after the introduction of "more efficient" European technology. This issue is analyzed in terms of the relationship of small-scale silver production to mineral extraction by the companies that controlled the mines of Porco during that decade. The persistence of this Indigenous technology, however, was rooted in conditions established in the nineteenth century with the beginning of industrial mining in Porco.

Chapter 2 focuses on the nineteenth and first half of the twentieth century, during which the industrial mining of silver, tin, and then zinc, dominated life in Porco. Settlement patterns recorded during archaeological survey revealed the development of a small agrarian population in the surrounding area as herders and agriculturalists moved to Porco to seek work in the mines. Some of these rural households also incorporated small-scale metal production into their economic repertoires as reflected in the appearance of cupellation furnaces and huayrachina remains adjacent to homesteads. The latter are identical, in terms of technology, layout, and social context to the facilities used by Carlos Cuiza. Somewhat later, alluvial tin extraction along the Todos Santos, a stream that runs to the east of the village of Porco, was begun by a newly formed mining cooperative. Small-scale silver production as well as tin cooperatives have historical roots in *kaqcheo*, a set of practices that began early in the colonial period.

The ways in which silver production was organized under the colonial regime are examined in chapter 3. Extractive institutions were formalized in the 1570s with the implementation of a series of policies spearheaded by Viceroy Toledo. With the implementation of the Toledan reforms, control over all aspects of the means of production shifted to Spanish *azogueros*, who replaced Native smelting and refining technology with large, capital-intensive stamp mills and employed forced laborers, called *mitayos*, in addition to wage laborers to work in them as well as the mines. This did not, however, eliminate smaller-scale production, as the archaeological record in Porco clearly demonstrates. Production, both large and small scale, was at its most intense and diverse during the late 1500s and continued, at a lower level, into the sixteenth and seventeenth centuries.

Chapter 4 examines the period between 1539, when the Spaniards took control of Porco, and 1572, when the Toledan reforms began to be implemented. Except for the first few years of exploitation under the Spaniards, mining in Porco was conducted primarily by Native laborers using Indigenous technology to produce silver from veins owned by the Spanish Crown, the Pizarros, and other conquistadors. Historical records document this boom, describing, albeit in a limited way, the labor force, mines, and mills that were controlled by economic elites. They also indicate that ore theft and household refining were commonly practiced. While later mining operations destroyed most of the infrastructure, some of the workspaces and housing used by Indigenous miners are preserved in the area surrounding the modern village. Overall, archaeological vestiges of smelting and refining facilities display a remarkable level of diversity that reflects their origins in both Native and European technological traditions as well as local innovation. Some of these technologies were adopted by later populations engaged in metal production at the household level.

Chapter 5 describes how production was organized in the southern Andes by the Inkas and their predecessors. Although the intensive reuse of Inka buildings in Porco by Spaniards makes it difficult to distinguish between pre-Hispanic and colonial occupations, Inka infrastructure can be discerned from the location and footprints of sites that were constructed by them. These reflect centralized control over a production process that was probably staffed by different kinds of workers, some of whom were mitayos. While no evidence has been found for dual scales of production in Porco under the Inkas, colonial documents relating to gold mining near present-day La Paz that were analyzed by Berthelot (1986) indicate that they often relegated mining by local communities to less productive deposits. The economic contexts and social meanings of silver differed radically from the ways in which the metal was used during Spanish colonial times, but similar tensions existed regarding access to mineral deposits.

Chapter 6 returns to the present to explore contemporary ASM in Bolivia, particularly the relations among small-scale producers, international companies, and state enterprises. The majority of miners who engage in ASM now belong to cooperatives that are formal economic entities recognized by the state. They were incorporated into party politics by the Evo Morales regime but nevertheless continue to have a conflictual relationship with the government as well as with large mining enterprises. The Bolivian case is then compared to ASM in India, Nigeria, and Ghana to identify similarities in the global processes that resulted in the marginalization of this sector and the attendant problems of poverty, environmental destruction, poor working conditions, and violence.

The book ends with a summary of key findings and a discussion of how a historical understanding of small-scale mining in Bolivia and other nations of the Global South provides insight into culturally specific trajectories as well as an awareness of the parallel political and economic processes that gave rise to artisanal and small-scale mining as a distinct economic sector. Key to this understanding is an analysis of the ways in which large- and small-scale mining are coproduced under colonial and now capitalist conditions.

A Note on Sources

Analysis of the social relations undergirding mineral production is essential to understanding the historical trajectory of small-scale mining. The constitution and deployment of the workforce, the nature of the technology employed, the ways in which workers and authorities who controlled the mines conceived of metals, the legal and economic frameworks that determined access to mineral resources, and the ways in which metal objects were distributed and used all shaped the nature of labor in Porco. The types of data utilized to investigate these phenomena depend on the period under examination and the scale of abstraction employed, in addition to the availability of different kinds of sources. The information that forms the backbone of this book was collected by the Proyecto Arqueológico Porco-Potosí, which was directed by the author.

Proyecto Arqueológico Porco-Potosí conducted fieldwork in Porco between 1995 and 2007. The field crew was composed of people who resided in the older, west end of town as well as undergraduates from the Universidad Mayor de San Andrés in La Paz and occasional students from the United States and the United Kingdom. A pedestrian survey of a 20-km² area surrounding Porco identified 156 sites, almost all of which were related to mineral extraction and processing and most of which were quite small. Larger residential sites occupied during Inka and colonial times were concentrated just

INTRODUCTION

to the north and northwest of Apu and Huayna Porco. A total of twelve sites were tested; eleven of these dated to the Inka or colonial periods, or more frequently, both, and one was used in the early twentieth century. Survey was also carried out to the southwest of Porco near the San Juan River. This survey identified twenty-two sites. One of these, Ferro Ingenio, is a colonial stamp mill adjacent to an early colonial site that had been occupied by Indigenous metallurgists (Van Buren and Weaver 2012; Weaver 2008). Mapping and testing of the site was conducted by Brendan Weaver (2008) as the basis of his master's thesis.

Survey was also carried out in the hinterlands of Porco in an attempt to locate pre-Inka sites associated with mineral production. The survey focused on Condoriri, a contemporary community surrounding a highland marsh, or *bofedal*, 10 km to the northeast of Porco. Eighty-two sites were located in a 25-km² area, and only one, the remains of a huayrachina used during Republican times, was unequivocally related to metallurgy. Lecoq and Cespedes (1996, 1997) had previously identified two large pre-Inka settlements on mesas to the northeast and south of the modern hamlet during reconnaissance of the region. These sites, Cerro Pukara (CS1) and Cerro Khollu (CS50), were mapped and surface collected.

Members of PAPP also conducted archaeometallurgical (Cohen 2008; Van Buren and Cohen 2010), faunal (deFrance 2003, 2012), paleobotanical (Goldstein 2006; Muñoz Rojas 2019), archaeomagnetic (Lengyel et al. 2011) and ethnoarchaeological (Van Buren 2003; Van Buren and Mills 2005) research on materials recovered during survey and excavation, and an archival investigation of early colonial sources (Presta 2008). The archaeological record provides insight into local practices, particularly the participation of individuals and households in small-scale metal production and the ways in which this activity was integrated into their social and economic lives. While a variety of data was gathered, the technology of smelting and refining is a particular focus of this analysis for two reasons. First, although mining is more familiar and has received the most scholarly attention, it is only the first step in a longer productive chain that entails the conversion of ore into usable metal. Second, the long-term exploitation of minerals, particularly precious metals such as silver, has resulted in the erasure of most archaeological evidence of earlier mining. In contrast, the facilities used to smelt and refine ore are relatively well preserved. They were usually built at some distance from the mines and were durable since the high temperatures needed to produce metal resulted in fire-hardening of the clay used in their construction. The features themselves reveal the nature of the labor needed to make and use them, and the settings in which they are found—public places exposed to the view of others, in workers' housing, or hidden near rural homesteads—provide insight into the social contexts in which they were utilized.

Relatively little archaeological research has been conducted in southern Bolivia. Pablo Cruz, however, has generated a considerable body of work on mining and landscape that has been used to situate Porco in relation to broader regional trends, especially during Inka times (Cruz 2006, 2009a, 2009b, 2022; Cruz et al. 2013).

Limited ethnographic work focusing on specific aspects of contemporary life in Porco was also conducted. Two cultural anthropologists, Maya Benavides del Carpio and Sofía Alcón, briefly visited Porco on four occasions between April and August 2004 to provide information about the schools and the relationship between educational practices and the local political economy. This was of special interest to PAPP because various outreach events were developed to educate teachers and students about archaeology in general, and our research in Porco, more specifically. In addition, two graduate students, Christy Eylar and Sarah Hoerlein conducted interviews with residents of Porco in 2005. Eylar (2007) employed a critical medical anthropology approach to assess variability in illness vulnerability among cooperative and company miners for her master's thesis.

Archival research on early colonial Porco was carried out by Ana María Presta (2008) in the Archivo General de la Nación (Argentina), Archivo Histórico de Potosí, Archivo y Biblioteca Nacionales de Bolivia (Sucre), and Archivo General de Indias (Seville and Simancas). For all periods published sources were also consulted to provide as thorough an account as possible of the history of the village and its relationship to the broader political economy. Unfortunately, historical sources that describe the southern Andes in the immediate post-conquest period are rare, which limits the utility of written records for understanding pre-Hispanic and early colonial Native societies in the region. Some of the key documents that do exist have been compiled and analyzed by Platt, Bouysse Cassagne, and Harris (2006) in their impressive volume *Qaraqara-Charka: Mallku, Inka, y Rey en la provincia de Charkas (siglos XV–XVII)*, which is referred to extensively in my examination of silver production at Porco under the Inka and early Spanish regimes. However, local practices in Porco must sometimes be reconstructed on the basis of what was written about Potosí, a larger mining center that generated considerably more documentation than did Porco. For instance, the now classic books by Assadourian (1980), Bakewell (1984a), Cole (1985), and Tándeter (1993) provide essential information about colonial labor regimes, and work by Platt (2000), Barragán (2017b), and Rodríguez Ostria (1989) has been fundamental to understanding kajcheo at various points in Bolivian history.

INTRODUCTION

The most pertinent ethnographies for understanding the working lives and belief systems of miners in southern Bolivia are Pascale Absi's (2005) *Los Ministros del Diablo* and June Nash's (1979) *We Eat the Mines and the Mines Eat Us*. The first provides an analysis of the world of cooperative miners in Potosí and their relationship with Cerro Rico, the mountain in which they work. Written in the first decade of the twenty-first century, it is used to inform the understanding of cooperative mining in Porco, although there are a few differences between the two cases. Nash's book covers some of the same ground from a different theoretical perspective but is focused on unionized company miners in Oruro during a politically charged time just before the military coup of 1971. While many elements described by Nash in Oruro are comparable to the situation in Porco, stark differences exist in the political trajectories of the two communities.

Much has been written about the relationship between historical and archaeological data in the interpretation of the past (Andrén 1998; Isayev 2006; Little 1991; Moreland 2001). The various sources of information used in this book are regarded as complementary in nature, and occasional contradictions between data sets are treated as opportunities for further investigation. The intent is to piece together as much information as possible to outline the trajectory of small-scale mineral production in Porco and examine the role of the participants in this sector of the broader political economy.

I

Small-Scale Metal Production at the Turn of the Twenty-First Century

AT THE TURN OF THE TWENTY-FIRST CENTURY, mining in Porco was characterized by multiple scales of production. These practices—large-scale mining and mineral processing by a transnational company, small-scale cooperative mining, and silver production at the household level—were intimately connected but also marked by economic competition and social tension. This chapter begins by providing a brief description of the physical and social landscape of modern Porco that is followed by an overview of the different ways in which mineral production was organized. As in many other mining centers in the Bolivian highlands, mineral extraction was dominated by a corporation that leased rights to less productive deposits to mining cooperatives that were sometimes required to sell what they produced to the company. From the perspective of the company, such an arrangement maximizes production while reducing the risks involved in directly investing in extraction. The cooperative members, on the other hand, gain access to mineral resources and the possibility of earning a living income, and, in exceptional cases, great wealth. This arrangement has ramifications beyond the workplace, namely the development of a stratified labor force with concomitant social and political differences.

In the second half of the chapter the vantage point shifts to a specific individual, Carlos Cuiza, whose involvement in the production of silver was shaped by both the skills and needs of his household and the larger political economy in which it participated. Observation of small-scale silver production by Cuiza, a former miner who lived in a rural homestead near Porco, provides insight into smelting and refining technology and its correlates in the archaeological record, and just as importantly, alerts us to the broader contexts in which such practices occur as well as the potential linkages between agriculture and mining.

Porco at the Turn of the Twenty-First Century

Porco is located at an elevation of 4,100 m in the Cordillera de los Frailes, a rugged range that flanks the eastern side of the altiplano in southern Bolivia. The climate is cold, arid, and windy, and the temperature differences between day and night or even sun and shade are extreme; a rose can bloom against a sunny wall while laundry hung in the shade of the same patio drips with icicles. The region is classified as dry puna, and the sparse vegetation consists primarily of small shrubs and bunch grasses. The surrounding landscape is a kaleidoscope of browns with a bright blue sky above, able to sustain small herds of llamas but too harsh for agriculture except for in pockets of alluvial soil adjacent to nearby rivers. People have been drawn here not because of the agricultural potential, but by the possibility of work in the mines.

FIGURE 1 Apu Porco (left) and Huayna Porco (right). Newly constructed buildings in the village of Porco can be seen at the base of Huayna Porco (Van Buren and Weaver 2012).

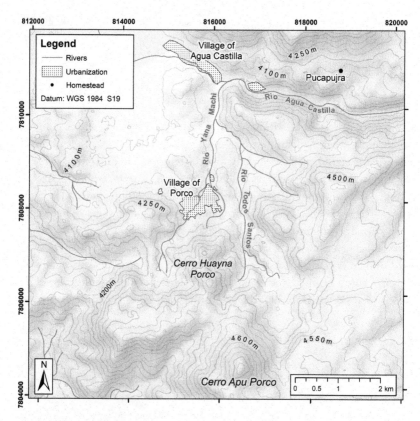

MAP 2 Location of Porco and nearby landscape features. Map by Brendan Weaver.

The village of Porco is situated at the base of Huayna Porco, a mountain riddled with the oldest mines, in a small basin sheltered from the strong winds that blow eastward across the altiplano creating white sand dunes on the lee sides of surrounding ridges. Apu Porco, a distinctive, flat-topped peak reaching 4,500 m in altitude, is located just to the southeast of the village and is the current focus of industrial mining operations. A small stream, the Río Yana Machi, runs through the settlement and empties into the Agua de Castilla River 3.5 km to the north where another village, also named Agua de Castilla, was built in the early twentieth century adjacent to the railroad that connects Potosí with the city of Uyuni. Another stream, Todos Santos, drains Apu Porco and enters the Río Yana Machi a kilometer or so before it reaches Agua de Castilla. The term *Porco* refers both to the village and to the municipality that it controls, which includes Agua de Castilla and six rural hamlets. This study focuses on the village of Porco and its immediate surroundings from the Río San Juan to the southwest, Agua de Castilla to the north, and the community of Condoriri to the northeast, the area in which we have conducted surveys and excavations.

In 1995, when Proyecto Arqueológico Porco-Potosí began investigating the history of mineral extraction in Porco, approximately 3,000 people resided in the village, almost all of whom were dependent on mining for their livelihoods. Most of the residents are of Indigenous descent and speak both Spanish and Quechua. The settlement was built along the Yana Machi, and in 1995 was still contained between two large rock outcrops that are referred to as *qaqas* in Quechua. The lower formation is called Mullupunku and is constituted by two large upright rocks between which the Yana Machi flows. The upper outcrop is called Wintuqaqa and was associated with a shrine to San Roque that had been dismantled by the time of our arrival. A *punku* is a door or entrance through which travelers pass, but it is also regarded as a portal to the dangerous world below. Qaqas, in general, are spiritually charged places associated with the underworld (Cruz 2006, 2012), and according to elderly residents these two outcrops were the sites of community rituals until about thirty years ago.

The village was not laid out in a rigid grid plan characteristic of settlements established by the Spaniards, but a typical plaza on what was the eastern end forms the civic-ceremonial core around which the offices of the mayor, town council, and traditional Indigenous authorities, as well as an elementary school, are arrayed; a large high school is situated downhill to the northeast. Residents identify a rectangular building a half block from the plaza as the original church; after a fire it was used as a social center, and the current church was constructed on the plaza. It is dedicated to Santa Rosa de Lima, the patron saint of Porco. In 1995, only the plaza, the soccer field near the high school, and one road in Porco were paved, and vehicles were so rare that dogs and children were unaccustomed to moving out of the street when they passed. There was one phone in town which could occasionally be heard ringing but was infrequently answered. Since then, the village has undergone a dramatic boom, driven largely by Chinese demand for metals. By 2018 Porco had over 5,000 residents; the streets as well as the Yana Machi were paved over and filled with cars and trucks; a market, new medical post, community center, and bank were built; and dozens of new houses and small stores were constructed, spilling beyond Mullupunku to the east.

Porco has a dual system of political organization that includes Indigenous authorities (*autoridades originarias*), a mayor, and a municipal council. In general, Indigenous authorities are responsible for internal affairs, while the mayor and municipal council are more directly engaged with relations

FIGURE 2 Village of Porco in 1997. Rock outcrop Mullupunku is located at center left, and Wintuqaqa at lower right. A covered portion of the Río Yana Machi runs through the center of town (Van Buren and Weaver 2012).

between the community and outsiders, including departmental and national institutions. However, there are institutional relationships that crosscut this distinction, with one, for example, being the role of the *corregidor* in certifying the good behavior of young men seeking to work in the company mines (Benavides del Carpio 2004).

At the turn of the century, the population was a mix of newcomers and families who had resided in Porco for many generations. The latter, called *originarios*, belonged to one of two kin groups: Jatun Ayllu (Ayllu Grande in Spanish) or Juch'uy Ayllu (Ayllu Chico). This dual form of organization is common in the rural Andes and undergirds access to resources, political leadership, and ceremonial life. In Porco, the autoridades originarias include a leader from each *ayllu* as well as from a few of the surrounding communities that are within the jurisdiction of the municipality. These leaders, called *kurakas*, are always accompanied by their wives who are also recognized as autoridades originarias. Each couple serves for one year, and the principal authority rotates between the two ayllus, with the leader from Jatun Ayllu being in charge one year, and the kuraka from Juch'uy Ayllu assuming this responsibility the next. Today, ayllu affiliation plays only a small role in the organization of everyday life. The lands belonging to each ayllu tend to be located in distinct zones surrounding Porco, although this spatial segregation breaks down within the village itself; interments in the cemetery, however, are clearly segregated (Benavides del Carpio 2004). Ayllu lands are marked by *mojones*, large piles of stones that indicate the boundaries of the community that are ritually reaffirmed each year. A set of three is located just to the east of Condoriri; one represents Porco ayllus, the second the ayllu from the neighboring community of Yocalla, and the third the hacienda Carma, which was the location of an earlier ayllu, Chilme. On the Domingo de Tentaciones, the first Sunday of Lent, the kurakas of the two ayllus in Porco make offerings of alcohol (*ch'allas*) at a small obelisk (*rollo*) in the plaza, and then one couple travels to these mojones to pour libations, while the other kuraka and his wife travel to the mojones at the other end of Porco territory to *ch'allar* as well. In this way they affirm the ayllu's territory and receive confirmation from the neighboring ayllus that they agree with the delimitation of boundaries. Families must pay a small fee or "*tasa*" to the indigenous authorities each year to maintain access to agricultural lands, pasture, and sources of firewood within their ayllu's territory. Theoretically, the kurakas can redistribute fields if they are abandoned, but this has not occurred recently.

In its general outlines, the organization and activities of ayllus in Porco are similar to those of the nearby community of Yura, 40 km to the southwest, as well as those of other rural villages in Bolivia. Throughout the Andes, the division between originarios and others—often categorized as mestizos—is common. In Yura they are called *vecinos* and are more closely affiliated with urban culture, better educated, and wealthier than originarios; especially in the past, they also tended to exploit them. The distinction in Porco is between originarios and newcomers, but, like the vecinos of Yura, the latter do not usually participate in the ceremonial life of the ayllus nor do they typically own land in the vicinity of the mines, although they may have fields in their natal villages. In contrast to the system of ayllus and autoridades originarias that Rasnake (1988) described in Yura in the 1980s, the organization in Porco is much simpler, probably because the population of originarios is smaller and does not engage in full-time agriculture. Some elements, though, are the same, such as the payment of the tasa, which was imposed by the Spanish state and continued after independence, the kurakas' responsibility for maintaining boundaries, and, especially, the continued importance of ayllus in the annual ceremonial cycle.

In Porco, ayllus are now most salient during the Fiesta of Santa Rosa, the village's patron saint day, which is held annually on the 30th of August, and the Fiesta de Candelaria, which is celebrated on the 2nd of February. Santa Rosa was the first Catholic from the New World to be canonized and is also the patron saint of Lima, Peru; Latin America; and the Philippines. The official Church account indicates that Santa Rosa was born in Lima in 1586 and spent time in a small nearby mining center where her father was an administrator, but Porqueños claim that she was born in Porco and left at an early age because she was treated badly by local residents. The songs sung to her in Quechua and Spanish by the *jailliris*, adolescent girls who dance in her honor, mention that she was born in Porco and ask why she abandoned them. Both ayllus claim her, and in the afternoon of the festival day each brings bulls to the plaza as well as bullfighters who participate in the bullfight and *corrida* (Franco Olmedo n.d.) and gains prestige based on the bravery of its animals (Benavides del Carpio 2004). In addition to the formal ceremonies in honor of Santa Rosa, the presence of the priest, who comes from Potosí to officiate, generates a flurry of marriages, baptisms, and masses for the dead, which are family affairs but ones in which many other residents participate. The festival of Santa Rosa, then, draws the community together but acknowledges the existence of the two ayllus to which long-term residents belong. Social and economic differences are also marked by who participates directly in the proceedings, and who watches the unfolding of the fiesta from a distance (Benavides del Carpio 2004).

The Fiesta of the Virgin of Candelaria is rooted more directly in a concern for agricultural productivity. The celebration is meant to enhance the growth of crops by driving away hail, summoning rain, and generally ensuring a good growing season. Each ayllu begins the fiesta independently, in this case within the social centers where they each have an altar to the Virgin who is repeatedly toasted by all present. The couple who is sponsoring the festival, the *pasantes*, are then decorated with crowns of flowers and young corn stalks that they carry on their backs along with beer bottles and a variety of agricultural produce. Troops of dancers—men dressed as condors or pumas and young women with white flags—begin in the social centers and then file outside led by the pasantes where they join the other ayllu. The dancers parade through the streets and then pause in the plaza where they enact a ritual that expresses the competition between ayllus; the male officials of each kin group take turns using a slingshot to try to pelt each other with small pears, and the ayllu who lands a shot gains prestige. This is evocative of the *tinkuy*, a ritual still practiced in some parts of northern Potosí that involves two ayllus battling each other until blood is spilled, thus fertilizing the land. Interestingly, the fiesta in Porco also involves a "friendly" tinkuy held on the second day during which the pasantes share a drink and an embrace.

The celebration of Candelaria is widespread in Bolivia and is, in fact, common in many parts of Latin America as well as Spain. What is noteworthy about the fiesta in Porco is that the ritual is centered on agricultural productivity, despite the village's 500-year history as a mining center. This reflects the widespread practice of income diversification in which both mining and agriculture contribute to a household's economic well-being.

A small survey conducted by Hoerlein in 2006 provides a window into the demographic characteristics and economic situation of households, particularly those located in the older western end of town. Her sample is heavily weighted toward those families because she made her initial contacts through the archaeological team, which included mostly long-term residents, and then used a snowball technique to identify additional people willing to be interviewed, many of whom were members of the local mother's club. Of the twenty-nine households about which she collected data, seven were headed by couples who were born in Porco, six were couples who had immigrated to Porco, and in the rest either the man or woman had been born elsewhere. This pattern is due in part to a company policy that requires miners to be residents of Porco or married to one; despite the difficulty and danger of the work, employment by the company provides a steady and, for Bolivia, a good income. The majority of those who had immigrated were from villages within walking distance, such as Belen, Carma, and Yura, or from the surrounding countryside. A third of the interviewed households owned land near Porco, including one couple who had immigrated; many of the immigrants owned land in their natal villages that they sometimes worked on weekends. Most of the production on these lands was for household consumption rather than sale.

Many families, but especially recently arrived workers, maintained a residence in Porco during the work week and returned to Potosí during the weekend to spend time with their wives and children. This was also true of the teachers, almost all of whom were outsiders (Benavides del Carpio 2004), and of the engineers who resided in Yuncaviri, the company mining camp, or sometimes lived in Potosí and made the daily commute to Porco. Even full-time residents traveled to Potosí a few times a month to shop, visit relatives, and attend to other business. Porco was—and still is—characterized by constant mobility, not due just to the ebb and flow of commodity prices that affect all mining towns, but because it is, in many ways, a satellite of Potosí.

Labor in Porco is highly gendered. Unlike in rural communities, masculine and feminine spheres are spatially delineated. Able-bodied men and youth work in the mines, and most women work at home at domestic tasks such as caring for children, preparing food, and doing laundry. The exclusion of women from mines results from national labor regulations, as well as company policies and current belief systems—particularly those held by men—regarding the appropriate place of women in the community. Not only is women's work essential to the maintenance of men's labor, but the presence of women in mines is thought to make ore disappear.

During the workday Porco becomes the domain of women who, when they have a lull in their tasks after they have delivered lunch to their husbands, sit on the curbs outside their homes to knit and talk. The mines, on the other hand, are purely masculine worlds. To my knowledge there are few female miners in Porco, although unmarried women and widows form a small component of the workforce in some other mines in the region (Lowe 2005). No pailliris, women who earn a meager living by sorting through mineral waste and selling the small quantities of ore that they recover, currently work in Porco, although a few of the women who were interviewed by Hoerlein said that they had worked as pailliris in the past.

Opportunities for women to work outside the house are thus limited, but many women maintain small stores in their homes that offer canned and dry goods as well as bread, or merchandise such as school supplies, used clothing, or small household wares (Benavides del Carpio 2004). They also raise herds of sheep and llamas, sell wool they spin and clothing that they knit, collect and sell firewood, rent rooms, make cakes, and do laundry for others. The data collected by Hoerlein indicate that while some women do not work to generate cash either because they are too busy caring for children or are among the very few whose husbands' incomes are sufficient, the majority of wives and single mothers do. These activities generate from 10 percent to most of the household income in cases when the man's work is irregular.

As Absi's (2005) research on the rituals and belief systems of cooperative miners in Potosí clearly shows, the work of mining is gendered not just in terms of the sexual division of labor, but also in the ways that mineral production and extraction are conceived. Cerro Rico, in Potosí, is regarded as feminine (Absi 2005) as are the mines themselves; the ore they generate is akin to the crops produced by Pachamama, a deity often glossed as "earth mother" but more accurately understood as the generative force behind all the earth's products (Absi 2005, 88). Men are able to locate and safely extract the ore created in the inner depths of these feminine bodies with the aid of El Tío, a deity represented in many mines as a large clay figure of a devil. The physical incarnation of El Tío is found in various forms in mines throughout the southern Andes. He is the owner of the mine and makes ore available to those who regularly offer coca, cigarettes, and alcohol; he also gives the necessary strength and courage to miners so that they can accomplish their work underground (Absi 2005, 108). The miners' relationship with El Tío as well as their own virility thus enables them to be successful. If they fail him, poverty, sickness, and even death ensue.

Many of the beliefs and practices that Absi described in Potosí are common in other mining centers such as Oruro, Huanuni, and Llallagua. Much of this ritual nexus also exists in Porco, but with interesting differences. Apu Porco, the mountain that contains most of the contemporary mines, is considered male, rather than female by local residents. When I asked Eloy Mamani, a cooperative miner who was born in Porco, if Apu Porco was female or male, he replied that the mountain is male and is married to Cerro Rico in Potosí. She is known as the "mamita de doce polleras"—the lady of twelve skirts. Polleras are traditional tightly gathered skirts that are sometimes worn layered, and Cerro Rico's twelve skirts are of different colors that are associated with twelve minerals. He went on to say that when people make a ritual libation in Porco, the first glass is for "el ser que es creador," or the creator, the second is for Apu Porco, and the third is for Mamita Santa Señora Cerro Rico. Bautista Ecos, Eloy Mamami's brother-in-law, then related a story that accounts for the paucity of silver produced by Apu Porco and the great richness of Cerro Rico. Apu Porco's "stinginess" is attributed to the mountain's marriage to Cerro Potosí to whom he gives all his silver. Interestingly, no stories are told about Huayna Porco, the smaller, "younger" mountain adjacent to Apu Porco, which was the location of the Inka and Spanish silver mines.

The second important difference between the beliefs held by miners working in Potosí and Porco is that the cult of El Tío is not as pervasive in the latter community. El Tío appears in some mines controlled by Porco Ltd. (Eloy Mamani May 25, 2018) and other cooperatives. He is absent from the company mines, as the administration prohibits the consumption of alcohol, which is so much a part of ritual practice. His cult and its probable emergence in the nineteenth century will be discussed in the following chapter. Instead of El Tío, some cooperative miners in Porco venerate *illas* of the mine (Bautista Ecos, May 24, 2018). Illas are commonly owned by agro-pastoral households in the Andes and are passed down from parents to children. They include natural objects that have the shape of animals or crops, found items such as artifacts, and carved figurines (Sillar 2017). They can also be small stone representations of llamas, alpacas, or sheep that embody the vital productive force of those animals that are used in ceremonies meant to ensure the well-being and fecundity of the herd (Flores Ochoa 1974–76). The term *illa* connotes purity, clarity, and abundance, and is often associated with silver. One twentieth-century Quechua–Spanish dictionary defines it as "stone that has been struck by lightning that is considered sacred, a rock outcrop split by lightening" (Lira 1973, 89, cited in Flores Ochoa 1974–76, 253, translation by author). Among miners in Porco, illas are pieces of pure mineral with distinctive shapes that form in empty cavities within a deposit. They represent the vital force of the ore and, when properly venerated, guarantee its continued abundance. Nevertheless, a new mining museum in Porco includes an elaborate statue of El Tío and features him in a promotional video on its website in an attempt to replicate the success of the mining tours that have been so popular in Potosí (Toro Montoya 2017). If these efforts to attract tourists are effective, El Tío may become more common in Porco in the future.

The intersection of belief systems surrounding agricultural productivity and mining has been described in detail by Platt (1983) in his exploration of Andean and proletarian consciousness in northern Potosí. Similar beliefs regarding the relationship between the two spheres are expressed in Porco during the fiesta of Señor Ckaccha, called in Quechua Tata Q'axcha Apu. Miners make a ch'alla to Tata Ckaccha every Friday, but their relationship to him is most salient during this ceremony that takes place during the first days of May and invokes the powers of two crosses, Tata Ckaccha and Tata Apu. These usually reside in chapels, the first on the slope of Huayna Porco, and the second at the foot of Apu Porco. According to Bautista Ecos (May 25, 2018), Tata Ckaccha is for miners and Tata Apu is for herders, agriculturalists, and people who make their living in transportation (who, before trucks became common, moved goods using llama caravans). They are brought down to the community center where they are dressed with garlands bearing miniature mining tools in silver or are decorated with the best produce of the season. Candles are lit at the base of the crosses, and everyone in attendance makes offerings of alcohol (Benavides del Carpio 2004). The men also talk and sing bawdy songs to the crosses, their communication facilitated by the extreme inebriation that is a common part of Andean ritual experience. On the third day, they are returned to their chapels, with the larger one, Tata Ckaccha, carried by men, and Tata Apu, the smaller one, carried by women. The sexual and procreative powers of these crosses were manifested most clearly by the graffiti depicting male and female genitalia found in the chapel of Tata Ckaccha after the fiesta in 2004 (Alcón 2004). Like El Tío, the crosses are invoked both for their ability to create an abundance of ore and to protect miners from the dangers of the mine, and more generally for health, fertility, and wealth. As Absi (2005, 131) argues is the case in Potosí, El Tío and the crosses are thus similar in their powers as well as opposites, being different incarnations of the same entity. In the case of Porco, the two crosses are related to different mountains and subsistence activities, in addition to different genders.

Tension between cooperative miners and the company has been reflected in conflict over the sponsorship of the fiesta of Señor Ckaccha. Tata Ckaccha is venerated by cooperative miners as well as employees of the mining company,

FIGURE 3 The cross named Tata Apu. Note the maize and tubers hanging from the cross; offerings of coca, alcohol, and flowers can be seen at the base. Llama blood has been thrown against the wall behind the cross (Van Buren and Weaver 2012).

and in the past sponsorship of the ceremony was rotated between Porco Ltd. and COMSUR. However, one year a decline in mineral prices had resulted in lower revenues, and nobody in the cooperative was willing to assume responsibility for the fiesta. When COMSUR offered to sponsor it, the cooperative members changed their minds, and a conflict ensued, resulting in two crosses: a Tata Ckaccha that is celebrated today only by Porco Ltd. and another that is more generally venerated.

The reciprocal nature of the relationship between the miners and the crosses is based on an ongoing cycle of sacrifice and reproduction that also shapes the lives of agriculturalists (Absi 2005; Nash 1979). The festival of the crosses is celebrated in many parts of rural Bolivia and expanded to include the mines. In the case of El Tío, though, the relationship is fraught with the immediate danger posed by the mines as well as the less likely prospect of striking it rich; making sacrifices in return for safety and prosperity is a regular ritual practice and a common element of daily discourse.

Miners in Porco (Eylar 2007, 109) and elsewhere in Bolivia (Absi 2005; Nash 1979) commonly refer to their work as "*sacrificado*," and this sacrifice is sometimes used to justify domestic violence, which appears to be fairly common in the village judging from the frequency with which it was mentioned in Hoerlein's interviews and our own discussions with local women. This impression is supported by Benavides del Carpio's (2004) description of the fiesta of Santa Rosa during which many men publicly asked the saint's pardon for the blows, suffering, and drunkenness to which they had subjected their wives. The connection some men make between the sacrifice of themselves in the mines for the sake of their families and their abuse of wives and children is explicitly indicated by the behavior described by the daughter of an alcoholic father who frequently beat her (Hoerlein n.d.). She reported that during these incidents he would say, "I work in the mine, what do you do here?" The brutal working conditions, fear, and the camaraderie that develops among the miners combined with the exclusion of women from such work seems to make integration into the domestic sphere difficult, in some ways similar to the challenges faced by men returning from war.

The nature of work in the mines thus shapes many aspects of the lives of families residing in Porco. Household practices, though, are not homogenous, and this diversity is due not just to individual differences, but to the ways in which mining is organized. Company miners tend to have higher and more stable incomes than those who work in cooperatives, and this economic distinction is associated with—and generates—social differences that pervade life in the village.

Dual Scales of Production in Porco

At the turn of the twenty-first century, life in Porco was shaped by COMSUR, the private company that controlled the mines. It was established in 1968 by Gonzalo Sánchez de Lozada, with minority shareholders that included Citibank, ADELA Investment Company, and Metal Traders Corps (Contreras and

Pacheco 1989, 62). Prior to forming COMSUR he had already acquired rights to the holdings of Empresa Minera Porco Ltda. This company, which was owned by two U.S. citizens, held concessions adjacent to the mines controlled by Compañía Minera de Bolivia (COMIBOL), the state mining company (Espinoza 2010, 178), which Sánchez de Lozada also leased.

Sánchez de Lozada unified and "rationalized" production to enhance efficiency (Contreras and Pacheco 1989, 62). The COMSUR operation in Porco subsequently became one of the most technologically sophisticated in Bolivia. In 1992 an expansion that included a new $10 million concentrator increased the daily capacity from 800 to 1,200 metric tons, with the output of zinc concentrate at 40,000 tons per year (Suttill 1993). COMSUR also supported community institutions and infrastructure by, for example, paying the salaries of about one-third of the high school teachers, maintaining the connection to the town's water supply, and providing technical training in a local mothers' club (Hoerlein n.d.)

Sánchez de Lozada, an American-educated entrepreneur popularly known as "Goni," served as the president of Bolivia from 1993 to 1997, and then again between 2002 and 2003. His second term was cut short when he resigned and fled to the United States after government troops killed at least fifty-nine civilians during the Bolivian "gas war," a period of massive public protest that crystallized around opposition to the president's plan to ship Bolivian gas through Chilean ports. In 2005 Sánchez de Lozada sold his shares of COMSUR to Glencore, a transnational mining and commodity trading corporation that in 2015 was the tenth-largest company in the world (Fortune 2015). The name of the Bolivian holding was changed to Sinchi Wayra, which means "strong wind" in Quechua, and later to Illapa, the Inka lightening deity (Espinoza Morales 2010, 223).

These technological and organizational transformations did not, however, result in the cessation of small-scale mining at Porco. As in a number of other highland mining districts in Bolivia, company miners work the most productive deposits that are under direct corporate control, while cooperative miners exploit less productive ones in the surrounding area. The two types of production are starkly different in terms of scale, organization, and social implications. However, the term *cooperative* is misleading in that the official members, or *socios*, share access to the deposit but do not actually cooperate in the extraction of the ore, nor do they pool the mineral produced. Instead, they each usually hire *peones*, day laborers who are excluded from decision-making and the other benefits of formal membership in the cooperative such as insurance (Michard 2008). In some cases the income of both socios and peones is determined by the amount and quality of ore extracted as well as current mineral prices, but while socios can occasionally become relatively wealthy, peones benefit only marginally during economic bonanzas (Absi 2010).

Three cooperatives operate in Porco: Cooperativa Minera Veneros, Cooperativa Minera Huayna Porco, and Cooperativa Minera Porco. The oldest is Veneros, which was founded in 1958 as Sindicato Minero Veneros Porco to work the alluvial tin deposits along the Agua de Castilla and Todos Santos Rivers. Shortly after this the Sindicato Minero Choque Carmona was founded and later became Cooperativa Minera Porco. Both Veneros and Porco were organized by ex-workers of the Empresa Minero Porco, which had gone out of business. They were renamed as cooperatives after a few years in order to join the National Federation of Mining Cooperatives (FENCOMIN). Cooperativa Huayna Porco is more recent, formed by ex-workers of COMSUR, which controlled the Porco deposits between 1969 and 2005. They attempted to join Cooperativa Porco but were rejected, ostensibly for lack of *"parajes"* or ore faces, so they formed a new cooperative and requested access to ore from COMSUR (Mamani and Ecos, June 1, 2018). In Porco, as in many other mining centers, unemployed miners created cooperatives to continue to have access to mineral resources and maintain their livelihoods.

Veneros ceased operations after the 1985 crash in the global price of tin. After commodity prices rebounded in the early twenty-first century, the cooperative regrouped and sought more productive concessions from the company, which at that time was Sinchi Wayra. By 2010 it consisted of fifty-eight socios, including ex-workers and widows, primarily from two families of Porqueños (Ayala et al. 2010). The Huayna Porco cooperative was established most recently, in 1989, and as of 2014 had approximately 98 socios and 350 workers overall (Amengual 2018). Its members exploit a variety of underground concessions including Huayna Porco, Santiago Alto, Pie de Gallo, and Ckacha Capilla. Porco Ltd., the largest cooperative, was founded in 1960 (Benavides del Carpio 2004) and in 2014 had approximately 254 socios and roughly 2,500 workers in total (Amengual 2018). Members of both Cooperativa Huayna Porco and Porco Ltd. work concessions on company-controlled property and are obligated to sell the ore they extract to the corporation, although workers exploiting more remote mines sometimes succeed in selling their minerals at higher prices in the markets of Potosí and Oruro (Benavides del Carpio 2004). The nature and organization of cooperatives will be described more thoroughly in chapter 6 when small-scale mining in Porco is compared to similar practices in other parts of the world.

Access to mineral deposits is also obtained in other ways, although these types of labor are less common and even more marginal. One form of extraction that entails a private sublease from the company appears to have

FIGURE 4 Recently constructed headquarters of Cooperativa Huayna Porco. Note Cooperativa Porco's new coliseum in the background. Photograph by the author.

become more frequent during the surge in commodity prices in the first decade of the twenty-first century; Porqueños call it "de los k'ara zapatos," a local colloquialism. This is closely related to "ck'ajche libre," which is ore extraction from faces that are leased from a cooperative, usually by retired miners. The very small scale of these activities, which barely yield enough to live on, does not represent a threat to either the company or the cooperatives (Benavides del Carpio 2004).

The contrast between cooperative and company, or "salaried" miners as they are called in Bolivia, extends beyond the organization of production. In the highland departments of Oruro and Potosí cooperatives have clashed with company miners over access to mineral deposits, and the relationship between cooperatives and the Bolivian state has become increasingly contentious. The emergence of these small-scale producers as a national political force (Marston and Perreault 2017) will be addressed in more detail in chapter 6.

From a local vantage point, the distinction between company and cooperative miners is expressed in a range of institutions and social practices. For instance, ritual differences distinguish cooperative and company miners. The former engage in ritual activity to increase the productivity of the mineral deposits as described above. Apparently, such practices can also be conducted from afar. A dozen horseshoe-shaped wind breaks were found during survey on the crest of a hill just to the south of Agua de Castilla. They all face Apu Porco, and each has a flat rock, or ceremonial *mesa*, in the center. A midden containing large quantities of ash, llama bones, and empty alcohol bottles had accumulated in front of the structures, called *adoratorios* in Spanish. A resident from Porco told us that they are used by cooperative miners from Agua de Castilla to venerate Apu Porco and to make offerings to ensure their safety and the productivity of the mines. Since cooperative work gangs are often composed of relatives, the adoratorios were reserved by families using charcoal to write their names on the mesas. These rituals are not conducted in company mines where work is closely regulated, and income is based on fixed salaries rather than the quality of the ore. Both cooperative and company miners, however, participate in community-oriented ceremonies.

The distinction between the households of company and small-scale miners is also reflected in the ways in which children behave and are treated at school, and differential access to healthcare. The latter two issues were investigated by PAPP members in 2004 and 2006, respectively. The village of Porco is an educational hub for the broader municipality, and PAPP organized events for teachers and students that were intended to communicate the nature of archaeological research as well as project results. In order to gain insight into how the educational system in Porco operated, two cultural anthropologists, Sofía Alcón and Maya Benavides del Carpio, conducted a brief study in the schools. Information about differences in access to healthcare was collected by Christy Eylar for her master's thesis. These studies found notable inequalities among families.

Distinctions between the children from company and cooperative households, and especially those of *k'ara zapatos*, were reflected in clothing and access to school supplies. Poorly dressed students were often teased and bullied, particularly among girls. Teachers knew which students were from company or cooperative households not just because of differences in dress, but because at the start of each school year they were required to provide a list to the company, which supplied school meals to the children of their employees (Benavides del Carpio 2004). None of the sixth-grade teachers who were observed singled out the children of cooperative workers for criticism, but two of the wives of cooperative miners who were interviewed mentioned that their boys had left school because of disparaging remarks made by teachers such as being called a "llamero," or herder, which is like being demeaned as a hick in English. The most common reason why people leave school, though, is lack of money. Interestingly, however, the only school teacher who was originally from Porco believed that children of fathers who worked for a cooperative were more disciplined and harder working than their more privileged peers precisely because they were "desperate" (Hoerlein n.d.).

Differences in wellness and access to healthcare were even more profound and also had intergenerational consequences. On the most basic level—food security—company and cooperative households tended to have distinct experiences. Of the people from cooperative households interviewed by Eylar (2007, 129), 55 percent reported that they had adequate food (defined as access to meat, vegetables, fruits, and dairy products on a regular basis), while 92 percent of the COMSUR families felt their nutrition was good. In terms of sanitation, 50 percent of cooperative families and 70 percent of company households had toilets, a situation that resulted in the contamination of outdoor areas throughout the village with human waste. Inadequate nutrition and poor sanitation made people more susceptible to illness, and when they became sick or were injured company and cooperative miners had recourse to different resources due to differences in income and health insurance. The worst off were uninsured cooperative miners who lacked access to Western medical care and did not have sufficient income to hire an Indigenous healer. Among the poorer households, acute and chronic illnesses led to a downward spiral of loss of employment, the need to spend scarce resources on health problems, and poverty that affected subsequent generations (Eylar 2007).

While the ways in which local institutions and everyday practices were shaped by the employment of the male head of household as either a salaried or cooperative miner were not the focus of sustained investigation in Porco, the research that was conducted and observations made during the course of working in the village clearly indicated a schism between the two groups, as well as pronounced differences between socios and their employees. This schism was not, however, absolute. Some of the miners in the households studied by Hoerlein worked for cooperatives before joining the ranks of company miners, and the reverse occasionally happened, particularly when a miner was let go by COMSUR because of injury or illness (Eylar 2007). Another example of linkages between the two groups is the case of a wife of a long-term company employee who participated in the meetings held by the mothers' club organized by the relatives of cooperative miners. Despite the somewhat permeable nature of the divide, however, the dual scales of production had effects that ramified throughout the community as well as shaping the lives of individual families.

The sometimes tense coexistence of both company and cooperative miners is found in other Bolivian towns, and cooperatives have been increasingly studied by social scientists (Absi 2005; Carrillo et al. 2013; Francescone

2015; Marston and Perreault 2017) as they have become prominent political actors on the national stage over the last two decades. This process has been stimulated, in part, by the migration of rural residents into mining centers whose growth has been fueled by an increase in global mineral prices. However, another, hidden, type of small-scale metallurgical activity that linked agricultural households with mining centers was discovered by PAPP in 2001: the artisanal production of silver by a rural household in the countryside outside Porco. The observations that we were able to make of this process facilitated our interpretation of the archaeological record and provided insight into the relationship between mineowners and workers.

Ethnoarchaeological Research in Porco: The Investigation of Small-Scale Silver Production

Two of the crew members who worked for Proyecto Arqueológico Porco-Potosí over several seasons were retired miners, Juan Equise and Dionisio Ecos. Conversation sometimes touched on the interpretation of smelting debris and other remains associated with mining and metallurgy, and at one point they recounted that their parents had used huayrachinas to produce silver in the 1950s. This report led to an attempt in 2001 to locate other elderly residents in the region who had witnessed the use of this small-scale technology. After two weeks of unproductive interviews, we were taken to the homestead of Carlos Cuiza, a retired miner who lived in the countryside near Porco. As we scrambled down the slope above his house, we unexpectedly encountered him working on a nearby ridge. He was, to our delight, repairing two small huayrachinas that had been damaged during the previous rainy season.

Huayrachinas, a type of smelting furnace that is oxygenated by the wind, were often mentioned in early colonial descriptions of Potosí because the Spaniards relied on this silver production technology—operated by Indigenous workers—for most of the first four decades after the conquest. In the 1570s, huayrachinas were largely replaced by mercury amalgamation, a process that relies on a chemical reaction between silver and mercury, rather than heat, to extract the metal from the ore. The last systematic description of huayrachinas was published by a North American mining engineer in the late 1800s (Peele 1893), and the technology was thought to have been forgotten during the following century.

Discovering that huayrachinas were still in use provided an opportunity to conduct an ethnoarchaeological study to better understand the relationship

between the production of silver using Native technology and the archaeological record and to assess how the process may have changed since colonial
times. However, a second, equally interesting set of questions arose as a result
of our interaction with Carlos Cuiza. Why had this small-scale technology
persisted over the course of 400 years? Why had it remained unreported in
the twentieth century? And, finally, why had it almost disappeared? These
two sets of issues will be addressed below, first by describing the process of
silver production, and then through an analysis of the broader context in
which it took place.

Indigenous Silver Production in Porco

Carlos Cuiza lived in a homestead, or *estancia*, called Pucapujra (also spelled
Pucapuca) which is 7 km to the east of Porco and 0.5 km to the south of
the road connecting Porco with Potosí. His household included his second
wife and two children; some of his adult sons by his first marriage were
miners in Porco, and Cuiza, himself, had worked in a cooperative when he
was younger. The household raised llamas and sheep and produced small
quantities of fava beans, potatoes, and other root crops. His wife occasionally
worked as a cook for the school in Condoriri, a hamlet located a few kilometers to the northeast. Clothing and some other essentials were purchased
in Potosí, but the family appeared to live close to a subsistence level. Cuiza
allowed us to observe the production of charcoal as well as four smelts and
two refining episodes on different occasions. Although the sample is limited
to the observation of just one person, another individual, Eloy Mamani, who
learned how to smelt from his parents, described an identical process. The
description presented here is organized in terms of the sequence of activities
required to produce silver, rather than the chronology of our observations,
and it combines information acquired during different visits (see Van Buren
[2003] and Van Buren and Mills [2005] for more detailed descriptions of
the smelting and refining processes).

Metal production is a fuel-intensive activity, but the municipality of
Porco—which includes Pucapujra—is dominated by shrubland steppe vegetation, and trees are scarce (Montes de Oca 1989). Vegetation consists primarily of thin bushes (*Baccharis* sp.), grasses (*Stipa* sp.), and cushion plants
(*Azorella compacta*), all of which can be used as fuel during some stage of metal
production. Cuiza prefered to smelt with charcoal made from *churqui* (*Prosopis*
sp.) a tree that grows in the lower, warmer valleys to the south, because it
burns hot, but on the occasion that we observed him making charcoal he had

determined that the purchase price was prohibitive. Instead, he decided to use *queñua* (*Polylepis tomentella*), the only locally available tree suitable for producing charcoal. This species occurs in small, discontinuous patches in inaccessible ravines and on mesa tops, a distribution that some biogeographers have attributed to agricultural disturbance and continued harvesting for firewood and building material (Kessler 2002). Cuiza noted that the number of queñua trees in the immediate vicinity had declined; however, he had reserved a small grove close to his house just for smelting.

The process began by chopping down six trees approximately 2.5 m tall, and then constructing a low, earthen platform to create a flat space for making charcoal. Cuiza used a handmade machete to remove the leaves and thick bark, called *sillphi*, and cut the trunk and branches into 30- to 50-cm-long lengths that he arranged vertically in alternating layers of thin and thick branches. This resulted in a solid dome in the center of which he placed *thaphallanta*, material from a bird's nest found in one of the trees. The pile was then covered with a series of materials: first, a layer of leafy queñua branches, next queñua bark, and then a layer of grass that had been collected nearby. This was capped with dark organic material that had accumulated at the base of the trees that Cuiza called *guano*. It consisted primarily of bark as well as the dung of llamas and birds. Cuiza then covered the entire dome with soil and placed cobbles along the base to stabilize it. He ignited the pile by inserting a torch made of dried *thola* and thaphallanta into the center. After eight days, during which a few more kilos of wood and a small amount of tire rubber were added, the process was complete. Cuiza scraped off what remained of the outer layers and spread the charcoal out to cool. He then separated the charcoal from the unburned wood; small pieces of charcoal were raked up and passed through a sieve to remove impurities (Cayo and Ulloa 2003). Cuiza began the process with 690 kg of queñua wood, which produced 151 kg of charcoal—enough for approximately sixteen huayrachina smelts.

The next stage in silver production was to smelt argentiferous lead ore in the two huayrachinas Cuiza had constructed on a nearby ridge 100 m to the southwest of his house. These small conical furnaces were built of clay and small cobbles on top of low rock pedestals that elevated them to better capture the winds that blow fiercely across the saddle. Their exposure to wind and precipitation leads to rapid disintegration that Cuiza attempted to forestall by embedding thin iron straps around the circumference of each and covering them with plastic during the rainy season. Nonetheless, he had to repair them each year and reported that after one or two years he would break them apart and build new ones. Cuiza sometimes referred to these furnaces as *"abuelas,"* which means "grandmothers" in Spanish, but did not comment on the use of

FIGURE 5 Carlos Cuiza repairing a huayrachina (Van Buren 2021).

this term. Eloy Mamani explained that they "are like grandmothers who cook in the kitchen" (Mamani May 25, 2018).

The huayrachinas had nine holes on each side for oxygenating the charge and were open at the top to allow the addition of ore and fuel and the dissipation of gases. Two openings were located near the base of the furnace on the north and south sides for removing slag and partially smelted ore, and a small tap hole for draining the liquid lead was made at the same level on the side. The sandy clay for constructing and repairing the furnaces was gathered from the quebrada near Cuiza's house, and the flat boulders that were used for building the unmortered pedestals were obtained from nearby outcrops.

The furnaces, while not enclosed in a building, were at the center of an informal but patterned workspace (Van Buren and Mills 2005, fig. 8). Just to the east and a bit downhill was a low, linear windbreak made of small, loosely piled boulders. This could be used as a shelter from the wind but, more importantly, kept the charcoal and mineral stored in the lee of the hill from blowing away. The metal tools used in the process, most of which were either made by Cuiza or by a blacksmith in Potosí to his specifications, were also stored close to the wall. Three stone anvils for crushing ore, litharge, and clay were located in a cluster a few meters south of the huayrachinas, and a shallow depression containing clay for the repair of the furnace was adjacent to them. The surrounding area was strewn with branches and grass that were used for fuel at various stages in the process, as well as discarded slag and furnace fragments. This conjunction of elements—the remnants of a windbreak and stone pedestals on a ridgetop associated with small pieces of slag and charcoal, as well as huayrachina fragments and sometimes ceramics eroding down the ridge—was common in the archaeological record around Porco and could be interpreted more confidently as the remains of huayrachinas after observing Carlos Cuiza at work.

Prior to smelting Cuiza first had to gather and process the necessary inputs in addition to the fuel. The objective of the smelt was to obtain lead that could later be used to refine silver ore, but analysis of the lead ore indicated that it also contained small quantities of silver (Cohen et al. 2008). Galena (lead sulfide) was purchased from acquaintances or in Potosí. In addition to ore, Cuiza added *acendrada*, or litharge, to the huayrachina. Acendrada is the crusty lining of the cupellation furnace that is used to refine silver and consists of lead oxide as well as silver that soaks into the lining. Incorporation of litharge into the smelt allows the sulfide ore to be reduced and is also a way to capture silver that was lost during the refining process. When Cuiza did not have enough acendrada from his own cupellation furnace, he sought out long-abandoned furnaces and extracted the linings from those. This is just one of the many ways in which archaeological sites associated with mining and metallurgy are reconfigured by the continual recycling of materials.

The initial step was to remove the waste rock, or gangue, from the lead ore, and then both the ore and acendrada were coarsely crushed on stone anvils using iron mallets. Once the inputs had been prepared and the huayrachinas were newly lined with clay, Cuiza set about charging the furnaces. First, he combined the ore with the acendrada in a ratio of 2:1 and dampened the mixture with urine. He next ignited ichu grass and burro dung in the base of the huayrachinas and plugged the apertures at the bottom of the furnaces with small logs. The chambers were then filled with alternating layers of mineral and either churqui or queñua charcoal, or a combination of both. Ch'allas, in this case offerings of cane alcohol and coca leaves, were made to the furnaces to encourage the success of the smelt. During the next eight hours and well into the night, Cuiza tended the furnaces, removing slag and partially melted ore from the base, adding charcoal and the mineral mixture with a shovel at the top, making occasional ch'allas, and occasionally rotating the stick that plugged the tap hole to allow the molten lead to drip into a small iron bowl below. By the end of this process, he had produced 4 to 6 kg of pure lead metal.

The next stage in the procedure was to use the lead produced in the huayrachinas to refine silver ore. The cupellation furnace that Cuiza employed for this task was located in a small adobe hut built into the side of a quebrada just to the south of the estancia.

The furnace, which was constructed of cobbles and clay, spanned the short length of the rectangular structure. It was a small reverberatory furnace that included a round hearth with an opening at the top and both sides, a chimney on one end, and a firebox that opened into the quebrada below on the other. The physical location of the structure provided a number of benefits; it protected the furnace from wind gusts that could cool the charge, allowed for the support of the chimney against the quebrada wall, facilitated ash disposal, and kept the entire process hidden from view.

Prior to refining, Cuiza repaired the furnace by covering it with a new coat of clay and then lined the hearth with finely ground *yareta* ash mixed with urine. This was tamped down with a smooth rock into a concave shape that he checked using a marble. He also instructed his children to gather llama dung, which was heaped just outside the structure. To begin refining, Cuiza placed lead metal produced in the huayrachina in the hearth and luted the top and one lateral opening with more clay. He then ignited a fire in the firebox using burro dung and thola, and once it was burning, he added llama dung through a small hole, a task that he continued throughout the entire

FIGURE 6 Cupellation hearth (small reverberatory furnace) used by Carlos Cuiza to refine silver (Van Buren 2020).

procedure. Refining also required a ch'alla, but in this case his wife brought in a paper containing offerings including coca leaves and molded sugar tablets, or *misterios*, purchased in the market in Potosí, which were added to the fire. This process, called cupellation, works because lead is easily oxidized and forms lead oxide that is absorbed by the porous lining of the hearth, leaving the silver, which does not readily combine with oxygen, behind. Silver can be lost, however, through cracks in the lining, and the offering safeguards the smelt from this possibility. The smelt is also protected by allowing only a small number of people to witness it; Cuiza noted that if bystanders who had not also attended the huayrachina smelt were present, the silver would become jealous (*celosa*), and disappear. Mamani (May 25, 2018) confirmed this and added that some people were destined to work with silver, and others made it disappear, just as within the mine itself. Once the lead metal had melted, Cuiza began to add large spoonfuls of finely ground silver sulfide. He continued to do this, as well as feed and stir the fire, make offerings of alcohol and coca, and remove slag from the surface of the lead bath until, nineteen or so hours later, a button of pure silver weighing approximately 150 g was all that remained in the hearth.

Observation of this entire process substantially enhanced our awareness of the factors that shape the artisanal production of silver and our interpretation of the archaeological record it generates, as will become clear in the following chapter. It also raised the question of why small-scale smelting and refining had continued into the twenty-first century, particularly given the enormous amount of time and effort that Cuiza expended and the relative inefficiency of the process with regard to the quantity of the final product (Cohen 2008). The persistence of this technology was clearly predicated on more than the continuation of cultural tradition or the expression of some sort of ethnic identity. With regard to the latter, in fact, at least some residents of Porco viewed Cuiza's production of silver in a very negative light, jealously complaining that he was enriching himself and refusing to teach others how to do the same. The evidence offered for this grievance was that he worked in secret at night, the faintly nefarious connotations of which might be related to the widespread belief in Andean mining communities that silver, wealth, and involvement with the devil are associated (Absi 2005; Nash 1979; Taussig 1980). So, engaging in silver production would only add to Cuiza's social marginalization as an impoverished, elderly, primarily Quechua-speaking *campesino* rather than enhance his status in the community. Instead of seeking a genealogical connection to long-standing tradition, this question needs to be addressed by enlarging the perspective to encompass the linkages between small- and large-scale mineral production in Porco and, more generally, the relationship between Carlos Cuiza's household and the broader political economy. Cuiza acquired the technical knowledge required to produce silver from his parents, but why, under these specific historical conditions, did he choose to engage in silver production?

Carlos Cuiza was both a campesino and a former miner who lived in the shadow of what was, at the time, the largest zinc-producing mine in Bolivia. He was familiar with both mineral extraction and farming and was acquainted with men who were still actively employed as miners. He was also a subsistence farmer with two young children and little access to cash, experiencing the rural poverty that is common in the Bolivian countryside. He was openly relieved when we arrived the second season to observe a smelt because his household was in an economic crisis, and we paid him for his time, purchased the required inputs, allowed him to keep almost all the final product, and gave him small gifts of food and coca. In retrospect, economic privation was most likely the reason he allowed us to observe him as he worked.

The need for cash was also the reason why Cuiza engaged in smelting. The precise amount of time that he spent on the process, from felling the trees to prying the silver out of the litharge, was not recorded, but a very conservative estimate that does not include the days during which the fuel was reduced to charcoal largely unattended or the collection of llama dung, is 66 hours. The yield of pure silver was approximately 150 gm, which would have been worth $36.82 in 2001, which was an unusual low point for silver prices, or, at the exceptional height of the market in 2011, $334.22 ("Silver Prices—100 Year Historical Chart" n.d.). Half of this went to the supplier of the silver, leaving Cuiza with $18.41 to $167.11 for his efforts. To put this in perspective, the minimum wage in Bolivia during that time was just under $200 a month. This comparison is specious, though, in that Carlos Cuiza had few if any other alternatives for generating income, so neither the inefficiency of the process, as measured by the yield of silver, nor the amount of time required for producing the silver relative to the money it generated seemed to be part of his calculus. The silver he produced was sold to jewelers in Potosí (his parents had sold it to the mint when it was still functioning), and the money generated by the sale was used to purchase necessities such as school supplies, clothing, matches, and other goods that the household did not produce itself.

Obviously, however, Cuiza would not have been able to smelt without access to the necessary inputs. The difficulty in acquiring charcoal was described above, but even more critical was the silver ore itself. Since we had no personal connections to active miners, we purchased ore in Potosí, but Cuiza acquired it from miners who had small quantities of high-grade ore that they illicitly pocketed during their work underground. This type of ore "theft," called *jukeo* in Bolivia, is common throughout the world, especially in mines that produce precious minerals such as gold, silver, and diamonds. When it is conducted by company miners in Porco, it is called "hacer dormir," which means "to put to sleep" (Benavides del Carpio 2004). In Porco both company and cooperative miners engage in jukeo, a practice that is facilitated by the nature of the silver deposits in the area. Even though the bulk of the ore that is now extracted consists of a mix of zinc, tin, and lead, as well as silver and antimony (USGS n.d.), small pockets of high-grade silver are sometimes encountered. These are often "stolen" by miners who pocket the ore or secret it in undergarments that are especially made for the purpose. The appropriation of this ore is illegal and can result in both the loss of employment and imprisonment. The illicit source of the silver smelted by Cuiza, and presumably by others who engaged in small-scale silver production, is probably the reason why there were no reports of this technology being used during the twentieth century.

The wariness associated with traditional silver production was made clear to us during an encounter with another family who apparently was learning the technique from Carlos Cuiza. During the pedestrian survey, a recently made structure with a new cupellation hearth similar to the one used by Cuiza was discovered near a homestead outside of Porco. The archaeological team asked the owner of the estancia about it, and she reported that it belonged to her son who was currently out of town. She suggested that they talk to him in Porco the following week. When two PAPP members went to his house, the man became extremely angry, denied owning the furnace, and threw them out; neighbors said that he had just been released from jail for jukeo. The secrecy associated with silver refining thus seems to be related to the source of the ore, which in some cases, at least, is legally defined as stolen.

Carlos Cuiza's decision to produce silver using traditional technology can thus be understood in terms of household economics as well as the relationship between this small-scale production and the large-scale mining operation that dominates Porco. As a campesino who could no longer work in the mines due to his age, Cuiza engaged in an ancillary economic activity that was used to generate needed cash based on his skills and connections with active miners in Porco. COMSUR exploited the highly productive mines in Apu Porco and leased others to cooperatives, creating access to underground workings that would otherwise be inaccessible. All these factors playing out at a specific historical moment promoted the use of traditional silver production in the shadow of one of the most technologically advanced mines in Bolivia.

Carlos Cuiza disappeared in 2005; after an interpersonal crisis he simply left, and his family did not know his whereabouts. With his departure, Indigenous small-scale silver production in Porco ended. When asked about small-scale smelting, Porqueños told us that he was the only one who still did it, and since no reports of such practices have emerged from other mining centers in the region, presumably the technology is now extinct. Its disappearance, as its persistence into the twenty-first century, raises interesting questions about the nature of technological continuity and change. During the smelts we observed, there were signs that Cuiza was encountering difficulties with the technology. The inefficiency of production relative to the time and fuel expended might be one indication of a problem, although this could also have resulted from the team's inexperience in selecting appropriate ores. Experimental data produced by Térygeol and Cruz (2014) indicate that the process can be more efficient than the PAPP observations suggest. More direct evidence of problems is the fact that Cuiza had difficulty getting both the huayrachinas and cupellation hearths to work properly. The first time we observed a smelt, he had constructed two huayrachinas that were in use simultaneously. One of the two smoldered and smoked but failed to reach a sufficiently high temperature to smelt the lead ore, so Cuiza eventually transferred the charge to the one that worked. He also had two cupellation furnaces for refining, one that he had inherited and another that he built using measured drawings of the first (Van Buren and Mills 2005). The new one did not operate properly, so he continued to use the furnace that his parents had originally constructed. Another indication of difficulties with the reproduction of this technology relates to the recently constructed cupellation furnace that was discovered during survey, which was described earlier in this chapter. According to the property owner, the furnace did not work despite the fact that Cuiza had been consulted for advice.

One way to understand the challenges that Cuiza faced is to view them not just as individual failures, but as a consequence of the absence of a technological community engaged in the same sort of practices (Schiffer 2002). Such communities can help practitioners solve problems by providing occasions for observation or by offering explicit advice. In the case of small-scale metal production, the lack of opportunities to observe other practitioners left Cuiza with limited resources with which to address technical problems. This was due, in part, to the secrecy associated with silver production, but also resulted from the simple fact that he was the last to use this technology, a situation that requires explanation at a broader scale of analysis.

Carlos Cuiza's case, in conjunction with archaeological evidence of metal production associated with early twentieth-century homesteads (discussed in detail in the following chapter), indicates that Native silver production was conducted by rural households in the vicinity of Porco as part of a diversified rural subsistence strategy. This technology was thus embedded in a demographic sector that has been steadily declining in Bolivia since the 1952 revolution. As rural populations have moved to towns in search of work, schools, running water, and other urban amenities, the countryside has been largely abandoned except for older individuals who are unwilling to emigrate or who have returned to their land after retiring, as is the case in many of the estancias near Porco. The construction of roads, the introduction of motorized transportation, and near-universal education have also facilitated access to cities where miners can sell high-graded ore to *rescatiris*, middlemen who purchase relatively small quantities of ore without paperwork indicating its origins. The social matrix in which small-scale silver production technology was embedded has disintegrated, resulting in its disappearance.

Conclusion

Cooperative mining as well as small-scale silver production in Porco can only be understood in relationship to larger scale enterprises. At the most fundamental level, access to ore is controlled by a company that has the legal backing of the Bolivian state. Less productive deposits are leased to cooperatives that do not have the capital to increase the efficiency or scale of production and sometimes are even prohibited from using large-scale machinery because of the potential hazards it poses to nearby galleries under company control. In the case of household silver production, the physical parameters of access to silver ore are even more apparent. Highly capitalized operations create below ground mines that sometimes contain small pockets of high-grade silver that is "stolen" by miners—both company employees and *cooperativistas*—while they work the surrounding face. The direct appropriation of high-grade ore by miners is one strategy they use to circumvent the economic and legal power exerted by mineowners, a practice that it is undergirded by their understanding of the sacrifice they are making in relation to the benefits that accrue to owners. This sacrifice is generally construed in terms of the reciprocal relationship between miners and the generative forces that create ore but is also understood as the result of economic exploitation; miners have a right to directly appropriate ore as part of the compensation for their work and the toll it takes on their health and well-being.

Household metal production in the first decade of the twenty-first century depended on the availability of high-grade silver ore that was illicitly obtained by miners. In the twentieth century ore may also have been obtained by pailliris who gleaned mine and mill waste, or directly from independent miners. Clearly, rather than being an organizational or technological vestige of the distant past, recent small-scale metal production in Porco was constituted in relationship to contemporary socioeconomic conditions at the local, regional, and global levels. It does, however, have historical roots in earlier practices. The following chapter will examine how these relations were established. Under what conditions did rural households incorporate small-scale metal production into their economic repertoires? How were these practices related to the development of industrial silver and tin mining? What was the relation between metal production and agriculture? In what contexts did cooperatives emerge? These questions will be investigated in the following chapter using archaeological data and documentary records about Bolivian mining in the nineteenth and twentieth centuries.

2

Small-Scale Metal Production in the Age of Industrialization (1825–1964)

THE HISTORY OF SILVER MINING in Bolivia after independence is the story of five decades of slow and uneven changes in production followed by a surge in output during the last quarter of the nineteenth century (Mitre 1981). In the early 1900s silver was rapidly replaced by tin as the primary export when the "tin barons"—three Bolivian entrepreneurs who together controlled 70 percent of the country's production—presided over its astronomical growth. It was also the time when militant mining unions, now icons of the Bolivian labor movement, emerged to fight back against the abuses that underwrote their wealth and ultimately succeeded in instigating the Revolution of 1952. Porco, however, appears to have been an island in a river of momentous change due to the modest size of its tin deposits and the continuing links between agriculture and mining.

The long-standing connection between mining and agro-pastoral activities was particularly important in the history of kajcheo because irregular, small-scale, and seasonal miners sustained themselves by maintaining access to agricultural resources, and in many cases engaged in wage labor only as a complement to agriculture. While mineowners frequently complained about the irregularity and indiscipline of the workforce, at many points this relationship benefited large-scale producers by providing flexibility in hiring, lowering investment in less productive mines, and shifting risk to the primary producers.

This chapter examines the development of industrial mining in Porco and the ways small-scale producers, most of whom had ties to the countryside, negotiated the process. It begins with the lull in production during the emergence of the Bolivian state and then describes the revitalization of silver

PRODUCTION IN THE AGE OF INDUSTRIALIZATION (1825–1964)   57

mining in the late nineteenth century when "modern" infrastructure, technology, and labor practices were introduced. The chapter then turns to the transition from silver to tin extraction in the early 1900s. Porco never produced tin at the scale of Llallagua, Huanuni, or Potosí, but some elements of its trajectory paralleled those of larger centers because all were controlled at some point by enterprises that introduced "modern" technology and management practices. Capital for technical improvements and the development of physical and financial infrastructure was provided by foreign sources. Employment in these mines appears to have attracted families who took up residence in the countryside around Porco and engaged in both mining and agricultural pursuits; some of them also smelted and refined silver on a household scale. The chapter then briefly considers the crucial role played by miners in the Revolution of 1952 and the subsequent nationalization of the mines and ends with the emergence of cooperatives in Porco during the mid-twentieth century.

Nineteenth-Century Silver Mining

In 1825, the year Bolivia won its independence from Spain, Simón Bolívar, "the great liberator," declared in the Decree of Pukara that all abandoned mines would become state property that could be sold. The collapse of the Spanish colonial regime opened the door to foreign investors, many of whom waited anxiously in Potosí on the eve of victory poised to buy up defunct silver mines (Lofstrom 1975; Ovando-Sanz 1965). Many were simply speculators, but others hoped to make the mines profitable again by the introduction of new technology and the application of labor discipline. The British were initially eager to invest in the Andes (Harvey and Press 1989), and they prepared meticulous reports describing the region. Foremost among them was John Pentland, a secretary of the British vice-counsel in Lima, who initiated a two-year survey of Bolivia in 1826 with the goal of producing a detailed map and an eye toward identifying worthwhile prospects for British investors. He described Porco as having been completely abandoned for some time (Pentland 1975 [1827], 78), and as such, it was available for purchase or rent by investors. This was attempted by Dámaso de Uriburu, an Argentinian entrepreneur who acquired the rights to all the unproductive mines in the province of Porco by using Bolivian citizens as fronts. He then distributed shares to these individuals and associated them in a company. His efforts were rewarded in 1826 when Antonio José de Sucre, Bolivar's second in command, approved the contracts of the Bolivian shareholders, but unfortunately, this came too late for Uriburu. The collapse of the British financial market in late

1825 made it impossible to secure the necessary capital to restart the mines, and the company was dissolved (Lofstrom 1973, 19–25).

The difficulties of resuscitating silver production in the province of Porco were also experienced elsewhere in the Andes. The mita, a system of forced labor used by the Spanish state to subsidize silver production, was officially abolished in Bolivia in 1812, and with the withdrawal of that labor force owners often decided to process tailings rather than continue with underground extraction. According to Platt (2000), this was accomplished by contracting with the Indigenous labor force, rather than directly employing workers. Illicit kajcheo, which had been widespread in the late eighteenth century, also remained important, and kajchas began to coalesce as an organized group that represented the individual interests of its members. In 1837 they made a proposal to the Gremio de Azogueros—the guild of mine and mill owners in Potosí—for tolerable working conditions and mutually beneficial practices. Specifically, they asked that (1) the mines be turned over to them from Saturday until Monday night after a review of the mining supports which they promised to respect; and (2) the ore be divided between the owner and kajcha, with the former being able to purchase the kajcha's portion at a fair price. Despite the benefits to both parties, the guild rejected the proposal, and ore theft increased as the century unfolded. Between 1830 and 1850 kajchas produced over 30 percent of the registered silver in the Potosí district (Rodriguez Ostria 1991, 33). Interestingly, mercury production in Huancavelica was also dominated by informal miners during this period, but for distinct historical reasons. After mercury was discovered in the seventeenth century, the Spanish state imposed centralized control over a highly localized mining complex until its catastrophic collapse in 1786. After that date, the *pallaqueo* system was instituted that allowed independent mining with a permit. Pallaqueadores were largely Indigenous and regarded with disdain by Spanish miners, who viewed them as destructive ore thieves and also worried about their impact on the availability of labor for more formal operations (Povea Morena 2012). In Republican times this evolved into the exploitation of numerous shallow deposits by miners who worked illegally and who steadfastly refused to engage in wage labor for the successive firms that attempted to "rationalize" production (Smit 2018, 115).

Bolivian entrepreneurs also explored the new business landscape during the decades after independence. Platt (2014) describes the variety of mining enterprises that operated in the Department of Potosí at the time, demonstrating that different configurations of capital, labor, and technology occurred in both small- and medium-sized operations. Many of the former involved a middleman who provided loans and supplies to independent

PRODUCTION IN THE AGE OF INDUSTRIALIZATION (1825–1964)   59

Native miners, sometimes relying on Chilean or Argentinean investors for the capital. The miners, or kajchas, gave a portion of the silver to the middleman and often sold him their share as well, thus securing money to make their tribute payments. The silver itself was either legally sold to the Banco de Rescates in Potosí or illicitly transported to Argentina as contraband. Langer (2021) argues that smuggling—which was conducted largely by Indigenous miners, muleteers, and caravan owners, although controlled at the top by influential merchants—enlivened the regional economy by distributing the benefits of silver production broadly. Porco was exploited in this way by kajchas during the mid-nineteenth century. In a detailed report on Potosí's mining industry that was compiled between 1841 and 1842, Porco was described as having eight "minas de caccheo" operated by 50 miners, as well as two hand-operated mills for pulverizing the ore. According to Platt's (2014) calculations each miner produced an average of 45 kg of high-grade, finely ground ore each week. While the larger, more formal mines listed in the report produced more, per capita this was a substantial return on the kajcha's labor.

Rodríguez Ostria (1991, 33) argued that kajchas were just one component of an informal economy that included *trapicheros* and ore thieves and that, through the absorption of unemployed workers, inhibited the development of a reserve labor force. Trapicheros ran small mills for beneficiating ore, and they, as well as rescatiris, advanced money and materials to kajchas either at a high rate of interest or with the agreement that they would be sold the mineral at lower than market prices. Trapicheros also offered salaried miners alcohol and money for stolen ore. Mineowners regarded these enterprises as "schools of depravity for the peon" (Rodríguez Ostria 1989, 134), places where competitors encouraged defiance of the regulations imposed by companies and the state.

An example of a rural trapiche was located during pedestrian survey on the south side of the confluence of the San Juan and the Cebada Cancha Rivers, 6.5 km to the southwest of Porco. The small mill complex consists of a double-chambered enclosure, a rectangular, gable-roofed structure, and two small, roughly constructed buildings. The larger, unroofed chamber in the first structure was used to mill the ore. The floor consists of well-worn bedrock on top of which rests a *quimbalete* for grinding. It is an oblong stone measuring 1 m long, with a curved lower surface. The top of the quimbalete is perforated with small holes to hold pegs that were used to attach a long pole to the stone. Two people would use the pole to rock the stone back and forth, and it is likely that, as in many trapiches of this sort, mercury was then used to amalgamate the crushed ore. This particular quimbalete has a cross pecked into it; the fact that the image is not worn suggests that it was made after the mill ceased operations. Two other quimbaletes are incorporated into the walls of the structure, one to close the doorway and another to patch a hole in the wall; a fourth is located outside the building. The blocked entrances indicate later use, probably by a herder. A quarry for producing these rocker stones is located on a steep slope just to the south of the site. The quimbaletes were hacked out of the rock outcrops and the surfaces finished as they were created. Quimbaletes in different stages of production were found in the quarry still attached to the rock face.

No excavations were conducted at the trapiche, and the lack of diagnostic artifacts on the surface of the site makes it difficult to determine the construction date. However, its relationship to a footpath that connects the site to a large stamp mill a few hundred meters to the east provides a clue. This path appears to follow the course of a canal that powered the stamp mill, suggesting that the path postdates the mill, which, based on the artifacts recovered there, was in use until the later eighteenth and early nineteenth centuries. Juan Equise, the owner of the estancia across the river from the trapiche, did not recall any stories of it operating. Since he was in his fifties when interviewed, the trapiche most likely dates to the mid- or late nineteenth century.

FIGURE 7 Trapiche adjacent to the San Juan River. Quimbaletes can be seen on the floor and in the walls (Van Buren 2020).

PRODUCTION IN THE AGE OF INDUSTRIALIZATION (1825–1964)   61

This rustic mill probably served miners who worked in the nearby Sora Sora mines, either as legal kajchas or as ore thieves, and constitutes a space in which Native workers were able to circumvent company and state control over the wealth they produced. They could only do so, though, because the Sora Sora mines had been worked on an industrial scale since colonial times and the infrastructure existed for the recovery of small amounts of high-grade silver by local operators.

Porco appears to have remained a backwater during the first fifty years of Republican rule. In 1851, a census published by José María Dalence noted that despite its former importance it was "a small place inhabited by a few poor miners" (Dalence 1851, 77) and later indicated that the mines were flooded, as were many other old mines in the area. The archaeological record tends to support this assessment since no remains dating to the early nineteenth century have been identified in the immediate vicinity of Porco, although it is likely that artisanal workings have been obscured by later industrial infrastructure.

Porco was, though, embedded in a network of roads that were used to transport silver from functioning mines in the Department of Potosí to Cobija, a port on the Pacific coast that was owned by Bolivia until its defeat in the War of the Pacific in 1879. An archaeological survey of the route conducted by García-Albarido (2022) identified the ruins of a hacienda, Juchuy Chaquilla, that was mentioned in historical sources as an inn or waystation. The site is located approximately 15 km to the west of Porco and lies within its current jurisdiction. The remains of a small adobe compound are situated on the edge of a bofedal that would have provided pasture and water for llamas and mules. A household 50 m to the southwest of the hacienda building includes a dense midden that is probably composed of the debris from meals prepared for travelers. Surface artifacts date to the nineteenth century, and include mold-blown bottles, white wares, and handmade ceramics.

A similar waystation is located on the same road in the community of Condoriri, which is to the east of Porco. Much of the site is still occupied, and the preservation is thus poor, but residents could still identify a kitchen, store, rooms for people to sleep, and others for storing forage, all arrayed around a large patio. According to Eloy Mamani, who lives nearby, three roads converged near the bofedal of Condoriri. The site served muleteers who transported silver from Potosí to Antofagasta; another such inn, or *tambo*, was located in Chanca, between Condoriri and Potosí, and the next in route to Chile was in the village of Yura. Peasants who resided nearby were forced to work for the innkeeper, a "Spaniard," until he left when the railroad was built, and animals were no longer used for transporting ore.

By the second half of the nineteenth century a new generation of mineowners without ties to the colonial silver industry and influenced by a modernizing ideology learned in Europe had emerged in southern Bolivia (Rodríguez Ostria 1991, 35). The "silver oligarchy" as they came to be known, included José Avelina Aramayo and his son Félix, Aniceto Arce, and Gregorio Pacheco. The Huanchaca Mining Company, started in 1830 by a member of the old mining elite, was sold to Arce in 1860 and led the way in production (Mitre 1981). The resurgence of silver mining in the early 1870s coincided with the implementation of liberal reforms that included the modernization of the currency system, an end to the government's monopoly of the purchase of silver ore, the elimination of protective tariffs, and attempts to privatize communal Indigenous lands (Larson 2004, 216). The conclusion of the War of the Pacific (1879–1884) also led to increased foreign investment. In fact, the first suggestion that large-scale work at Porco had resumed is the formation of Compañía Tornohuaico by Isidoro Aramayo and Ciriaco Gironás in 1884. This concession, covering 30 ha, was situated along the vein of the same name that is located just south of Porco (Centro de Estudios de Potosí 1892).

Additional evidence that the mines at Porco had been resuscitated comes from the diary of J. B. Williams, a Cornish miner who supervised work at Porco from 1884 to 1887. Williams was one of hundreds of Cornish mine captains who were enticed overseas by British companies with the promise of steady work at good wages during a time when English mining was on the decline, in part because of cheap tin imports from South America (Harvey and Press 1989). His laconic account of events in Porco speaks directly to the challenges faced by owners and supervisors in imposing discipline on the Indigenous labor force (Rodríguez Ostria 1991). The fundamental problem, from their perspective, was simply getting people to work. For instance, on July 19, 1885, Williams wrote, "I went down town again pretty early but could not get anyone to work, but after pay succeeded in getting 17 to start for the mine, but when they got up on the mountains 7 started to run like deers and when we got to the mine we only had 9. I sent one of the dependentries back to tell Mr Pascoe, so he mounted his mule and captured 3 and sent them up here, which I kept in the mine 3 days and 3 nights" (Gale and Taylor 2009).

This incident reflects the power of the mine captain to physically coerce workers, but also indicates that the rules of the game were contested. Rodríguez Ostria (1991) argued that a shortage of labor was the largest impediment to the development of Bolivian mining in the nineteenth century. This was due to the cessation of the colonial mita (Espinoza Morales 2010, 48) as well

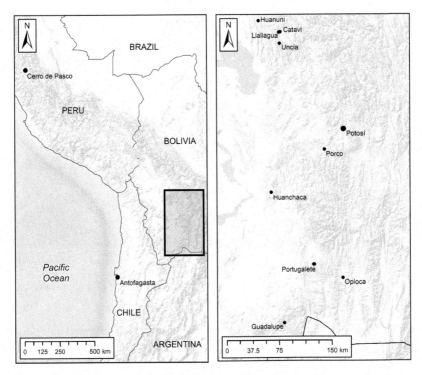

MAP 3 Location of mines mentioned in text. Map by Brendan Weaver.

as the destruction caused by the War of Independence. However, he also attributed the labor bottleneck to profound differences in the understanding of the nature and value of time. Employers increasingly demanded that workers conform to a schedule established to maximize productivity, but the potential labor force was comprised primarily of peasants who were members of indigenous communities or *colonos* who worked on haciendas (Rodríguez Ostria 1991, 30). These laborers were often available only on a seasonal basis, participated in fiestas of various types during the work week, and frequently drank so heavily on Sunday that they failed to report for work on Monday. An obvious attempt to encourage adherence to an industrial schedule in Porco was the erection of a sun dial in the village plaza. It was noted by Williams in his 1884 diary and appears in a photograph taken twenty-three years later along with a man on horseback who was most likely a mine administrator (Wright 1907, 323). Marking time in this way apparently had little effect, as Williams complained frequently about the failure of workers to show up at the mines. For example, on August 30, 1885, he wrote: "Feast Sta Rosa. A grand procession parading the Plaza, dressed in all kinds of hideous colours

FIGURE 8 Sun dial (center left) in plaza of Porco (Wright 1907, 323, public domain).

and fashion, more like a Circus than anything else," and on the next day: "No men at mine today. I hear they are all drunk at Porco so I don't expect we shall get any men this week" (Gale and Taylor 2009).

Scholars (Contreras 1986; Langer 1996; Platt 1983) concur that peasant participation in the mining economy was the primary reason why Andean miners did not follow the same route toward proletarianization as workers in more developed countries. Contreras examined the case of Cerro de Pasco, an important silver mining center in central Peru, but much of his analysis also applies to southern Bolivia. However, he argues against the notion, posited by Rodríguez Ostria (1991) and other historians as well as contemporary observers, that the backwardness of mining at that time was due to an overall lack of permanent skilled labor. Instead, he makes a convincing case that given the conditions faced by mineowners—particularly the elimination of the mita, a partial reduction of tribute requirements, and the abolition of the *reparto*, or forced sale of goods to Indigenous households—employing a fluctuating labor force for the extraction of ore was a rational and efficient way to reduce costs. The withdrawal of state backing in combination with the resultant rise in wages and a lack of capital to support miners year-round or to invest in technology to replace them led owners to employ a seasonal workforce, both in the mines as well as for transporting the ore to mills. It also resulted in their acceptance of partial payment in high-grade ore, called *"la huachaca"* in

PRODUCTION IN THE AGE OF INDUSTRIALIZATION (1825–1964)   65

Peru, which was equivalent to the ore-sharing arrangements made in Bolivia (Contreras 1986, 96).

The largest percentage of peasants who migrated to Cerro de Pasco, both men and women, came from the surrounding area, but approximately half originated in other departments. These were places with similar climates, but more importantly, they had a history of mining and were not dominated by haciendas. Immigrants were free to leave the land and were probably familiar with some aspects of mining. Furthermore, these agrarian households were organized to simultaneously engage in multiple tasks (e.g., pastoral, agricultural, and domestic) and support each other by exchanging labor which was helpful when family members were absent (Contreras 1986, 130–31, 146). People usually immigrated during the agricultural off-season when there was an excess of labor locally and worked for one to three months before returning home. A decline in the labor force after 1854, when tribute was entirely abolished in Peru, indicates that at least part of the desire for work stemmed from the need to pay this tax (Contreras 1986, 152–54). The fact that campesinos continued to migrate to Cerro de Pasco after that date, though, shows that cash to pay for such things as fiestas, church services, alcohol, coca, dyes, and textiles had become a necessity for rural households.

In Bolivia, Native tribute continued into the 1870s. Gil Montero's (2014) analysis of mining in Lípez demonstrates its importance in motivating Indigenous employment in the mines and mills of San Antonio del Nuevo Mundo, not just in the nineteenth century but also during the apogee of silver production during the 1600s. In addition to avoiding the consequences of non-payment, Native communities also regarded the provision of tribute as a means to safeguard access to land (Platt 1982).

The nineteenth-century boom in Bolivian silver mining occurred between 1872 and 1895, an unlikely period given that first Germany, and then the United States and other industrial nations shifted from silver to the gold standard. However, local conditions, especially changes in state policies, made silver production profitable for many in Bolivia. The silver oligarchy and other merchant-miners finally had enough political influence to prevail against protectionists, and in 1872 legislation was passed that allowed the export of raw silver. Silver producers could get more for their product on the free market as well as avoid the taxes that had been associated with selling their silver to the national bank, a requirement imposed by previous regimes (Langer 1989, 18). The boom, though, did not last long, and Bolivian silver production declined sharply in the 1890s as demand for tin, which was used in the manufacture of tin cans and coating for electrical wire, increased. The key role played by kajchas in the silver economy continued for a decade or so in the tin mines before production was reorganized during the modernization of the mining industry (Rodríguez Ostria 2014). Kajcheo, though, continued to be practiced when conditions favored small-scale mining or when large operations chose to outsource the risk associated with working less productive deposits.

The Industrial Mining of Tin

The "age of the tin barons" began in 1900 with the discovery of a fabulously rich vein in the La Salvadora mine in northern Potosí, and tin—as well as the people who mined it—shaped the trajectory of Bolivian history for the next eighty-five years. Industrial mining and attendant forms of labor discipline began in the 1800s but became prevalent during the first decades of the twentieth century (Absi and Pavez 2015) when Bolivia was the second-largest producer of tin in the world. Tin became Bolivia's most important national export and remained so until 1980. During this period, tin miners also became an important force in national politics.

The tin barons Simón Patiño, Mauricio Hochschild, and Carlos Victor Aramayo came from very different backgrounds, but their personal histories converged during the first three decades of the twentieth century when they became the largest producers of tin in Bolivia and were counted among the wealthiest men in the world. Their companies dominated national production, and their influence on Bolivian politics was as outsized as their fortunes even though they never held office. Patiño was the wealthiest and most famous of the three, in part because he was a Native Bolivian who became a key figure in the world of British finance, a reversal of the subordinate role usually played by Latin American entrepreneurs.

The tin barons introduced modern technology and systematically enacted labor practices that had only been sporadically attempted in the past. As one Bolivian historian noted, Patiño's name "represents for tin what Ford represents for the automotive industry. He is the only multimillionaire who escaped from Latin American mediocrity to insert himself in British finance, the heart of European capitalism until the first world war" (Sergio Almaraz 1967, quoted in Espinoza Morales 2010, 75, author's translation). Patiño's business practices, however, were not unlike those of other large companies; he generated his fortune by exploiting poorly paid laborers who worked in miserable conditions. Unions that were created to improve the lives of miners were vehemently opposed by companies controlled by Patiño and his peers.

Members were fired and jailed, and in the worst incidents, the army was mobilized to suppress "agitation," an action that sometimes resulted in violent confrontations during which soldiers killed protesting miners (Smale 2010).

It was Aramayo rather than Patiño, however, who was involved in the modernization of tin mining in Porco. Industrialization arrived with the railroad in 1912, the same year that Porco Tin Mines, Ltd. was first advertised on the London Stock Exchange with £125,000 in capital (*Mining and Scientific Press* 1912, 538). Porco Tin Mines was one of hundreds of British freestanding companies that invested in the Andes at the turn of the century and that were the immediate predecessors of multinational corporations (Miller 2000). Porco Tin Mines acquired the complex from Arturo Arana, an entrepreneur from Sucre who produced both silver and tin, which were processed in a ten-stamp mill in Agua de Castilla (*Mining and Scientific Press* 1912, 538). The Aramayo Francke Company appears to have been associated with the enterprise, although the nature of its involvement is unclear (Singewald and Miller 1917). The concession included 400 acres of mining properties and thirty acres adjacent to the Agua de Castilla River with associated water rights (*Weekly Sun* 1912, 3). By 1915 a concentration plant was under construction at the site, and the complex was reported to be "one of the most up to date in Bolivia, the plant including stamps, sand and slime tables and a Hardinge mill for regrinding" (Bullock 1915, 421). An aerial ropeway transported the ore from the mines to the mill, and the resulting concentrate was then moved by rail to Antofagasta, Chile, where it was shipped to New York (Henderson 1916). An early photograph shows the mill and ancillary structures (Singewald and Miller 1917); these were dismantled in the 1960s, but the stone foundation of the mill can still be seen.

A report made by North American geologists in 1917 noted that "Porco Tin Mines Ltd. is the only operator in the district, and its property includes the whole of the mineralized area of Apu Porco and a large part of Huayna Porco, but it is mining only the tin veins of Apu Porco. The mine offices are situated in a ravine between the two mountains on the north side of Apu Porco at the tunnel of the old Pie de Gallo mine, which was the most important of the silver mines on Huayna Porco" (Singewald and Miller 1917, 331). Agua de Castilla became a settlement almost equaling Porco in size as a result of its proximity to the railway, and the mill complex eventually developed into Campamento Yuncaviri, a gated camp housing managers and engineers. Porco Tin Mines' operation was thus centralized, relatively large scale (the mill was processing fifty tons of ore per day in 1917 according to Singewald and Miller), and legally precluded mining by others in the immediate vicinity without the company's permission.

FIGURE 9 The Agua de Castilla mill completed in 1915 (Singewald and Miller 1917, 29, public domain).

Some sense of the nature, but not the size, of the labor force can be garnered from a report prepared in 1916 by G. M. Henderson, an engineer who was sent to assess the Porco operation as a possible investment opportunity. In addition to describing the mines, calculating the value of the ore relative to the cost of extraction, and specifying the machinery that was already in place, Henderson listed the types of laborers that were employed and how much they were paid. A simple hierarchy characterized work in the mines themselves: miners worked in gangs under bosses who reported to foremen. Three other types of laborers are also listed: carmen and shootmen who moved the ore out of the mines, workers who ran the aerial tram that transported the ore to the mill, and "women sorters," or pailliris, who separated ore from gangue. Foremen received 200 bolivianos per month, while pailliris, the lowest-paid laborers, earned 1 to 1.2 bolivianos per day; the daily wage for miners was 2.5 bolivianos. The situation in the mill was more complicated as there were diverse positions, such as mechanics, carpenters, and blacksmiths, which required more skill. These men earned 3 to 4 bolivianos per day, the same as the mill foremen. The lowest-paid workers were "boys" who earned only 0.5 or 0.8 bolivianos daily, followed by various types of unskilled laborers who received 1.5 and 2 bolivianos. The best compensated person in the mill complex was the storekeeper who, rather than earning profits from sales, was paid a salary between 150 and 200 bolivianos a month. In the end, though, Henderson recommended further examination

PRODUCTION IN THE AGE OF INDUSTRIALIZATION (1825–1964)   69

of the deposits to ensure that sufficient reserves existed to yield a return on any future investment.

While the extant documents provide a relatively clear view of mining operations from the perspective of management, they include no observations of the miners or the community in which they lived. In fact, a map of Porco published in the *Times* in 1912 depicts the mines, aerial ropeway, railroad, mill, and water source, but excludes the village. The only exception is Singewald and Miller's (1917, 330) dismissive description of Porco as a small Indian village that was "a most primitive and picturesque place, consisting entirely of crude houses built of boulders collected from the stream and hill slopes and covered with thatched roofs," an image that is not entirely accurate as a photograph taken a decade earlier shows the church as well as plastered and whitewashed buildings around the plaza (Wright 1907, 323). The only archaeological remains that might be associated with this period in the village's history consist of a tall adobe chimney that was built against an outcrop on the southwestern edge of town where it was used to roast tin ore. It is located next to a flat area that had been cleared to make an informal soccer field and is now the site of a museum. A woman who lives nearby recounted that her grandmother told her that foreigners had lived there in houses that looked plain from the outside but had curtains and elegant furniture within. Whether this was her grandmother's observation or a recollection of a story that she had heard from her ancestors is unclear. The fact that the entire area was leased by Porco Tin Mines Ltd. in 1912, and the facility was not depicted in the *Times* article published the same year suggests that it was used for processing tin somewhat before that date.

Archaeological research does provide some insight into the lives of Porqueños, particularly those who resided in nearby estancias. The establishment of rural homesteads around the village during the nineteenth and early twentieth centuries is suggested by data acquired during the archaeological survey of the area surrounding the village, including a small stretch of the San Juan River that lies within the municipality's jurisdiction. The pedestrian survey revealed that this area was occupied by households engaged in agro-pastoral pursuits at only two points in history: the Late Intermediate Period that preceded Inka occupation of the area and, much later, during the nineteenth and twentieth centuries. A total of ten estancias belonging to the second group were identified, and these cluster in two areas: near the streams descending from Cerros Apu and Huayna Porco and running north toward Agua de Castilla and along the Río San Juan. These sites are comprised of one to four rectangular structures constructed of stone or, more recently, adobes, and probably housed nuclear or small extended families. The domestic trash surrounding these homes includes plain and lead-glazed ceramics, bottle glass, and a variety of other items indicative of recent occupation such as tin cups, shoes, spoons, and recycled lard cans; one also contains fragments of *botijas* (Spanish storage jars) and Panamanian majolica, which indicate an early colonial component. Many are associated with small corrals, and the estancias in the San Juan drainage are located near abandoned agricultural terraces or small riverside fields encircled by stone walls.

The lack of an earlier agro-pastoral occupation and the temporal correspondence between the use of these sites and industrial mining in Porco strongly suggest that the latter enabled the former. While sustaining a purely agro-pastoral community in the vicinity of Porco would be difficult, if not impossible, miners could have raised llamas and crops to supplement their diets, sell in town, and provide a buffer against the vagaries of employment in the mines. Today, only the elderly reside in estancias for long periods, but in the past, prior to the availability of electricity, running water, and especially schools in Porco, entire families did so, at least for some parts of the year. The number of households who depended on both mining and agriculture for their livelihoods may never have been sizable, but the population would certainly have been larger than the archaeological data suggest both because currently occupied estancias were not inspected and because villagers today report maintaining estancias on ayllu land far beyond the area covered by the survey.

Langer (1996), in his discussion of nineteenth-century mining in Bolivia, divides mining operations into four types: (1) mines located in the high altiplano in areas that were sparsely populated by herders, (2) mines near large urban centers such as Potosí, (3) mines close to Indigenous communities, and (4) mines near haciendas. Porco, like the much better studied Huanchaco operation at the Pulacayo mines just to the west (Mitre 1981), falls into the first category, although the village appears to have been occupied by a small number of miners throughout the preceding century. But, while Pulacayo eventually became a company town, Porco took a different path. The miners there developed the very modest agrarian potential of its hinterlands, allowing the movement between mine and field characteristic of other areas where agricultural settlement preceded the establishment of mines.

As discussed in the previous chapter, the close interface between agriculture and mining in the Andes is reflected in belief systems as well as settlement patterns. The persistence of an agricultural cosmovision in the context of contemporary mining has generated a great deal of interest from scholars. Much of the debate has focused on the cult of El Tío, whose presence in industrial mines seems incongruous to outsiders and thus has received special

PRODUCTION IN THE AGE OF INDUSTRIALIZATION (1825–1964)

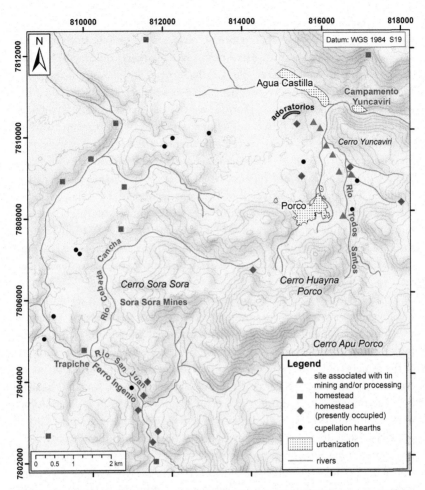

MAP 4 Location of homesteads and cupellation hearths identified during survey. Map by Brendan Weaver.

attention. El Tío is usually represented as a naked man with an erection, devil's horns, pointy ears, and cloven hooves, his arm outstretched and his mouth open to receive offerings of cigarettes, coca leaves, and alcohol. During the *k'araku*, a ritual performed twice a year and sometimes after serious accidents, miners also provide him with the heart of a sacrificed llama. These offerings are rooted in a principle of reciprocity that pervades many social and supernatural relations in the Andes. Work teams of miners make sacrifices to El Tío to encourage him to reveal his riches as well as to protect them from injury and death. Individuals may also make secret agreements with El Tío to enrich themselves.

June Nash (1979) conducted an ethnographic study of tin miners in Oruro during the 1970s, when political consciousness among Bolivian miners was at its peak. She was interested in how workers combined premises drawn from different realms—the family, agricultural communities, mining unions, the church—to produce worldviews that gave meaning to life and shaped action. Nash (1984) argues that rather than creating a syncretic belief system organized into a single hierarchy of ideas, Indigenous ways of thinking allow for the coexistence of apparently contradictory worldviews. She contends that potential dissonance is mitigated by temporally and spatially segregating different types of ritual practice; in Oruro, as in much of highland Bolivia, the veneration of Pachamama and El Tío takes place on Tuesdays, Fridays, the week of Carnival, and the month of August, while Sundays and saint's days are reserved for Christian worship. Spatially, rituals for El Tío such as weekly ch'allas and the k'araku are performed underground, while Christian rituals are restricted to aboveground contexts, or at least to level zero in the mine.

One of Nash's goals was to understand the emergence of a revolutionary ideology among workers who simultaneously held fast to beliefs and practices that some scholars and activists considered irrational. Employing an anthropological perspective shaped by dependency theory, she found that the ideology of the miners could not be understood in terms of dichotomies such as "modern" and "traditional." Nash (1984) argues, rather, that the worldviews held by these miners resulted from the specific historical and cultural conditions that prevailed in Bolivia, including its position as a dependent country. Ritual practices also shifted as the relations of production changed. Prior to the 1952 revolution, mineowners often participated in the k'araku, purchasing the sacrificial llamas and distributing gifts of jackets and skirts in exchange for lumps of high-grade ore. The reciprocal relations evoked by this exchange reduced the sense of alienation and motivated workers. Teams of miners were paid for the quality of the ore they extracted, and as a result, El Tío was venerated as a source of wealth. Witchcraft against competing teams was common. However, when Nash was living in Oruro in the 1970s, workers were compensated by tonnage rather than the mineral content of the ore they produced (Nash 1979, 162–63). The participation of managers in ritual activities had largely ceased, witchcraft was no longer apparent, and El Tío was regarded more as a protector against accidents than as a provider of wealth.

All scholars would agree that the relationship between miners and El Tío is an expression of a general understanding of reciprocity between people and the earth, represented by various spiritual entities, that was commonly held by agricultural communities in the Andes. Tristan Platt (1983) has also

PRODUCTION IN THE AGE OF INDUSTRIALIZATION (1825–1964)   73

argued for the continuity of more specific pre-Hispanic religious principles regarding the underworld, or *ukhupacha*, into the present. He analyzed rituals conducted in agrarian contexts as well as small and large mines in the province of Chayanta in northern Potosí to investigate the degree to which the consciousness of industrial miners was underwritten by or resulted from a rupture with traditional Andean precepts. Platt's (1983) findings suggest that religious notions originating in agricultural communities were transferred to the mines in a process that he calls "transformational continuity." He argues that the cult of El Tío is essentially a much-elaborated expression of the campesinos' belief in the subterranean divinity called Pachatata. In the mines, El Tío and his consort, Pachamama, bring wealth and well-being, just as Pachatata, along with Pachamama, are responsible for fecundity in the world of agriculture. Platt thus rejects Nash's notion that the ritual practices of Indigenous campesinos and miners are segregated by time and space since he found that in northern Potosí the principles undergirding the different practices were essentially the same. From this perspective, syncretism can be understood as the almost superficial incorporation of "foreign" elements into a belief system whose underlying structure remains constant.

While their work is shaped by different theoretical perspectives, Platt and Nash concur with regard to many elements of their analyses. They both also reject Michael Taussig's (1980) argument about the emergence and meaning of El Tío. Taussig compared the significance of the devil among cane workers in Colombia, where he conducted ethnographic research, with the cult of El Tío in the Andes, basing his understanding of the latter largely on the work of Nash as well as that of other scholars. He explicitly framed his analysis in terms of classic Marxism in which precapitalist modes of production are contrasted with capitalism. In the former, workers control the means of production and organize their own labor to produce goods that are valued in terms of their usefulness in different realms of life. Within capitalism, people work for the owners of the means of production in exchange for money, and the goods they produce are likewise valued in monetary terms. In the latter case these objects—as well as the labor invested in producing them—are regarded as commodities divorced from the actual social relations in which their production is embedded. According to Taussig (1980, 17), the devil represents "an evil and destructive way of ordering economic life . . . what it means to lose control over the means of production and be controlled by them" under particular historical conditions that, in the Andean case, were associated with the industrialization of mining.

Platt's (1983) assessment of Taussig's argument as reductionist and unrelated to concrete Andean realities is accurate. In particular, Taussig completely de-historicizes the Andean case by contrasting an idealized model of pristine peasant communities characterized by reciprocal relations with an evil capitalist mode of production, when, in fact, Andean Natives have been participating in the market for five centuries, sometimes with great success. However, Taussig does consider two aspects of El Tío that Platt and Nash do not examine in any detail: (1) his association with the extremely negative aspects of the Christian devil, and (2) the widespread development of similar belief systems among Indigenous Americans.

While the reciprocal relationship between miners and El Tío is clearly rooted in Andean precedent, his demonic features have developed since the Spanish conquest. Pachatata is a local name for the spirit that presides over ukhupacha, but this being is more generally known in the region as Supay. Based on a philological analysis of these terms Taylor (1980) argues that prior to the arrival of Europeans the word *supay* referred to an aspect of the soul of the dead that resided with other ancestral spirits from the same ethnic group in what is now known as ukhupacha. Over time, ukhupacha became the Christian hell where nonbelievers suffer for eternity, and Supay was transformed into the devil who presided over it. Taylor suggests that the process of demonization was driven largely by the Catholic Church, whose practitioners believed that the Native populace was being led astray by pagan beliefs inherited from their ancestors.

The equation of Supay with the Catholic devil and his transformation into El Tío must be understood as an Indigenous process that resulted in meaningful ritual practices under certain historical conditions. Taylor's linguistic research indicates that the demonization of Supay was already underway in the sixteenth century, and certainly the colonial mines would have facilitated the equation of ukhupacha and hell. Pre-Hispanic mining included the use of tunnels but usually took place in pits and trenches that were open to the sky. Under the Inkas, tunnels did not exceed 70 m in length, while by 1573 galleries in Cerro Rico had reached depths of 200 m (Salazar-Soler 1997b). These hot, dark spaces filled with sulfurous fumes and echoing with dripping water and falling rocks surely induced fear and suggested the European notion of the underworld. Their ownership by rapacious Spaniards with an insatiable desire for silver would also have contrasted with pre-Hispanic attitudes toward the precious metal. Inka control over forced laborers was not benign, but neither was it mercilessly exploitative. The Inkas provided housing, food, and tools for miners and required them to work only a few months of the year. Perhaps as important, they shared a similar cultural orientation with their subjects, one aspect of which was the use of silver to signify status and evoke religious beliefs rather than as a means of exchange. Silver was held in

PRODUCTION IN THE AGE OF INDUSTRIALIZATION (1825–1964)   75

high regard because of these connotations, not because it could be endlessly accumulated to acquire a vast array of goods and services, an entirely foreign practice in a society that lacked markets like the Inka Empire. However, even in the sixteenth century many Native workers participated in mining on behalf of their communities to earn the silver necessary for paying tribute, and some individuals also smelted silver and sold it in the ore market in Potosí. Indigenous participation in a mercantilist economy in which the use value of silver was subsumed by its exchange value thus occurred quite early.

Surprisingly, despite these profound changes in economic relations and working conditions, El Tío does not appear to have taken physical form under the Spanish regime. Systematic examination of a variety of documentary sources by Salazar-Soler and Langue (1997) and Orche and Amaré (2011) revealed no references to El Tío during colonial times, suggesting a rupture between the current cult and pre-Hispanic practice. Perhaps the campaigns against idolatry that were waged by the church during the seventeenth century inhibited the public expression of beliefs connecting Supay and mineral extraction (Orche and Amaré 2011), or maybe ritual centered on smaller, portable representations, such as the clay figurines of Pachatata and Pachamama used in Chayanta (Platt 1983) or those described by Salazar-Soler (1987) in the Julcani mine of Peru. Salazar-Soler and Langue (1997) and Absi (2005, 125–26) concur with Taussig (1980) that the cult of El Tío most likely emerged during the nineteenth century concurrent with the development of industrialized mining.

In addition to the physical instantiation of El Tío as a voracious Christian devil, another characteristic that sets him apart from Pachatata or Supay is that individuals can make a private bargain with him to increase their own wealth. Attributing personal accumulation to an individual's pact with the devil is widespread in Latin America and is generally understood by anthropologists to reflect concern with the abrogation of social ties in the community, family, or workplace, the kind of dissolution that tends to result from the penetration of capitalist relations. Van Vleet (2011), for instance, describes stories of devil possession that are associated with the conversion of individuals from Sull'kata, a village in northern Potosí, to evangelical Protestantism and their migration to the cities to pursue opportunities for economic advancement. In another case, Nugent (1996) provides a detailed historical account of the economic and political processes in Chachapoyas, Peru, that led community members to attribute the success of "foreign" merchants to contracts with the devil. Nugent makes the important point that these beliefs are not universal but arise in specific socioeconomic contexts. Unfortunately, information about El Tío in the nineteenth and early twentieth centuries is lacking, making it difficult to specify the conditions under which the cult emerged. Judging from ethnographically documented cases of similar phenomena, we would expect that the elaboration of the cult occurred in a period of rapid economic change during which teams of miners were compensated by the quality of the ore they produced. As Platt (1983) has argued, the ubiquity of the devil in different historical contexts cannot be mechanistically attributed just to precapitalist reactions to the market and in this case is rooted in long-standing beliefs in the underworld. However, the demonic, public nature of El Tío and his ability to enrich individuals at the cost of human life is relatively recent. As Taussig contends, El Tío conserves aspects of the reciprocal relations that undergirded the moral economy of Andean communities, but also acknowledges their abrogation—with attendant costs—when individual miners attempt to accrue wealth on their own.

The implications of this analysis for understanding the history of kajcheo and the specific historical trajectory of Porco are twofold. First, the cult of El Tío was most likely created by kajchas whose economic well-being depended on access to productive veins of ore. Reviews of colonial sources have revealed the absence of references to El Tío, thus suggesting that this process occurred during industrialization in the nineteenth century. Second, while El Tío is present in Porco, the veneration of illas is also important, perhaps because of the long-standing relationship between miners and agriculture. The fact that J. B. Williams, the Cornish foreman who lived in Porco in the 1880s, did not mention such a cult is suggestive. He worked in the mine on a regular basis and, given his pejorative descriptions of local rituals, would certainly have noted the presence of El Tío if he had encountered the cult; either it was hidden from him or was not practiced in Porco at that time.

Small-Scale Silver Production in the Shadow of Industrial Tin Mines

Rodríguez Ostria (1989) and others (Barragán 2015, 2017b; Platt 2014) have examined key aspects of small-scale production during the nineteenth century, but archaeological survey has revealed household production that occurred on an even more modest scale. The archaeological record at Porco indicates that despite the measures taken by companies to impose labor discipline, miners and their families continued to circumvent them in ways that are not described in historical documents, probably because it occurred at a household level that was not visible to outsiders. A pedestrian survey of the area surrounding the village revealed silver-processing features associated with rural estancias within easy walking distance of the mines. These features usually consisted of huayrachina remains on a nearby ridge as well as small cupellation furnaces and, in a couple of cases, stone-grinding platforms. Ten furnaces were located, most situated in quebradas or rock outcrops close to the homesteads described above; one was dated to the colonial period on the basis of surface ceramics, four were without diagnostic artifacts, and five were used during the twentieth century. Two of the latter were excavated. The best-preserved set of features is located at the confluence of the San Juan River and the Cebada Cancha, 7 km to the southwest of Porco. It consists of a huayrachina on a hill overlooking an occupied estancia, a cupellation furnace that was constructed against a large boulder near the home, and a small stone grinding platform for preparing the ore. Both the huayrachina and cupellation hearth were excavated, and a radiocarbon sample on charcoal from the former dates to the twentieth century (10 + 50 BP – Beta-177732; $\delta 13C = -25.5$ o/oo). Juan Equise, mentioned earlier as the current owner of this estancia, did not remember any of these features being used but had observed his parents smelting in a huayrachina on a ridge just outside Porco. The second furnace excavated is located approximately 4 km to the northwest of Porco in an unusual rock formation called Chaco Allana Kullko. An archaeomagnetic sample from this site yielded a date of 1870–90 (Lengyel et al. 2011). However, part of a steel truck spring, which was probably used to introduce silver ore into the hearth, was discovered next to the furnace. Since motor roads were first constructed near Potosí in the early 1900s this find suggests a somewhat later date.

The nature and spatial configuration of these features is very similar to silver production technology recently used by Cuiza in Pucapujra, and their association with rural households located in the shadow of an industrial mine suggests that they were employed in much the same manner. The estancias associated with cupellation hearths are located adjacent to bofedales or small patches of agricultural land. While more productive than the surrounding countryside, these resources were not sufficient to sustain entire households throughout the year. These families probably engaged in smelting as a means of diversifying their income from agro-pastoralist activities and wage labor in the mines. The ore could have been obtained legally by kajchas or palliris, or illicitly from miners who high-graded. The locations of most of the cupellation hearths in places that were hidden from view suggest the latter, although technical demands, namely, the need to support the narrow chimney of the furnace and to protect it from strong winds, may also have been factors in determining their placement. This interpretation is bolstered by the last published description of huayrachinas, written by Robert Peele, a

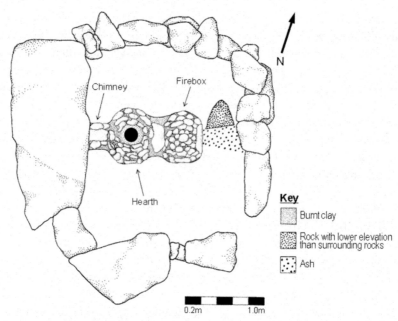

FIGURE 10 Excavated cupellation hearth located near the home of Juan Equise, at the confluence of the San Juan and Cebada Cancha Rivers. Illustration by the author.

North American mining engineer, at the end of the nineteenth century. Peele (1893) described their use near Porco and provided a photograph of a local man with two of them. He was most interested in the technical operation of the furnaces but noted that they were used to smelt ores that were obtained either by gleaning old mine tailings or by theft. He did not describe cupellation furnaces but was aware of their existence as he mentioned that "litharge obtained from the native cupelling furnaces" was a component of the charge. Although Peele produced the only detailed account of huayrachinas from this period, a number of engineers also observed functioning huayrachinas in southern Potosí, López, and northern Argentina during the late nineteenth century (Boman 1908, 554–55).

The huayrachinas described and illustrated by Peele are almost identical to the ones used by Cuiza a century later, but there are also some interesting differences. The ores smelted by the men observed by Peele included galena (lead sulfide) as well as high-grade silver ores such as silver sulfide and ruby silver. In contrast, Cuiza smelted lead sulfide mixed with litharge in order to produce pure lead metal that was later used in the cupellation hearth to refine silver ore (Cohen 2008; Van Buren and Mills 2005). In both cases, though, the metallurgists preferred argentiferous to pure galena because it augmented

FIGURE 11 Photograph of man with huayrachinas near Porco (Peele 1893, public domain).

the amount of silver produced during the subsequent refining stage. Another difference is that the furnaces measured by Peele were a bit larger than those constructed by Cuiza (Van Buren and Mills 2005, table 2). These divergences in form and practice suggest that high-grade silver ore was more abundant or more accessible in the nineteenth century than it was in the first decade of the twenty-first century and thus would have yielded a greater return for the time spent smelting.

Labor Mobilization and Mining Unions

From the inception of industrial mining in the mid-nineteenth century to the Great Depression, Bolivian miners protested many of the same types of maltreatment: poverty-level wages, long shifts, abusive supervisors, and high prices in company stores. However, the conceptualization of these problems and the nature of the protests changed as modern management practices replaced patron-client relationships, and workers—especially the small core of specialized wage laborers who resided in urban centers such as Potosí and Oruro—were exposed to Marxist analyses of their place in the world economy (Lora 1977; Smale 2010). The transformation of labor relations occurred during the 1920s and 30s, concurrent with the harsh economic conditions created by the Depression and the Chaco War (1932–35). It was during this decade that the militant mining unions for which Bolivia is famous were born.

The onset of World War I created an economic crisis in the mining sector that was followed by two decades of instability, with sudden downturns followed by recoveries, all of which were caused by shifts in international demand. Drops in the price of tin led to wage depression and massive layoffs that ignited protests by the miners. These were often forcefully quelled by police at the behest of mining administrators. Trade organizations that were independent and to the left of the governing Liberal Party began to emerge after World War I as a result of these conditions as well as ideological influences from Bolivian intellectuals and interaction with radical Chilean mine and railroad workers (Lora 1977, 108, 117; Smale 2010, 69).

On May 1, 1923, a transformative event in Bolivian labor history occurred in Uncía, the location of Patiño's most productive mines. After years of conflict and many attempts to organize, workers founded the Federación Obrera Central de Uncía (FOCU). The Tin Company of Llallagua and Patiño's other large enterprise, La Salvadora Mining Company in Catavi, refused to recognize the federation, and the miners prepared to strike. In mid-May the army was deployed to the area where it was well housed and generously fed by the mining companies (Smale 2010, 127). The FOCU, in an attempt to get backing from labor organizations throughout Bolivia, sent emissaries to federations in all the major cities, a move that prompted the government to declare a national state of siege. On the morning of June 2, the police and military began to arrest federation members, including its president, and a crowd gathered in the plaza to demand their release. By evening their ranks had been swelled by miners ending their shift, and the crowd became more vociferous. Although accounts differ about exactly what happened next, witnesses agree that the military opened fire with a machine gun, killing at least six people and injuring ten. The federation's leaders were imprisoned or deported, and the organization eventually dissolved (Lora 1977, 118–27).

The Uncía massacre quickly came to symbolize the struggle of labor to overcome the combined forces of capitalism and the Bolivian state and epitomized the violent oppression of miners by government forces that occurred episodically over the next few decades, most notably at the Siglo XX-Catavi mining complex in 1942 where an attack on striking miners by the army left

PRODUCTION IN THE AGE OF INDUSTRIALIZATION (1825–1964)   81

hundreds of workers dead. In reaction, miners formed the Union Federation of Bolivian Mine Workers (FSTMB), which became the vanguard of organized labor in Bolivia for the subsequent four decades. In 1946 the FSTMB, led by members of the Trotskyist Revolutionary Workers' Party (POR), issued the Thesis of Pulacayo which called for an armed revolution led by the working class, among other, more specific demands. In 1951 the reformist Nationalist Revolutionary Movement (MNR), allied with POR, won the national election, but the ruling military regime annulled the vote. Thousands of armed workers, many of them miners, marched to the capital demanding that the elected government be instated. The Bolivian National Revolution of 1952 had begun; within three days the military had been ousted, and the MNR, with Victor Paz Estenssoro as president, took control (Klein 1971). Radical changes ensued during his first term, with agrarian reform, universal suffrage, and nationalization of the major tin mines among them.

Six months after the revolution began, Paz Estenssoro established the Bolivian Mining Company (COMIBOL) to direct operations at the 163 mines that had been nationalized. COMIBOL was not, however, just another government agency that administered the mining sector, but a twelve-year experiment in worker co-management. The FSTMB was charged with representing workers' interests; laid-off miners were employed, wages were increased, social benefits were improved, and company stores were subsidized. However, the lack of investment in industrial improvements that had begun under the tin barons and continued under COMIBOL, combined with large financial outlays, the loss of technical expertise with the start of nationalization, and other factors resulted in the company being on the verge of collapse by 1960 (Burke 1987). The experiment lasted only until 1964 when a military coup terminated the MNR government, and the co-management of COMIBOL was abolished. The next two decades in Bolivia were dominated by military juntas, and, ironically, it was only after Paz Estensor was reelected in 1985 and responded to the crash in global tin prices that COMIBOL was gutted, though not entirely eliminated.

Neither documents nor oral history suggest that workers in Porco engaged in the protests and unionization efforts that characterized other mining centers. The reasons for this are difficult to determine. Three factors, though, may have mitigated such participation. First, as Henderson's (1916) assessment of Porco's potential suggests, tin deposits, and thus corporate investment, were small in scale. Second, a description of the Porco mines in the early 1960s states that they had been worked by the *pirquín* system, another term for small-scale mining or kajcheo (Contreras and Pacheco 1989, 61–62). This practice did not tend to foster protest or unionization. Third, the miners

FIGURE 12 Recently erected statue in Porco of a miner breaking his chains, with a rifle in one hand and a hammer in the other. Photograph by the author.

who worked in Porco were still closely connected to the countryside, a factor that, as historians have argued, inhibited the development of an independent proletariat that recognized their predicament based on the type of Marxist analysis that was disseminated in larger mining centers. This history is indirectly reflected in the public art displayed in Porco. Almost every mining center in southern Bolivia has a sculpture of a miner with a pneumatic drill or hammer in one hand and a rifle in the other that was erected to commemorate the crucial role played by miners in the 1952 revolution. However, Porco's main plaza lacked statuary of any kind until the transformation of the village during the recent commodity boom when a statue of a man performing the traditional condor dance was placed on the north side. Only in recent years has a figure of a miner with a gun and hammer been installed on top of Mullupunku. This suggests that the evocation of the national revolution has only become important recently, perhaps with the influx of miners from other parts of the country.

Mining Cooperatives

Large-scale tin mining was a very profitable business in Bolivia during the first decades of the twentieth century, but symptoms of decline began with the world economic crisis of 1929 (Capriles Villazón 1977). Mines closed, and the Chaco War against Paraguay (1932–35) deepened the recession. Unemployment was rampant, and returning soldiers could not find formal work in the mines. To make a living many turned to independent mining as well as outright ore theft (Absi 2005, 27). Barragán (2017b) has examined the context in which kajcheo came to be recognized by the state during the five years following the war's end, a process that set the stage for the development of cooperatives in succeeding years. Key to this was the Constituent Assembly of 1938. Participants included a variety of workers and intellectuals who, in the wake of the war, shared a critique of individualist liberalism and the socioeconomic power wielded by the tin barons. They argued for a regulatory, corporatist state that acted on behalf of social interests, especially those of former combatants and workers. In this context, the question of what to do with the miners of Potosí was resolved by leasing abandoned mines to kajchas within a system controlled by the state, resulting in first the development of syndicates, and then the creation of cooperatives over the following decades.

Absi's (2014) study of the very first mining cooperatives in Potosí argues that these coops were initially created not by the unemployed, but by kajchas who worked under company auspices. As during other periods of Andean history, miners were engaged in a variety of ways during the first half of the twentieth century. For example, the Compañia Minera Unificada de Potosí not only employed salaried workers but also hired miners to accomplish specific tasks through monthly contracts; for instance, drillers were sometimes paid for the selective extraction of ore from a specific vein. In addition, the company engaged kajchas who were assigned a particular ore face or waste heap (in the case of pailliris) and required to give one third of the concentrated ore they extracted to the corporation, and to sell the rest to the company at rates that were below market price. In some respects, these kajchas were like other laborers in that they were assigned a place to work and were required to clock in. They also defended the interests of the companies they worked for because their patronage allowed them access to productive ore faces. So, for example, when tunnels intersected in the honeycombed workings of Cerro Rico, kajchas would violently resist the incursions of miners from other companies. However, the struggle to control the commercialization of the ore they produced in order to earn a fair price led to the formation of the first mining cooperatives in Bolivia. More commonly, however, cooperatives were created by the unemployed.

The first mining cooperative in Porco, Cooperativa Minera Veneros, was given rights to the alluvial deposits along Río Todos Santos, a small stream that originates in Apu Porco. Todos Santos has been visibly altered by both large- and small-scale mining. Contaminated by acid rock drainage from the large workings above, the water is described as "sour" and undrinkable by residents. The archaeological survey identified six sites related to the small-scale extraction of tin along the banks of the Todos Santos. Three of these are

FIGURE 13 Facility for dressing alluvial tin ore located during survey near Todos Santos River. Photograph by the author.

tunnels driven into the alluvium to extract tin, two are complexes for washing and sorting the tin-containing sediment, and one is a large grinding stone associated with waste generated by triturating tin ore. In addition, the remains of a 250-m-long canal were found along the western side of the river below which the sediment was scoured to bedrock. A local resident reported that this had been done to hydraulically remove and sort tin-containing deposits, but how exactly this was accomplished is not clear. Hydraulic mining was a well-known strategy for recovering ores from alluvial deposits in western North America but was usually employed in areas with abundant water. Its use by cooperative miners in Porco was innovative but environmentally destructive, although not nearly as problematic as the drainage of acidified water from the hard-rock mines in Apu Porco.

As discussed in the previous chapter, the formation of Veneros was quickly followed by the establishment of Cooperativa Minera Porco; Cooperativa Huayna Porco was formed almost thirty years later. They were created by unemployed miners rather than kajchas, and both exploit hard-rock deposits that contain a complex of zinc, tin, and silver.

Conclusion

The two centuries following independence were marked by enormous changes in Bolivia's mining sector, with a brief resurgence in silver extraction followed by the production of industrial metals—first tin, then zinc, and most recently "complejo," a mixture of the three minerals. This shift was accompanied by the rapid adoption of industrial techniques and, during the 1930s, the emergence of unions shaped by a Trotskyist vision of labor and social change. The process culminated in the 1952 Revolution that saw unionized miners on the vanguard of a radical restructuring of the sector which included nationalization of the largest mines and the institution of worker co-management. The experiment ended in 1964 with the first in a succession of military regimes, followed, in the 1980s, by the implementation of neoliberal policies by elected governments.

Small-scale mining, both legal and illicit, generated a large portion of the silver and tin that was recovered in Bolivia between independence and the Depression and supplied households with an important source of cash income. These ores were recovered by kajchas who worked in a variety of ways but, perhaps most frequently, within a share-cropping system in which *rescatiris*, or middlemen, provided advances, and then, in exchange, received a portion of the ore as well as rights to purchase the remainder. Cooperatives

86 CHAPTER 2

arose during the 1930s, with membership increasing as each successive wave of unemployment followed the rise and inevitable fall of mineral prices. Over time they absorbed most of the miners who in prior years would have become kajchas; independent, small-scale mining thus became institutionalized and, eventually, recognized by the state. Perhaps surprisingly, it has been the co-operatives rather than unionized workers who are employed by large mining companies that have engaged in violent protests over the last few decades; however, while assuming the aggressive stance characteristic of the militant unions of years past, cooperatives lack their social and political vision.

The relationship between small- and large-scale mining over the last two centuries was characterized by both mutual interdependence and tension. During the nineteenth century large-scale operators' need for labor and low-risk strategies for exploiting less productive deposits forced them to accept ore-sharing as a means of attracting workers. A reserve labor force with mining skills could also be tapped when high mineral prices warranted an increase in formal employment, a factor that was increasingly important in the subsequent century. On the other hand, small-scale miners struggled for access to high-quality mineral deposits. To a large extent they depended on the physical infrastructure left behind by previous mining operations, and for legal access they required leases or other agreements with mineowners. This relationship developed almost immediately after the Spanish conquest, and as will be seen in the following chapters, Bolivian independence did not radically transform it.

3

Silver Extraction Under the Colonial Regime (1573–1825)

THE CONQUEST OF PERU IN 1532 was a more protracted affair than is usually portrayed due to resistance by Native Andeans as well as ongoing conflict among Spaniards. By the 1560s, much of the political strife had been quelled, but the rich surface deposits of silver from Potosí that had filled the coffers of the Spanish treasury since their discovery in 1545 were exhausted. In response to this crisis, King Philip II appointed Francisco Toledo as fifth viceroy of Peru, an official who is recognized as one of Spain's most skilled colonial administrators, and one whose policies had a profound impact on Andean communities. His mandate was to create a stable political and economic order that would facilitate the generation of revenue that could be used to fund the colonial government as well as various enterprises in Europe, most of them bellicose in nature. The reforms implemented in the 1570s by Toledo systematized the extraction of resources from the Native population and resulted in a dramatic reorganization of the political economy of the southern Andes. The creation of institutions that provided the framework for resource extraction during much of the colonial period has been the focus of an important body of scholarly research (Bakewell 1984a; Cole 1985; Mumford 2012; Tándeter 1993; Wernke 2007), with somewhat less attention paid to its corollary, namely the development of practices intended to circumvent the new economic regime (Assadourian 1980; Barragán 2015; Tándeter 1981a; Zulawski 1987). The different scales of production present at Porco, including the development of kajcheo, and the diverse types of technology associated with them are the focus of this chapter.

Viceroy Toledo implemented two policies that were key to rejuvenating the declining mining sector: he encouraged the adoption of the patio process,

87

and he institutionalized the mita, a forced labor draft that was loosely based on Inka precedent (Assadourian 1992). The combination of new technology and a constant supply of cheap labor enabled Potosí to become one of the most productive silver mines in the world. The patio process was a method for extracting silver by combining it with mercury to form an amalgam; the mercury was purchased from the state which controlled the distribution of this crucial input. The ore was first pulverized in an *ingenio*, or stamp mill and then combined with mercury in stone-lined bins or a patio, after which the mercury was removed, leaving pure silver behind (Craig 1993). This process was suitable for extracting silver from large quantities of low-grade ores, and its adoption quickly led to the revitalization of silver production in Potosí (Assadourian 1992).

The construction and operation of a mill complex was costly, although the price varied depending on the type of technology used. As Gil Montero and Téreygeol (2021; Kennedy 2021) make clear, ingenios could be composed of different components depending on the place, time, and nature of the deposits being worked, as well as the financial capacity of the owner. In Potosí, where reservoirs had been constructed to power the mills, the grinding mechanism consisted of a large masonry housing, or *cárcamo*, for the wheel to which a substantial wooden axle was attached. As the wheel rotated, cams lifted vertical shafts affixed with metal-shod stone stamp heads and then released them. The falling stamp heads crushed the ore on top of a flat stone anvil. In addition to the mill, the owner—called an *azoguero* from the Spanish word for mercury —had to build an entire complex that supported the technical process as well as the workers and administrators who engaged in it. As Assadourian (1992) argued, azogueros could obtain all the necessary inputs, with the exception of iron, from internal, rather than European sources. Wood, however, was a scarce resource on the altiplano, and as industrial and domestic demand for fuel increased the countryside was stripped of the few trees it could support (Gade 1999, 68; Moore 2010); in 1599 a visitor reported that no trees existed within twelve leagues (approximately 68 km) of Potosí (Ocaña 1969 [c. 1599–1608], 167). The single largest expense in the construction of an ingenio was, in fact, the wooden axle of the waterwheel made from large timbers that were hauled from the lowlands to mining centers by Indians or oxen. According to Bakewell (1984b), in the early 1600s a single axle cost 1,300 to 1,650 pesos, the equivalent of a medium-size house, while the price of an entire ingenio ranged between 10,000 and 50,000 pesos. The prohibitively high cost of mill complexes resulted in the concentration of this technology in the hands of a few wealthy azogueros, almost all of whom were of European origin.

Toledo's second goal was to alleviate the labor shortage in the mining industry. By the time he arrived, some Indigenous communities were already sending members to Porco and Potosí to acquire silver for making tribute payments. Toledo expanded and regularized this system. The new regulations were first implemented in 1573 but underwent revisions over time. The system required native communities in sixteen *corregimientos*, or provinces, that extended from the outskirts of Cuzco, south to what is now the southern border of Bolivia, to send between 13 and 17 percent of their adult male population to Potosí annually. They were recruited by their kurakas, Native leaders who were in charge of *parcialidades* that consisted of one or more ayllus. A little less than two-thirds of the mitayos were assigned to mills and the remainder to the mines; in both cases they were allowed two weeks of "rest" for every week they worked, although the rest period was usually spent engaged in wage work or the sale of products they had brought from home (Gil Montero and Zagalsky 2016).

The mita was based on the assumption that the social landscape that Toledo observed in the 1570s would continue to exist unchanged under the new economic system that he helped establish and in the face of population loss resulting from introduced diseases, exploitation, and conflict. One of the unexpected and most disruptive consequences was the constant drain on the population and resources of the rural communities that supplied mitayos. Entire families laden with agricultural products for subsistence or sale in Potosí accompanied mitayos, providing yet a further subsidy to the mining industry (Assadourian 1980, 36; Stavig 2000). Worse, the demand for labor was constant even in the face of declining rural populations, forcing poorer community members who could not pay for substitutes to return to the mines more frequently. Those who did report for the mita were required to work longer hours and often for two weeks rather than one; family members frequently had to help men complete tasks that could not be finished within the allotted time (Tándeter 1991). As a result, many mitayos fled to other villages where they were exempt from the mita, and others remained in the mining center after their turn was up to work as "free" laborers (Cole 1985, 26). These men, called *mingas*, were paid more than forced laborers and were usually assigned to more skilled and less dangerous jobs, but as Zagalsky (2014) notes, mitayos frequently worked as mingas during their two weeks of rest. Both these strategies for avoiding the mita, however, led to further demographic declines in the countryside.

Toledo included two related provisions to supplement the low weekly wage paid to mitayos: the right to work in the mines for their own benefit on weekends, and the right to a portion of high-quality ore (Cole 1985, 7–17).

These practices refer to kajcheo—although the term was not used at the time—and were intended to accomplish the same goal, namely, augmenting a low monetary wage with silver extracted by the wage worker. García de Llanos, in the dictionary of mining terms he compiled in the first decade of the seventeenth century, referred to this practice as *achurani*, from the Quechua verb meaning "to give to each his own portion or that which belongs to him" (Llanos 2009 [1609], 2). Each mitayo was allowed to take a small load of ore, an *achura*, that weighed approximately two *arrobas*, or 23 kg. Llanos noted that while common in earlier times the practice had largely disappeared by the 1590s because of the decline in the quality of silver deposits. In the decades after he wrote, however, the illicit form of kajcheo became a key strategy of extraction and generated much conflict in Potosí.

Capital requirements for the construction of ingenios meant Native people lost control over the productive process and were reduced to forced or wage labor in the same settings where they had once been independent workers. Azogueros became the powerful nucleus of an emerging bourgeoisie who appropriated the wealth generated by Native labor and provided a portion of it to the Crown in the form of a tax referred to as the "royal fifth." That, at least, was how the system was supposed to work and, for the most part, did. From the beginning, however, Native Andeans, as well as Spaniards, found ways to circumvent or exploit the new order.

The Colonial System in Porco

The vast silver deposit in Potosí is said to have been discovered in 1544 by Diego Guallpa, a *yanacona*, or personal retainer, who worked for a European mineowner smelting silver in Porco. Indigenous miners and European overseers from Porco were among the first to join the rush to Potosí, and the status of the earlier center declined as the lucrative new mines became the focus of the imperial economy. However, the deposits at Porco continued to be worked during the following century and a half by both large- and small-scale producers, and the diversity of technologies used to produce silver reflects these differences in scale as well as experimentation with new techniques.

Probably the largest seventeenth-century investment in Porco was made by Antonio López de Quiroga, a fabulously wealthy mine and mill owner. His most lucrative holdings were in Potosí, but in about 1669 he decided to include Porco in his investments. Apparently, the mines there had been abandoned for quite some time because of flooding, but López de Quiroga, inspired by the riches said to have been recovered by the Pizarros, believed

EXTRACTION UNDER THE COLONIAL REGIME (1573–1825)   91

that he could make them workable again by constructing an adit, a gently inclined horizontal tunnel that would drain and provide access to the silver deposits. Over the course of twenty years he poured over 300,000 pesos into its construction, and in his attempt to advance the work he is credited with the first use of blasting powder in an American silver mine. However, the money he spent and the technological innovation he applied resulted in only a modest return on his investment (Bakewell 1988, 74–76). Evidence of this enterprise was not identified in Porco, most likely because the adit was reused by subsequent miners. There are no known archaeological traces of mining activity in Porco during the following century.

However, insight into Spanish production in Porco during the late sixteenth and first decades of the seventeenth century can be derived from both the historical and archaeological records. Luis Capoche's (1959 [1585]) well-known account of Potosí and a later set of unpublished documents that list the assignment of mitayos in the first decades of the seventeenth century (A.G.I. Charcas 55, ff. 1–18) provide information about mineowners, Native workers, and infrastructure during this period. In 1585 Capoche sent a report describing the history and current condition of Potosí and surrounding mines to the new viceroy, Hernando de Torres y Portugal. Like many other Potosinos, he was motivated by chauvinistic pride in the city's past and a desire to preserve its crucial place in the Peruvian economy. As a clear-headed millowner, though, he was also aware of the way in which other Spaniards would depict Potosí as teetering on the brink of collapse in an attempt to extract more mitayos and lower mercury prices from the Viceroy (Hanke 1959, 47–48).

By the time Capoche wrote, many of the mines in Porco had already flooded, and the number of vecinos, or Spanish residents, had declined from about one hundred to forty (Capoche 1959 [1585], 125). He described the town as financially ruined because of the poor yield of silver ore, and noted that the smelting furnaces no longer functioned, although Indians continued to operate a few huayrachinas. He did, however, mention that two mills had been constructed in a nearby quebrada and operated year-round because of the good water supply. Capoche's account includes lists of mineowners in Potosí and other nearby mining centers. In Porco he identified three veins in which claims, measured in *varas* (units about 80 cm in length), had been made. This is probably the mine now called Hundimiento that is located on the northern flank of Huayna Porco, just to the southeast of the village. "Hundimiento" suggests ruination, and according to a story recounted by Bautista Ecos (personal communication 2018), the mine got its name from an event that occurred during colonial times. A miner was required to work during the fiesta of Misericordia, a celebration that took place on the second Sunday after Easter. He told the owner that he could not work that day because he was in charge of the fiesta, but the owner insisted. So, according to the legend, his wife and relatives carried out his obligations, and after the mass there was the usual procession from the church to the hill of Santiago, which is between the village and the mine. Just as the procession reached the top, the mine collapsed, killing hundreds of people working within, and a black bull emerged from the swirling dust and ran toward the west (or north—people disagree about the direction) taking the silver with him. Ever since, the mine has been called Hundimiento and the area to the west of it, Misericordia. The legend speaks directly to the conflict between the demands of the Spaniards and the ritual obligations of the miners who resisted having their social and spiritual lives subsumed by claims on their labor. The refusal of the owner to recognize the vital importance of the worker's involvement in a community ritual resulted in a catastrophe for all.

Capoche (1959 [1585]) described seven holdings in what is probably now Hundimiento, two of which belonged to the Crown and the church, respectively, and a third to Francisca Pizarro, Hernando's niece. The rest were owned by Diego Beltrán, Juan del Campo, Juan Vejel and company, and Diego Alvarez. These mines ranged from four to one hundred *estados*, or approximately 8.5 to 213 m in depth. Two other veins—the "vetas de Zoras" had been recently discovered by an Indigenous man named Alonso Zora, who may have been from the Soras, a group located to the north of Lake Poopó, and who had died sometime prior to 1585. This deposit most likely corresponds to a ridge now called Sora Sora 4 km to the southwest of the village. Capoche listed thirty-five holdings claimed by seventeen individuals as well as the Crown in these two veins. He described four as pit mines and others that were worked by shafts or where shafts were under construction. Only three, though, had been excavated to any depth, probably because the claims were new. With only one exception—the younger siblings of Alonso Zora—the owners were European men.

Variation in the number of varas owned by individuals was pronounced. Not including the Crown, who held 240 varas, the combined length of mining claims ranged from 10 to 150. These fall into three categories: large claims ranging from 60 to 150 varas, medium holdings between 35 and 60 varas, and small mines of 20 varas or less. The latter were held primarily by men who shared claims with others, while the larger holdings were owned by individuals who had their own mines as well as shared claims. Similar diversity in the size of operations is found in the distribution of mitayos to vecinos in Porco that was ordered by Viceroy Montesclaros twenty-nine years later.

By 1600 the number of vecinos residing in Porco had declined to just thirty (Ocaña 1969 [c. 1599–1608], 182), and those who remained com-

EXTRACTION UNDER THE COLONIAL REGIME (1573–1825)   93

plained that they were being impoverished by the shortage of mitayos. Correspondence regarding their complaints and official efforts to augment the mita assignment was identified in the Archivo General de Indias in Seville and transcribed by Ana María Presta (A.G.I. Charcas 55, ff.1–18). The earlier documents include three reassignments of mitayos that were made by Viceroy Montesclaros between 1614 and 1615 as part of his broader attempt to increase tax revenues (Latasa Vasallo 1998). These redistributions suggest that silver mining was still an important activity in Porco during the first decades of the seventeenth century, although on a modest scale. The documents include the names of recipients, the number of mitayos assigned, their ethnic group, and, in the case of the first reallotment, descriptions of some of the recipients' holdings. Twenty-three vecinos were assigned a total of 486 mitayos over the course of three distributions. By far the largest number, 101, was allotted to Jhoan de Estrada, who was described as having the most substantial operation in Porco. His holdings included a sixteen-stamp mill; furnaces for smelting high-grade ore; additional furnaces to process *lamas*, the finely ground amalgam; a *desacedero de hierro* for pulverizing iron; and mines. Diego Beltran received the second largest contingent, sixty-seven, for work in his two-stamp mill. Beltran was also the only vecino listed in the 1614 document who had holdings in the first Porco mine as well as the vetas de Zoras. The mills owned by Beltran and Estrada were described as being located in the Quilcata Valley, a name that refers to a stretch of the San Juan River situated approximately 8 km to the west of the village of Porco; today a small settlement named Khelkhata is located just where the river bends toward the east and flows in the direction of Ferro Ingenio. Two other vecinos, Bartolome de Belasco and Francisco Ruis Cavello, owned stamp mills in Agua de Castilla as well as mines, and received forty-seven and forty-four mitayos, respectively. Their mills were probably located in Yuncaviri at the same place where a mill for processing silver and tin ores was constructed in the nineteenth century. These four mills are the only ones mentioned in the documents. Three other vecinos were assigned twenty-three to twenty-five mitayos each for mine labor and the processing of ore; allotments to the remaining men averaged a little less than seven mitayos apiece, and the nature of their holdings was not indicated. Clearly, the category of "large-scale" mining enterprises is itself an abstraction in that it encompasses operations of very different sizes. All these individuals, however, enjoyed an entitlement to subsidized labor provided by the state, and many would have augmented this workforce with wage laborers.

These documents also provide detailed information about the ethnic composition of the mitayos assigned to Porco. The largest contingent in the

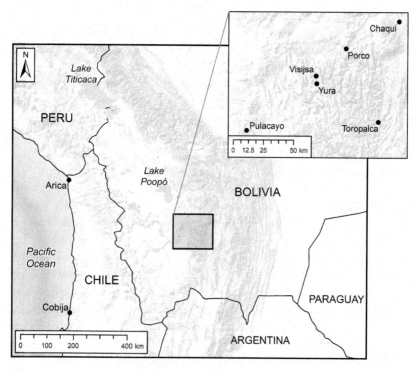

MAP 5 Location of key places mentioned in text. Map by Brendan Weaver.

redistributions of 1614 and 1615 was from Carangas (129 or 38 percent), a few hundred kilometers to the northwest of Porco. An additional 136 (41 percent) came from nearby provinces: Acachaques (present-day Achacachi) on the southeastern edge of Lake Titicaca, Quillacas and Asanaques to the south and southeast of Lake Poopó, and Soras, Casayas, and Capinota to its north. Smaller numbers of workers were assigned from communities closer to Porco, including eighteen men (5 percent) from Colo, Caquina, and Picachures 55 km to the north of Potosí; twenty-six (8 percent) from Chaqui, which is 25 km to the east of Potosí; and fourteen (4 percent) from Visijsa. The Visijsas were an ethnic group that occupied the area around Porco at the time of the conquest and were reduced, or resettled, by the Spaniards in the towns of Chaqui, Toropalca, and Yura, the latter just 34 km to the south of Porco. The only mitayos who came from lowland areas were ten from Cochabamba (3 percent), which is located roughly 250 km to the north; these people were probably associated with highland groups that controlled agricultural land in the lower elevation province.

The redistributions made by Montesclaros constituted a minor revision of the official, normative framework for labor recruitment established by Toledo that was already being subverted in practice. The documents suggest the ways in which the system was distorted by Spaniards seeking access to state subsidies. In 1625 the vecinos in Porco reported that of the 623 mitayos who had been assigned to the mining center by Toledo, only 250 were showing up, despite the redistributions that Montesclaros had made a decade earlier. Apparently, some were being redirected by officials in Potosí to participate in the mita there, and others had been temporarily diverted to work in the countryside but had never been returned. Contending that Toledo had personally visited Porco and had made the original assessment on the basis of its richness and importance, the vecinos requested a royal cedula requiring that the assignments made by Montesclaros be carried out (A.G.I. Charcas 55, ff. 1–2). They also argued that the repartimiento, or distribution of mitayos, to all mining centers should be equitable, rather than favoring Potosí. While the specific circumstances of Porco's decline relative to Potosí's success were unique, the case reflects a broader struggle over labor that was occurring throughout the Andes. Viceroys privileged the assignment of mitayos to mines and mills and resisted their diversion to other enterprises to maintain the flow of silver to the Crown. Spaniards with businesses outside the mining sector, however, often attempted to augment their workforce with these government-subsidized laborers (Gil Montero and Zagalsky 2016).

A few hints in the correspondence with Montesclaros as well as in Capoche's report suggest that Porco may have attracted Spaniards engaged in the diversion of mitayos into other enterprises, specifically the transport of goods between Potosí and the Pacific port of Arica. In his description of the village, Capoche stated that clothing and other merchandise off-loaded in Arica passed by Porco on its way to Potosí, and that many of the mitayos assigned to the mines ordinarily worked moving these goods, presumably by llama caravan. He may have been referring to the mitayos from Carangas as the communities in that province were dedicated to llama herding and transport (Medinacelli González 2013), and the road to Arica passed through it (Beltrán 2016). The Carangas took full advantage of their pastoral skills and geographic location after the Spanish conquest. They owned the only good grazing land on the road between Potosí and Porco, in Condoriri, as well as pastures near Tollojchi (Nicolas 2018, 95).

Capoche also noted, with, perhaps, mock surprise, that four or five wealthy men who earned their living by transporting merchandise, mercury, and silver bars between Potosí and Arica happily resided in Porco despite the particularly harsh climate. And just before he described the vecinos who held claims near that settlement, he stated "At present the mines that are being exploited in Porco are the ones that I list here, or at least with this title they are given Indians" (Hanke 1959, 126). In fact, the reassignment of mitayos described in the 1615 document indicates that mitayos were withdrawn from three individuals (including Doña Teodora de Bargas, the only woman on the list of recipients) because they did not reside in the village. The wealthy Spaniards who lived in Porco, then, were conveniently located close to highland pasture as well as the road connecting Arica with Potosí, had access to mitayos who specialized in moving products by llama caravan, and could divert them to work transporting goods without attracting official notice.

While Spaniards manipulated the mita for their own profit, Indigenous individuals as well as entire communities attempted to avoid it altogether. The monetization of the mita, a process by which Natives subject to forced labor could pay for a replacement, emerged almost immediately after the Toledan reforms, and by the first decades of the seventeenth century one-third to one-half of the annual quota was met by the provision of silver in lieu of laborers. These *indios de plata*, or silver Indians, as they were called, could be used to hire mingas to work in the mining industry, or the money could simply be pocketed for other purposes (Zagalsky 2014). Either way, the practice represented a direct monetary subsidy of private Spanish enterprises by Indigenous communities but also enabled Natives to avoid the worst abuses of the colonial system. Saignes (1985a) showed that the degree to which this strategy was employed varied across ethnic groups. The difference can be seen even within the Charka federation, a loose coalition of ethnic groups that occupied much of the central part of Bolivia at the time of the conquest. This large population was divided into two halves: the Qaraqara, who resided closest to the mining centers, and the Charka, who lived to the north.

By 1617, the Qaraqara provided only 17 percent of all the mitayos demanded of them in person and paid for the rest in silver. In contrast, the more distant Charka met almost all their obligations in labor. Saignes (1985b) attributed this pattern to the different financial resources available to these communities and their kurakas, which, in turn, can be related to their proximity to Potosí; populations close to mining centers usually had the opportunity to earn enough revenue by selling products or their labor in these urban markets to meet their mita obligations as well as a separate tribute that was levied in silver. For instance, a record of agricultural production by the Visijsa settled in Chaqui indicates that by 1611 nine of the eleven ayllus were producing garlic, cabbage, and barley for the market (del Río 1995a). Other Qaraqara communities relied on the sale of wild resources to acquire funds.

EXTRACTION UNDER THE COLONIAL REGIME (1573–1825)   97

The 1610 document analyzed by Saignes (1985b) states that the Qaraqara obtained silver by selling firewood, charcoal, and *ichu*, a bunch grass used for thatch and kindling.

Another common strategy for evading the mita was flight, or migration, a subject that has attracted a great deal of scholarly attention due to its effects on the organization of rural as well as urban life. Natives living in the catchment of the Potosí mita often fled to Indigenous communities at lower elevations that were exempt from forced labor. There they became *forasteros*, outsiders who, in theory, no longer had the obligations and rights associated with ayllu membership and thus lost access to land. Many migrated to mining centers such as Oruro, which were not assigned mitayos and where the pay was often better than in Potosí. Still others became *yanaconas* who forfeited the rights to community resources conferred by kinship in exchange for being free of the labor tax. Yanaconas worked as agricultural laborers on Spanish haciendas, and many became craftsmen in urban centers (Weaver 2008). While the degree to which yanaconas were entirely cut off from their communities of origin has probably been overstated (Saignes 1985a), "absenteeism" due to

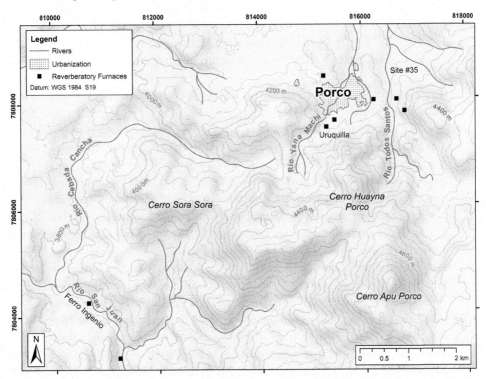

MAP 6 Location of sites mentioned in text. Map by Brendan Weaver.

population loss caused by migration and disease posed a serious challenge to kurakas, the Native leaders who were responsible for delivering mitayos to the Spaniards.

The frequent manipulation of the mita system established by the colonial government suggests that the official records of mining activity do not always reflect actual practice. However, the archaeological record does support the existence of both large- and small-scale operations in Porco. The best evidence for large operations comes from the portion of the San Juan River, or Khelkhata Valley, that is within the jurisdiction of the municipality of Porco. This area is approximately 8 km to the southwest of the village and separated from it by rugged terrain, which includes the Sora Sora ridge. Archaeological survey identified the Sora Sora mines as well as Ferro Ingenio, a large mill complex that is most likely the ingenio that was owned by Jhoan de Estrada. In 2023 a second, smaller mill complex was located a few kilometers to the west of Ferro Ingenio. A brief inspection of the site suggested that it was somewhat later in date, but it could have been constructed over an earlier ingenio built by Diego Beltran.

Large-Scale Mining and Milling in the San Juan Valley: Sora Sora and Ferro Ingenio

The mines at Sora Sora consist of two formal adits and numerous pits and tunnels that extend 700 m along an east–west-trending ridge at an elevation of about 4,200 m; a small number of huayrachina fragments are scattered along the crest. The adits, which have vaulted, masonry entrances in the colonial style, probably correspond to the two veins described by Capoche (1959 [1585]) and are located at the western end of the ridge. Stone buildings were constructed at different points in time on both sides of a quebrada that runs along the southern base of the ridge. These buildings and associated features can be divided into three sectors (Weaver 2008). Sector A is located at the top of the drainage in a shallow basin where a spring emerges in the ravine, near a small stand of queñua trees. The zone includes two kinds of buildings. One group is composed of individual structures that incorporate boulders or rock outcrops, including five small huts and an irregular wall and associated foundation that may have enclosed a workspace or corral. Two of the huts have tiny, terraced patios in front of them, and one still has an intact doorway with a stone lintel that measures 1.2 m in height. These buildings most likely served as sleeping quarters for individual miners. The second group of buildings is more formal in nature and includes three rectilinear multiroom structures, two of which, Structures 1I and 1J, are located on the north of the quebrada, and one, designated Structure 1A, on the southeast. The latter is composed of at least five rooms, four of which have stone sleeping platforms, in addition to an outdoor kitchen area protected by a wall and marked by an ash deposit. Surface artifacts included a fragment of yellow majolica, amethyst glass, a tin can, and animal bone; a large quimbalete was located outside the building. Structure 1I is similar in layout, although it includes a nicely built room with niches in each of three walls and had a double-pitched roof. Artifacts associated with Structures 1I and 1J include botija fragments, a green glazed handle with a serpentine appliqué that has been found at seventeenth-century sites in the area and decorated Indigenous wares consistent with styles found at the colonial site of Ferro Ingenio. Green and manganese decorated majolica and small fragments of thin green glass, both of which also occur at early colonial sites, were also present. Based on the surface artifacts, buildings in Sector A appear to have served as residences for miners during early colonial times—contemporaneous with Ferro Ingenio—and then again in the early twentieth century. The basin was attractive because it provided relatively flat ground, water, and firewood.

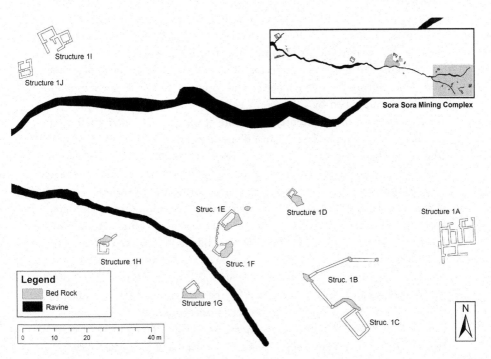

FIGURE 14 Sector A of Sora Sora. Map by Brendan Weaver.

Sector B is located downslope from Sector A and consists of five rectilinear buildings on the north side of the ravine and a circular structure on the south. The function of the latter is enigmatic; it is extremely well made, with the wall still standing to a height of 1.8 m and five niches in the interior and a narrow door; perhaps it was used as some sort of storage facility for ore and tools. The rectilinear structures to the north were built on large tailing heaps close to a mine entrance, indicating that they were constructed at some point after the initial exploitation of the mineral deposit. Eroded botija fragments were found in the tailings, suggesting that colonial miners first exploited this section of the vein. While most of the buildings appear to have been roofed living spaces, one building includes a large, walled patio that was used as a work area or corral.

Sector C encompasses the colonial adits in addition to two large, well-made buildings, one on each side of the ravine. The structure on the south side was probably entirely unroofed, and most likely served as a storage facility as well as a corral for llamas or mules used to transport ore. The building on the south side consists of a row of seven rooms and two smaller ones that are arranged perpendicularly to them. Three have sleeping platforms, and a long wall, built after the complex was constructed, creates a sheltered patio space for some of the rooms. This building may have served as a dormitory for miners, or more likely, for the supervisors and engineers who worked at the mine. No diagnostic artifacts were identified in this sector.

The adits, tailing heaps in Sector B, and the mining camp in Sector A were in use during the colonial period and correspond to the types of mineral exploitation described by Capoche in 1585. Like most mines, though, Sora Sora was worked intermittently over time as ore prices rose and fell, new technologies were applied, and demand for different kinds of metals emerged. Regarding the latter, some of the well-preserved buildings, particularly in Sector C, may be related to silver or tin exploitation in the nineteenth century. Antimony became an important metal during the twentieth century; it was used during World War I for hardening lead ammunition and later for manufacturing car batteries and other industrial applications. A local resident who lives in the San Juan Valley remembered a few men who briefly and informally mined antimony at Sora Sora around 1992, but, according to him, they were not responsible for constructing any of the buildings. Earlier exploitation of antimony is suggested by the presence of amethyst glass in Sector C. Sun-colored amethyst glass was most commonly used around the time of World War I. Two U.S. geologists who visited Porco in 1917 noted that there were many antimony mines in the region during the preceding few years and that these were "small, crudely worked properties, generally

EXTRACTION UNDER THE COLONIAL REGIME (1573–1825) 101

operated by Indians." Indigenous prospectors would take samples to individuals capable of financing an operation who then legally claimed the mine and "allowed" the miners to extract the ore. The hand-sorted mineral was sold to the owners in 100-lb loads delivered to the railroad in Agua de Castilla and when resold on the international market yielded profits of up to 50 percent (Singewald and Miller 1917, 331). Antimony extraction at Sora Sora may have been organized in this way, but without excavation of the buildings at the site, the possibility that they were initially used for the relatively large-scale extraction of this or other minerals cannot be ruled out.

The mines of Sora Sora almost certainly generated the ore that was subsequently processed in Ferro Ingenio, a stamp mill that is located on the bank of the San Juan River, 2 km to the south of the mines. Excavations and architectural survey carried out in 2006 and 2007 by Brendan Weaver (2008) at the site of Ferro Ingenio revealed multiple occupations, the industrial core of which are the remains of a water-powered stamp mill. On the basis of surface artifacts, including a four real coin minted in 1739 (categorized by Menzel 2004, 348, as Po-358), the construction of the ingenio was initially dated to the middle of the eighteenth century (Van Buren and Weaver 2012). The Montesclaros document discussed above, however, indicates that the mill was in operation by at least 1614; the archaeological data suggest that it was then reused during the next century, possibly in response to a change in tax law that reduced the "royal fifth" to the *diezemo*, or tenth, which generated increased investment in the rehabilitation of old mines and the opening of new ones (Garner 1988).

Ferro Ingenio has all the elements of a typical colonial stamp mill (Bakewell 1994). However, the disposition of facilities within the complex was more dispersed, since it was built in a rural setting and not contained within a walled compound as were urban ingenios (Gisbert and Prado 1990, 24–31). The mill building, which was constructed of stone, measures 60 by 9 m and is partitioned on the west end to form a room used for storage or other purposes. The structure would probably have been roofless so that the dust produced during milling could more easily disperse. Water was diverted from the San Juan River upstream and conducted to a wheel that was housed in a masonry *cárcamo*, part of which is still standing. Stamp mills were characterized by how many *cabezas*, or heads, they had (on one or both sides of the wheel) as well as the number of *mazos*, or stamps, on each head. The 1614 Montesclaros redistribution described Estrada's ingenio as having two heads with eight stamps on each. This accords with the architecture at Ferro Ingenio, as the mill building has sufficient space on both sides of the cárcamo to accommodate two heads. A large quimbalete, or rocker stone that was used to crush ore

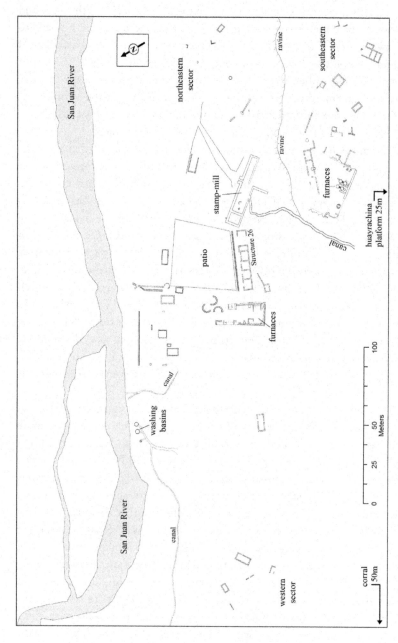

FIGURE 15 Ferro Ingenio. Mill complex is at center right. Map by Brendan Weaver.

EXTRACTION UNDER THE COLONIAL REGIME (1573–1825)   103

manually, was also found in the mill house; as Weaver (2008) suggests, this may have been employed to comminute smaller quantities of ore that were intended for smelting, rather than amalgamation. A large patio paved with river cobbles is situated to the west of the mill, and a narrow canal that runs along the southern, upslope side of the patio provided water for mixing with the amalgam and to the washing tanks that were located just to the west.

The Montesclaros document indicated that Estrada's ingenio included six furnaces for refining *negrillos*, silver sulfide ores, and thirty more for lamas, the amalgam produced by the patio process. Two batteries of furnaces were identified at Ferro Ingenio in separate rectangular enclosures that were dug into the hillside. The complex on the southeast side of the site contained approximately seven reverberatory furnaces that were constructed in a row along the southern wall of the depression, while the number of furnaces in the complex located to the southwest of the patio was impossible to calculate due to the poor state of preservation; a few additional furnaces were located in other buildings, but the chronological relationship of these to the rest of the site is unclear. Given the physical proximity of the two sets of furnaces to the mill and patio, respectively, it is likely that the complex to the southeast was used for negrillos, and the one to the west, closer to the patio, for lamas. As Weaver (2008) argued, Ferro Ingenio appears to have employed distinct technologies for different processes. Silver chlorides, locally called *pacos*, and pure native silver, called *tacana*, were usually encountered on the surface, in the upper reaches of mines, or in pockets within a lower vein, and were most efficiently refined by smelting. Negrillos, however, were found at lower levels and could be processed by smelting or amalgamation. The decision to refine these ores using one or the other process was shaped by the nature of the minerals, as well as the availability and cost of inputs—mercury, salt, iron, and copper sulfate for amalgamation and fuel, and either litharge or lead for smelting (Guerrero 2016).

The individuals who supervised the mill probably resided in an adobe building consisting of five contiguous rooms with entrances overlooking the patio. The walls are well preserved, but aside from arched niches in a few of the rooms, no interior features are apparent on the surface. A 1- by 2-m unit excavated to the southeast of the building revealed a domestic midden that spanned several centuries of use. Weaver's (2008) analysis of the excavation found that the upper three layers contained more recent artifacts mixed with older material, probably washed down from earlier deposits located upslope of the unit. Artifacts include Panamanian majolica, fragments of provincial Inka vessels, and botijas, all of which are found at early colonial sites, as well as cream and pearl wares that were produced in the late eighteenth and early nineteenth centuries. The first and second layers also yielded five hexagonal black glass beads that date between 1675 and 1800 (Deagan 1987, 174), a mother-of-pearl button, pieces of shoe leather, a cactus-spine needle, and a silver *tupu*. The latter two items, in particular, suggest the presence of a woman at the site, and one of the leather fragments appears to be from a child's shoe. A pocket of ash in Levels 2 and 3, the product of a discrete depositional event, contained a small, open handbell, a metal pendant with green glass inlay, and underglazed green and red transfer-printed wares that are characteristic of the early nineteenth century; no refined white earthenwares were recovered below Level 2. The material from this unit, while mixed, indicates that the mill was used in the late sixteenth and early seventeenth centuries as well as the late eighteenth and early nineteenth centuries, but the occupation was probably not continuous.

The ethnic composition of the group of mitayos allotted to Jhoan de Estrada reflected that of the workers assigned to Porco as a whole; most came from Carangas, while the others were drawn from six different groups located between the southern shore of Lake Titicaca and Potosí, with the exception of four people from the nearby community of Chaqui to the east. If they served in person, they would have first gathered with their wives and, perhaps, older children on an appointed day in a designated town within their home province. There they would have received some silver as well as customary provisions (for example, dried potatoes, quinoa, coca, or maize depending on the province) and been seen off with a solemn ceremony reminiscent of funerary rites (Nicolas 2018; Platt 1983). After first traveling to Potosí where they would have been divided among azogueros, they would have walked to Porco and then to the Khelkata Valley. In 1619 a royal cedula was issued requiring that azogueros compensate the mitayos for their travel time at a rate of half a day's wage for each day traveled, but they usually paid only for the return trip (Nicolas 2018, 47).

Extrapolating from Capoche's (1959 [1585]) account of the assignment of mitayos in Potosí, roughly a third would have been sent to work at Sora Sora and the remainder to Ferro Ingenio. Nicolas (2018) describes the tasks assigned to each mitayo. *Barreteros* were responsible for cutting ore with an iron rod and were the most skilled workers. In the late sixteenth century many of these men had previously been *indios de vara*, independent miners responsible for supervising small teams of workers; after the Toledan reforms this task was most often accomplished by mingas. The ore they removed was broken into smaller pieces by *brociris*. The second large category of workers in the mines were *apiris* who carried the ore on their backs to the surface in 25-kg loads by candlelight; in Potosí they made as many as twenty-five trips per day. This unskilled job was usually assigned to mitayos, since mingas often refused to do it. During the first decades that the system was in place, mingas working as barreteros earned up to three pesos per day, while mitayos received only 2.5 pesos a week (Cole 1985, 25–30), well below the cost of living in a mining center where the price of food and other goods was extremely high. In addition to these jobs, women and some men sorted ore at the mouth of the mine, separating the gangue, or waste from the mineral which was transported to the mill by llamas. These pailliris were independent workers who gleaned the tailings and sold the little that they found for a pittance (Jiménez de la Espada 1965 [1836], 372–85).

Workers assigned to mills usually earned about 25 percent less than miners (Salazar-Soler 2002). Nicolas (2018) has described the organization of work in these contexts, and archaeological remains at Ferro Ingenio, as well as descriptions of the amalgamation process itself, suggest additional tasks that were required. Once delivered to the mill, the ore was unloaded and then ground in a quimbalete or fed under the stamps by teams of five mitayos, called *serviris*, per mill head. Manually triturated ore would then be moved to the bank of furnaces just above the mill, while the mechanically pulverized mineral would be carried to the patio; both would be sieved to remove large particles. Smelting and the assessment of the correct quantities of salt, iron, and copper sulfate used in amalgamation required the knowledge of an experienced worker or supervisor; mixing the amalgam with hoes, rakes, or bare feet was probably a less skilled task but, according to a contemporary observer, required more experience than one might suspect (Llanos 2009 [1609], 119–20). The mixture, once amalgamated, would be washed in the tanks adjacent to the patio and then placed in a canvas bag so that the mercury could be squeezed out. The remaining *pella* was pounded into a mold by a *golpeador* and delivered to the battery of furnaces uphill from the tanks to drive off the mercury, which was recovered in ceramic or iron vessels called *capelinas*. Ancillary tasks necessary to support the entire process would have included the supply of fuel, water, and other inputs, construction of new facilities, repair of old ones, and periodic cleaning. The silver, once produced, would be stored as *piñas* until enough had accumulated to be assayed and taxed at the Caja Real in Potosí, or transported directly to Arica via a roughly paved road that runs north along a stretch of the San Juan River and then joins the main route to the Pacific coast.

In both the mines and the mills, mitayos and mingas would have worked alongside people from different ethnic groups who spoke different languages. This was due to the assignment of mitayos from multiple communities to individual Spaniards, a practice that may have been intended to undermine the development of solidarity among workers. While the state's use of "ethnic" or kin groups to organize labor and extract taxes reinforced local identities, ethnic mixing in workspaces and urban centers generated new social categories: Spaniards, Indians mestizos, mulatos, and a number of other types that were classified according to "racial" admixture into different *castas*. Salazar-Soler (2002) has described this process in Potosí where thousands of Indigenous workers from different communities interacted with each other as well as enslaved people of African descent, Spaniards, and occasionally people from other parts of Europe. Among miners and mill workers, a new argot rapidly emerged that combined words from Quechua, Aymara, and Spanish to describe the technology and tasks that were specific to silver mining. Pieter Muysken (2017), a linguist, suggests that the early division of labor in Porco and Potosí can even be discerned in the terms listed by García de Llanos (2009 [1609]) in his early mining dictionary. Quechua words are frequently combined with Spanish ones and are often associated with tasks accomplished by yanaconas, many of whom had been Quechua-speaking Inka retainers. In contrast, Aymara, sometimes combined with Quechua, more often describe the work of mitayos who most frequently were employed as apiris, moving ore from the rock faces to the mine entrance.

Cole (1985) has provided a detailed description of the terrible conditions under which mitayos labored in Potosí, including confinement in the mines during the work week, physical abuse, the imposition of a quota system, and the constant danger posed by falls, cave-ins, and diseases like silicosis and pneumonia. Coercive methods for recruiting and retaining workers increased during the late colonial period resulting in a collective legal appeal by mill workers in Oruro and Paria for relief (Gavira Márquez 2006). While many of the same circumstances would have prevailed at Sora Sora, some aspects of miners' day-to-day experiences were probably distinct due to the nature of the mines and their geographic isolation. The shallowness of the workings, particularly in the years immediately following their discovery, meant that miners did not have to endure the heat, flooding, and pitch darkness that characterized deep shafts, nor did apiris have to climb successive ladders to deposit their loads at the mouth of the mine. Miners may also have slept in the huts near the workings, or perhaps even in the other structures, rather than spending the entire week in the mines. This may, however, have been even less comfortable, given the frigid temperatures and fierce winds that prevail outside.

While mining required back-breaking physical labor in dangerous underground tunnels—conditions that induced fear and anxiety, at least in workers new to the job—ingenios posed a different set of hazards. The two most common were injury from moving parts and exposure to dust that caused

EXTRACTION UNDER THE COLONIAL REGIME (1573–1825)

silicosis which, before the use of blasting powder, was a more serious problem in the mills than the mines. They also produced a constant, deafening noise (González-Tennant 2009). More insidious, though, was exposure to lead, mercury, and other heavy metals that could occur not just in the mill itself, but also in nearby housing (Kennedy 2021; Kennedy and Kelloway 2020, 2021). Lead fumes were generated by smelting silver ores along with metallic lead or litharge. The dangers of lead exposure were not known at the time, but health effects include anemia, abdominal pain, and muscle wasting; in severe cases it can also damage the neurological, renal, and hematologic systems and impair physical and cognitive development (Sanborn et al. 2002). Poisoning can result from inhaling the fumes and dust or inadvertently consuming lead in contaminated food. Exposure to mercury could occur during all steps of the amalgamation process, and at least some of the risks associated with inhaling fumes were understood at the time. Robins and Hagan (Robins 2011; Robins and Hagan 2012; Hagan et al. 2011) have documented pervasive mercury contamination in Huancavelica and Potosí and have described the potentially devastating effects not just on workers who came into direct contact with the element or its compounds but also on nearby residents who breathed the vapor that ingenios generated. Effects depend on the type of compound and the way in which it is absorbed, and symptoms can take years to develop. Acute poisoning results in the loss of sensation in hands and feet, uncontrollable shaking, and impaired vision among an array of other symptoms, sometimes followed by death due to respiratory failure. Intoxication resulting from chronic exposure results in the loss of teeth, weight loss, tissue degeneration, and ultimately symptoms associated with the deterioration of the nervous system such as shaking and loss of muscle control; psychological disturbances are often associated (Robins 2011, 107–8). While books and magazine articles often erroneously state that "millions" of Indians died in the mines of southern Bolivia, the health effects of working in the industry extended far beyond deaths from cave-ins and falls and were only occasionally noted (Gavira Márquez 2003).

Opportunities for theft existed at all points along the chain of production, as is reflected in the work of Juan Pérez Bocanegra, a Franciscan priest who published instructions for how to administer the sacraments to Native people. The section on confessions is organized by commandment, and for the eighth and ninth commandments (on theft and coveting the property of others) he provides a fascinating list of questions related to the types of fraud that could be committed by individuals practicing different trades. Questions intended for Indians who worked in the mines and mills ask whether they had stolen high-grade ore from the mine itself, while transporting and milling it, or, as amalgam, from the patio or washing basins (Pérez Bocanegra 1631, 286–89). Supervisors and millowners also had opportunities to either steal silver outright, or, in the case of azogueros, to avoid payment of the royal fifth by selling untaxed silver to foreign or local merchants; rescatiris, individuals who purchased silver ore from small producers, and "thieves" also avoided taxation. The isolated location of Ferro Ingenio and its proximity to a road that led to the official port of Arica as well as the smaller harbor of Cobija would have facilitated the movement of untaxed metal; in both places silver could be sold to French or other vessels engaged in contraband trade along the Pacific coast.

The theft of silver extended even to the officials employed by the Crown to oversee its control. Gavira Márquez (2008), for instance, describes the involvement of the Spanish administrators in charge of the Caja Real of Carangas in various types of fraud related to the mining industry during the 1700s. The most famous case, however, was the Potosí mint fraud in the mid-seventeenth century. Complaints about the adulteration of Potosí's coins with copper had arisen as early as the 1630s and increased in frequency during the following decade. When King Phillip IV attempted to pay his foreign creditors, Genovese merchants complained that the currency was debased, and in 1648 the king sent an official to the viceroyalty to investigate (Oropeza 2013). The resulting scandal reached the highest administrative levels in Potosí and ended in 1650 with the execution of the royal assayer, Felipe Ramírez de Arellano, as well as Francisco Gómez de la Rocha, a wealthy silver merchant. Although only two men were executed, dozens more were involved, ranging from slaves who worked in the royal mint to the highest-ranking magistrate in Potosí (Lane 2017).

The illicit appropriation of silver was pervasive in the formal, large-scale sector of the mining industry, extending from the point of extraction to the manufacture of coinage. It was the appropriation of ore and partially refined silver acquired during the earlier stages of this process, though, that promoted the development of a parallel or informal economy (Tándeter 1981a; Barragán 2017a) associated with small-scale production. This was done both legally and illicitly, depending on the type of access that the laborer had to the means of production.

Small-Scale Production in Porco

Ferro Ingenio and Sora Sora are examples of formal operations that required considerable capital investment in infrastructure and benefited from the use of forced labor provided by the state. Small-scale independent production in

EXTRACTION UNDER THE COLONIAL REGIME (1573–1825)   109

Porco under the colonial regime is best represented by Site 35, a modest metallurgical complex at the foot of Cerro San Cristobal just to the east of the road that connects Agua de Castilla to the mines in Apu and Huayna Porco. The site consists of six rectangular foundations, two quimbaletes with associated grinding platforms for triturating ore, and two crudely made buildings that contain facilities for refining silver. On the southern side of the site, a broad terrace was built against the hillslope and buttressed on the north side by a dry-stone wall. A test unit yielded only a few sherds, but analysis of a soil sample from the excavation revealed small fragments of cinnabar, the mineral from which mercury is produced (Muñoz Rojas 2019). This area was, perhaps, a workspace for processing ore. A vertical mine shaft with footholds hewn into the side is located above the site just below the peak of San Cristobal.

The excavation of three structures at Site 35 in 2002 yielded a range of tools and technologies utilized in silver refining as well as small quantities of domestic debris. Structure 1, which had a well-preserved rectangular foundation, was altered twice during the course of its occupation; a stone step was placed below the entrance on the interior of the structure, and a narrow partition was built across the width of the building. Ceramics consisted mostly of jars, but fragments of cooking vessels and serving bowls were also found. A small percentage of the sherds are from provincial Inka vessels, a type that appears to have lasted until approximately the mid-seventeenth century in this region (Van Buren and Weaver 2014). A cached set of grinding stones—a small *batan* and netherstone—were found beneath the floor. Archaeobotanical (Muñoz Rojas 2019) and faunal analyses (deFrance 2012) identified a small quantity of camelid bones, as well the seeds of quinoa, lentils, and cactus, and, surprisingly, fragments of some type of crustacean, perhaps crawfish from the nearby Río Todos Santos. These remains indicate a diet that included native and Eurasian domesticates, as well as wild species.

Materials associated with metallurgical processes tended to be concentrated in the south side of Structure 1. These included a small hearth built against the wall as well as enigmatic cigar-sized fired clay cylinders with tapered ends. They were heavily burned, but their function is unknown. Small pieces of slag, charcoal, and camelid excrement, or *taquia*, that had been used for fuel, were also recovered during the analysis of soil samples (Muñoz Rojas 2019). The contents of Structure 1, like most of the buildings excavated at Porco, reflect the interdigitation of domestic and metallurgical activities that occurred during colonial times. Structures 3 and 7, however, are workshops that were devoted primarily to the production of metal.

The foundation of Structure 3 was constructed of large cobbles and boulders arranged in a rough L-shape, with the eastern side of the long axis of the

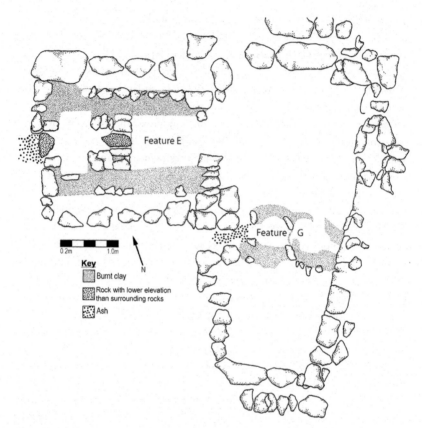

FIGURE 16 Structure 3 at Site 35. Feature G is a cupellation hearth of the type used to refine silver. Feature E is a rectangular reverberatory furnace with an unknown function (Van Buren 2016).

building consisting of a large rock outcrop. This configuration accommodated two types of metallurgical furnaces. The short end of the L contained a rectangular reverberatory furnace, while a small cupellation hearth had been constructed perpendicular to the long end of the L; the chimney of the hearth was supported by the rock outcrop and an opening in the northern wall allowed ash to be removed. While the function of the rectangular furnace is not clear, the cupellation hearth is identical to the *tocochimbos* found in the late nineteenth- and early twentieth-century estancias described in the previous chapter and to the cupellation hearth used by Mr. Cuiza to refine silver.

Structure 7 has a roughly made oval stone foundation that may have been surmounted by an ephemeral superstructure. A carefully constructed open hearth was built into the northeastern end of the structure. The floor of the

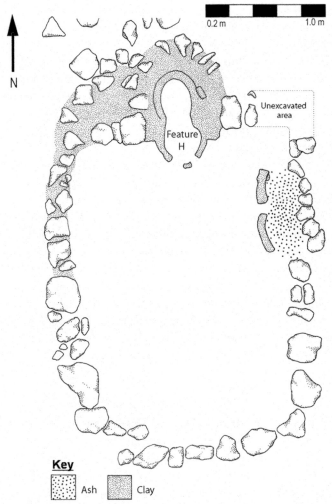

FIGURE 17 Structure 7 at Site 35. Feature H is a metallurgical hearth of unknown function. Illustration by the author.

hearth slopes to the south and empties into a circular depression dug into the floor of the building. The function of this feature is not understood; it was, perhaps, related to the production of lead that was subsequently used in the cupellation hearth to refine silver.

During work at the site, a burial was encountered eroding out of a sand dune just to the east. The individual was interred in a seated position within a simple pit, and only the upper portion of the skeleton was preserved. The position of the body and the presence of a pair of *tupus* indicated that the individual was an Indigenous woman, probably middle-aged or older given the wear on her teeth. She was found with a Nueva Cadiz bead and most of a red-slipped jar.

Archaeomagnetic samples from the hearth in Structure 7 yielded a date of 1650 to 1800 (Lengyel et al. 2011); the provincial Inka sherds and the Nueva Cadiz bead (Smith and Good 1982; Lapham 2001) recovered from the burial, as well as a chevron bead and hawksbell (Mitchem and McEwan 1988; Deagan 2002, 145), found in the L-shaped structure suggest that the first part of this range—or perhaps earlier—is most likely.

Site 35 appears to have housed a small residential population—perhaps just one or two families—that was engaged in the production of metal. Like Ferro Ingenio, the operation was vertically integrated, with mineral extraction, trituration, smelting, and refining being carried out in a limited space, but in this case probably by the same people. The small hearths and furnaces would have been appropriate for processing the ore produced by a modest family operation acting independently. Low artifact density and diversity suggest a short-term, seasonal occupation, an interpretation that gains support from the recovery of a cached set of grinding stones hidden under the floor of one of the structures. The residents of the site were probably independent workers who—judging from the visibility of the complex from the adjacent road—may have been legally exploiting the small mine in Cerro San Cristóbal.

Mining, Labor, and Ore Sharing

No information is available regarding the illicit appropriation of ore at Porco during colonial times, but the practice is well documented in Oruro and Potosí. In both of those centers, and presumably Porco as well, ore sharing—or theft, depending on one's perspective—was central to the organization of production. Ore sharing was a key tactic used by workers to supplement their wages and by owners to attract labor. In Carangas gleaning waste heaps and recovering ore from abandoned mines—referred to there as jukeo—provided an alternative to the paltry wages and abusive treatment associated with employment by azogueros in the late eighteenth century (Gavira Márquez 2014). As Barragán (2015, 2017a) emphasizes, the contested nature of the practice resulted from differences in how property was conceptualized, as either the product of labor or private property legally acknowledged by the state.

Zulawski (1987) examined the case of seventeenth-century Oruro to explore why an industrial proletariat failed to emerge in that context even

EXTRACTION UNDER THE COLONIAL REGIME (1573–1825)   113

though the azogueros there did not receive mita workers and thus relied entirely on mingas, or wage laborers. From its founding in 1607, workers were attracted by relatively high wages as well as the right to remove a piece of ore for themselves. This was regarded by owners as an unfortunate but necessary means of subsidizing low wages and attracting workers without expending scarce capital. During the first decades after the town's establishment, professional Spanish miners were hired to oversee the process, and they attempted to minimize theft at all stages of production. Their success was limited, though, in part because workers would return to the mines over the weekend to extract ore for themselves. This practice became more prevalent after 1680, when Viceroy Conde de Monclova, in an attempt to increase revenue, relaxed regulations so that ore of unknown origin could be processed and sold. The change of policy resulted in an increase in the number of trapiches, hand-operated mills in which "stolen" or "shared" ore was refined. The expectation that ore would be shared was probably reinforced by the labor shortage caused by a major epidemic in 1720 which further slowed the demographic recovery of the Native population. Luis Capoche (1959 [1585]), observed that even by the time he wrote in 1585 mingas would not work without the right to ore because the low wages did not compensate them adequately for the hard labor and high risks they faced in the mines. After examining the demographic characteristics of forasteros and yanaconas in Oruro, Zulawski (1987) concluded that a proletariat dependent on wage labor did not emerge because most forasteros were from nearby agricultural communities where they could return when facing economic hardships. Tándeter (1981a) and Barragán (2015), however, suggest that the direct appropriation of ore by underpaid or unemployed miners played a key role in inhibiting the development of an industrial working class in Andean mining centers.

While the direct appropriation of ore was also common in Potosí, it was not until the eighteenth century that the term *kajchas* was used to describe "weekend miners." Tándeter (1981b) provides a detailed description of the role of kajcheo in the mining economy at that time. Kajchas contracted with trapiche owners (or rescatiris) who could advance them the funds to purchase tools, candles, mercury, and other goods necessary for mining in addition to allowing them to use their mills for processing ore. The trapicheros charged high prices, particularly for the mercury which was marked up 50 percent over the usual rate, and they also had the right to the *relaves*, the leftover amalgam of silver and mercury that adhered to the mill after it was cleaned out by the kajcha. The volume of ore processed by the kajchas was low relative to the quantity milled in the ingenios, but because it was hand-selected and thus very high grade, the amount of silver produced by these small-scale entrepreneurs—of which there were an estimated 4,000 in 1759—reached over a third of total production during the mid-eighteenth century.

People from a variety of castas, including *indios*, mestizos, criollos, mulattos, and some *españoles*, became kajchas, united primarily by their common interest in removing ore for their own profit, a right that they defended vigorously and violently, much to the dismay of mineowners and civic authorities. According to Pedro Vicente Cañete, who proposed a revised mining code in 1794, the kajchas in Potosí were organized into three types of crews according to ethnic identity: *cacchas*, *gaurinas*, and *ancoamañas*. Cacchas were Indians who had fled from the mita or who were forasteros, guarinas were criollos from Potosí, and ancoamañas were mestizos. Each crew included some individuals with mining experience, and leaders were selected on the basis of whether they had the knowledge and means to arrange fiestas devoted to the Santa Cruz (Martire 1977)—an early indication of the relationship between kajcheo and festivals honoring the cross. Cañete probably exaggerated the formality of kajcha organization because he proposed to use it as the basis for assimilating them into a more orderly, legal system of mineral exploitation, but the categories he identifies provide evidence for the range of people involved in the practice.

As Tándeter and others have pointed out, attitudes towards kajchas were ambivalent. They were regarded by many as unruly, violent thieves who damaged the internal mine supports in their unregulated search for high-grade ore. Complaints about the destruction of infrastructure and the resulting danger to miners were voiced by many azogueros. However, even Spaniards like the chronicler Arzans Orsúa y Vela (1965 [c. 1705–36], 3:201) also viewed kajchas as tough, honorable men worthy of respect who "violently remove metal on holidays, although they work with the force of their own hands and risk their lives" (3:201). The most renowned was Augustín Quespi, a kajcha "captain" who had been trained in arms by a Spaniard and led bands of men into the mines on the weekends. According to Arzáns, he was a generous and devoted Christian, but was famed for his violent exploits and particularly the maltreatment of guards and azogueros who impeded his access to the mines. A small man with almost superhuman strength, Quespi was repeatedly arrested, beaten, and imprisoned. In the last incident recounted by Arzáns (3:381), which occurred in January 1735, the captain and his kajchas had been arrested and were being brought to jail when residents of the Native parishes rose up and attacked the party. Quespi managed to escape amid a rain of sling stones, with the sound of church bells clanging and women screaming adding to the overall chaos. The Indigenous response to Quespi's arrest suggests the incipient sense of collective identity among kajchas that

EXTRACTION UNDER THE COLONIAL REGIME (1573–1825)   115

Abercrombie (1996) argues was the basis for an emerging plebian class. This sensibility was maintained throughout the eighteenth century, culminating in midcentury with a violent demonstration in Potosí after a young kajcha had been killed by a guard protecting a mine. This provoked exaggerated fears of an armed uprising against Spanish rule during the Carnival festivities of 1751 (Abercrombie 1996).

Discussions among azogueros and civic authorities about how to control the kajchas were commonplace during the eighteenth century (Martire 1977; Barragán 2015) and peaked during the protests by kajchas described above. In response to the 1735 event, authorities considered razing all the trapiches to eliminate the facilities on which kajchas depended for both credit and processing their ore. They decided against this, however, because Crown revenues would drop if this source of production were eliminated (Barragán 2015). Similar measures were rejected in 1752 for much the same reason, but also because of the difficulty of maintaining a sufficient work force without the practice of kajcheo. Large- and small-scale mining enterprises were thus intertwined with regard to the maintenance of a labor force as well as the ways in which kajchas gained access to minerals, which were primarily by exploiting ore faces that had been exposed by the large enterprises for which they worked during the week. Owners considered deploying the power of the state to control their competitors, but the overall shortage of labor—due to their refusal or inability to provide reasonable wages—forced them to maintain their contradictory and fraught relationship with the kajchas.

Small-Scale Mining and Technology in Porco

The archaeological and historical records suggest that small-scale technologies for grinding and smelting ore not only persisted after the Toledan reforms but diversified. This expansion was the result of continued interest in the processing of small quantities of high-grade ore, an interest that was fueled within the Indigenous population by the demand for silver to meet tribute obligations, pay for substitute mita workers, and, for some, to purchase goods in the market economy. The creation of new technologies was fostered not just by demand, but also by the interaction of people from different backgrounds with varying degrees of experience with mining and metallurgy.

Barragán (2015) points to the importance of trapiches in creating an economic space in which small-scale, frequently Indigenous, miners could operate. As noted in the previous chapter, trapiches often consisted of quimbaletes that were operated on bedrock or a large flat stone, usually within a small enclosure. The ground ore could then be smelted or amalgamated using a process similar to procedures employed in the large ingenios. Quimbaletes function according to the same principles as *batanes*, the smaller rocking stones that were used in Indigenous households throughout the Andes to process food. Interestingly, they occur infrequently in pre-Hispanic mining contexts (De Nigris 2012). In her early survey of metallurgical sites, Lechtman (1976) observed that quimbaletes were widely dispersed in the Andes and tended to be very similar in the size, shape, and dimensions of the holes that accommodated the pegs used to lash the poles onto the grinding stone. This uniformity, combined with the lack of references to such stones in early documents, suggested to her that quimbaletes were created during early colonial times and introduced at various mining centers by Spaniards. The large sample of quimbaletes that have been identified by archaeologists over the last few decades, however, indicates that they are not very standardized. The fact that both quimbaletes and batanes are rocked in a similar manner implies that the former was predicated on domestic food processing technology that was scaled up to increase capacity. Most likely, quimbaletes were first designed by Indigenous workers who were familiar with batanes and who, along with European miners, introduced them to mining sites throughout the Andes.

Another type of small mill noted by Alvaro Alonso Barba (1992 [1640], 128–29) as an alternative to the quimbalete is what he calls simply a "trapiche." Alonso Barba was a miner, metallurgist, and priest whose treatise, *Arte de los Metales*, describes in detail the many techniques that were used in what is now southern Bolivia to process different types of ore. Although he only illustrates the bottom half of the mechanism that he calls a trapiche, he describes it as being similar to an *atahona*, or what today is called a *tahona* in Spanish, or Chilean mill in English. Such mills consist of a lower bedrock or paved floor on which a stone wheel is rolled in a circular fashion. The stone is affixed to a beam that is attached to a pivot anchored in the center of the floor. The beam is moved by a mule, horse, or ox walking in circles around the periphery of the mill (De Nigris 2012). As Barragán (2015) notes, this technology was derived from Roman mills that produced olive oil or flour and entailed the use of European animals that were expensive to maintain. No such mills have been found near Porco, but historical sources indicate their use in Potosí, and archaeological examples have been reported from Chile, Argentina, and Peru (De Nigris 2012). The use of milling technologies derived from European and Andean traditions is a clear reflection of the coexistence of two technological styles; in the case of trapiches, however, historical evidence indicates that they were employed by people of Spanish as well as Indigenous descent (Gil Montero and Téreygeol 2021).

EXTRACTION UNDER THE COLONIAL REGIME (1573–1825)   117

Smelting and refining technology also diversified during early colonial times, in part because there was a continued need by large-scale producers for furnaces to treat high-grade minerals that would otherwise suffer losses if processed using the patio method, but also because small-scale producers often depended on the exploitation of modest quantities of high-quality silver ore. Identifying the functional and historical factors underlying this diversity is challenging because the purpose of some of the archaeological features is still unclear, as are the historical traditions from which they were derived. Huayrachinas continued to be used to smelt ore (Cohen et al. 2010) and, as discussed in chapter 4, were an Andean technology that was probably introduced by the Inkas; when mentioned in historical texts, these furnaces were associated with Indigenous workers. The origins and deployment of other smelting and refining technologies used at the same time are less clear.

Relatively large reverberatory furnaces, with hearths measuring 1 m or more in diameter, were one of the most common ore-processing facilities found at Porco. Reverberatories are configured so that the mineral being processed does not come into direct contact with the fuel. This is most often accomplished by constructing a firebox adjacent to the hearth from which it is separated by a partition. The hot air flows over the partition and into the reaction chamber where it is reflected downward from the domed roof and concentrated on the hearth. The same principles guide the construction of *tocochimbos*, which are, in essence, small reverberatory furnaces.

PAPP members identified eight relatively large reverberatory furnaces (excluding those associated with Ferro Ingenio), five of which were excavated during the 2003 and 2005 field seasons. The best preserved is located on the east side of the site of Uruquilla, or "Porco Viejo," which is located just above and to the southwest of the modern village in an area that is publicly visible. It is situated in a shed-like rectangular building (Structure 10), with the southeast side consisting of three crude masonry pillars. This arrangement would have supported the roof, allowed for the circulation of air in what would have been an extremely hot space, and provided access to the quebrada below. The primary chamber of the furnace is circular and measures 1.4 m in diameter; an oval firebox is located on the southeast side of the chamber and the ash from it could easily have been disposed in the quebrada. An inclined chimney is attached to the northwest side of the furnace and extends beyond the wall of the building. The chamber itself was covered by a domed roof, which, according to local residents, was intact until recently. Furnaces of this type were called "dragon furnaces" in the seventeenth century due to the amount of ore that they consumed and the fact that their distinctive chimneys looked somewhat like tails (Alonso Barba 1992 [1640], 142–43). A similar,

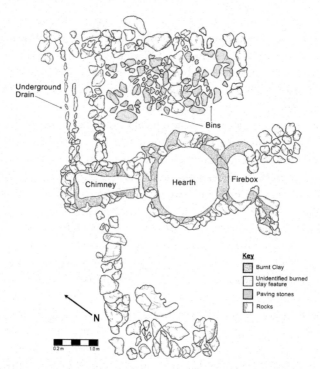

FIGURE 18 Reverberatory "dragon" furnace in Structure 10 at Uruquilla. Illustration by the author.

undated furnace is located outside our survey area, near an estancia approximately 8 km to the northwest of Porco. The dome on that furnace is partially intact and has two openings in the side (Cohen 2008, 242).

Excavation of Structure 10 yielded few artifacts but did reveal information about the construction of the complex and some associated features. The furnace appears to have been constructed first and the building erected around it. The building also included two roughly paved bins, perhaps for the temporary storage of fuel, litharge, or other inputs that had to be kept dry. Immediately below the pavement, excavators encountered damp, ashy sediment that yielded early colonial ceramics, a weight, a large drop of lead metal, and fragments of a tupu, suggesting that the furnace was constructed after the initial colonial occupation of the site. Another feature that was discovered in excavation units just outside the shed is more difficult to interpret: a narrow, stone-sided channel is located perpendicular to the furnace just below the occupation surface. It runs from the northern corner of the chimney to an extension of the northeastern wall of the shed but does not open

EXTRACTION UNDER THE COLONIAL REGIME (1573–1825)   119

into the furnace. Its purpose is unknown, although ventilation or drainage are possibilities. On the southwestern side of the furnace, a shallow channel begins at a poorly preserved basin situated near the door of the chamber and curves east. It is unlined but contains ashy sediment and flecks of charcoal. This was most likely used to tap liquid slag during the smelt. A clay feature (Feature LL) in the west corner of the building was probably employed at some stage in the smelting process, but preservation was too poor for its function to be determined. Archaeomagnetic samples from the hearth floor yielded date ranges of 1775 to 1900 CE for the furnace and 1640–1775 CE for the clay feature (LL) within the structure. The discrepancy is most likely due to the poor magnetization displayed by samples from the site or, perhaps, problems with the master curve, which was the first calculated for this region (Lengyel et al. 2011). It is also possible that the furnace was reused after the facility was initially constructed.

Three additional reverberatory furnaces, UR10, UR11, and UR12, were excavated on the slope just to the southeast of Uruquilla at the foot of Cerro Huayna Porco, an area that would have been visible to people walking to the mines or pasturing their animals. They were constructed in a row just a few meters apart. Only the foundations remain, and based on differences in preservation, it appears as if UR12 were built first, then UR10 and 11, perhaps using materials scavenged from UR12. Archaeomagnetic samples taken from UR10 yielded a date of 1675 to 1760 CE (Lengyel et al. 2011).

Unlike the furnace in Structure 10, UR10 to 12 had rectangular fireboxes constructed on the east or west sides of the hearths; the fireboxes of UR10 and 12 had stone grills that were used to support the fuel, while the firebox of UR11 had a clay grill perforated with round holes. Only UR11 was well enough preserved to be able to discern the complete footprint of the feature. These furnaces conform closely to the descriptions and illustrations of reverberatory furnaces in Alonso Barba's treatise (1992 [1640], 138) and are also roughly similar in plan to colonial furnaces found by Angiorama and his team in northwestern Argentina (Angiorama and Becerra 2010; Angiorama et al. 2015). However, those reverberatories vary in the details of their construction, and a number have distinctive conical chimneys connected to the hearth by a short underground tunnel. As is the case in the Porco region, they also differ in terms of the overall context, with individual furnaces reflecting small-scale mining and larger complexes resulting from greater investments in infrastructure by organized companies.

Structure 10 at Uruquilla was unusually clean, and no slag appropriate for analysis was recovered. Samples of slag and vitrified furnace fragments were, however, collected from the dragon furnace identified to the northwest of

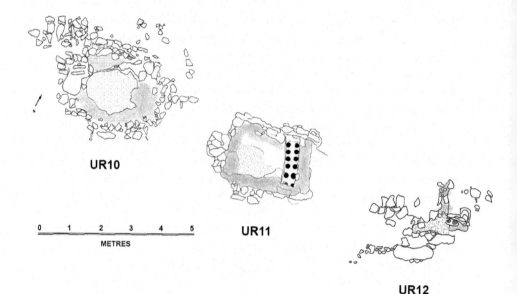

FIGURE 19 Reverberatory furnaces (UR10, UR11, and UR 12) excavated at Uruquilla (Van Buren and Cohen 2010).

Porco, and UR10, UR11, and UR12. These were analyzed by Claire Cohen at the Institute of Archaeology, University College London, using optical microscopy, SEM-EDS, and XRF. All are lead silicates containing lead and zinc sulfides and metallic prills. The presence of sulfur in the majority of the prills indicates that the lead ore was sulfidic, probably lead sulfide, and the high levels of lead in the slag and silver in the metallic prills suggest the production of a silver/lead alloy. All of the reverberatory furnaces at Uruquilla thus appear to have been used to smelt unroasted argentiferous galena, as described by Alonso Barba (Van Buren and Cohen 2010). Thus, like huayrachinas, the reverberatory furnaces processed argentiferous lead, which produced a lead-silver bullion that required further refining. These results indicate that rather than being linked in a single chain of production, huayrachinas and large reverberatories were used for the same purpose. The decision to use one or the other technology may have been based on the quantity of ore that was being smelted, the availability of resources for constructing the furnace and employing workers, or cultural preference.

Site 35 also indicates the range of technology that was used at any one time to produce silver on a small scale, although, unfortunately, the functions of two of the features—the hearth in Structure 7 (which will be discussed further in the subsequent chapter) and the rectangular reverberatory furnace in Structure 3—are unknown. Perhaps more significant than the variety of technologies employed at the site, though, is that it housed the earliest known cupellation hearth identified at Porco. This type of furnace, which is almost exactly like the one used by Carlos Cuiza and associated with the Republican era estancias surrounding Porco, is also a reverberatory furnace but on a diminutive scale, with hearth diameters averaging 40 cm. Unlike the larger reverberatories, however, these furnaces were used to refine silver rather than to smelt argentiferous lead ore.

The cultural origins and history of these cupellation hearths as well as the larger reverberatories are debatable. While there is mounting evidence that cupellation was practiced in the pre-Hispanic Andes (Schultze et al. 2009, 2016), traces of reverberatory furnaces used for this purpose or any other in pre-Hispanic times are scant. The only evidence to date is a furnace excavated in the Escaramayu complex near Pulacayo, a mine 90 km to the west of Porco, that was also exploited during colonial times (Lechtman et al. 2010; Cruz et al. 2022). Radiocarbon dates on material immediately adjacent to this furnace, which is similar in form to UR 11 at Porco, suggest that it was used between the nineth and thirteenth centuries CE. The excavators believe that it could have been employed to roast, smelt, or refine copper ores, evidence for which is abundant at the complex in which the furnace is located (Cruz et al. 2022).

Additional evidence in support of the identification of reverberatories as a pre-Hispanic technology includes: (1) the lack of archaeological or a substantial body of documentary evidence for such furnaces in Europe prior to Spanish expansion; (2) the widespread use of reverberatories in the southern Andes immediately after the conquest; (3) the use of natural draft rather than bellows; and (4) perhaps most intriguingly, a document dated to 1635 in which the author declares that he had discovered the "secret" of Indigenous smelting for which he provides an illustration that is very similar to the furnaces found at Pulacayo, Porco, and other places in the southern Andes (Cruz and Téreygeol 2020). Based on these factors the excavator, Pablo Cruz, and his colleagues (2022) argue that the reverberatory furnace was, in fact, an Andean invention that was later diffused to Europe. While this reconstruction of events is plausible, the absence of such furnaces at sites like Tarapacá Viejo and El Abra that have yielded abundant evidence for Late Intermediate Period and Inka metal production, is surprising. Additional finds of well-dated reverberatory furnaces that were constructed prior to the Spanish conquest would help support an interpretation of pre-Hispanic use.

Another possibility is that reverberatory furnaces originated in Europe shortly before the Spanish invasion and were introduced to the Americas in an attempt to maximize silver production (Van Buren and Cohen 2010). The early history of reverberatory furnaces in Europe has not been fully explored, but they were discussed by Agricola, a German metallurgist, in his classic exposition on mining and metal production that was published in 1556. Agricola (1950 [1556], 493) described reverberatories used by Hungarians and Poles to separate silver from lead, and this tradition could be the ultimate source of the technology found at Porco, perhaps arriving via a somewhat surprising route. The House of Fugger was an extremely influential German banking and merchant company that operated throughout Europe—including Hungary and Poland—in the late fiftteenth and sixteenth centuries. One of their most lucrative strategies was to make long-term loans to the ruling elite, including the Hapsburg kings, which were secured against income-generating properties such as mines. Often the terms stipulated that the Fugger company would receive the income produced by these resources until the loan was fully repaid (Meadow 2002), and thus the Fuggers developed firsthand knowledge of metallurgical processes that were particularly well developed in Germany at that time. In 1528 Carlos I—whose position as Holy Roman Emperor was secured by bribes paid to the electors by his grandfather Maximilian on the basis of a loan from the Fuggers—asked the House of Fugger to provide experts in mining and metallurgy in order to improve the production of silver in the American colonies. Metallurgists were sent to the Caribbean and Venezuela, and many ended up in New Spain where they introduced the use of a Castilian blast furnace followed by cupellation in a reverberatory furnace to produce silver (Bakewell 1984b). While the details of this very conscious act of technology transfer are not known, the procedure may have been similar to the better documented introduction of mercury amalgamation by Bartolomé de la Medina in Mexico in 1554. At the behest of the Fuggers (Mira 2000), Medina, who learned the technique from a German in Seville, traveled first to Mexico City where he resided for a year in the home of an acquaintance that became, as one historian (Probert 1997) describes it "silver amalgamation headquarters" as miners visited and learned about the new method. He then demonstrated the process to mineowners from throughout the region in a beneficiation plant he had constructed for this purpose in the village of Pachuca (Probert 1997). This period of explicit teaching was followed by years of experimentation and the exchange of knowledge among practitioners.

Almost a century later, Alonso Barba (1992 [1640], 136–38, 142–43) described reverberatory furnaces in great detail. In contrast to the European writers, he emphasized their use in smelting and, in fact, noted they had previously been used only for refining. He provided instructions for making

EXTRACTION UNDER THE COLONIAL REGIME (1573–1825)   123

reverberatory furnaces for smelting ore that could also be used, when constructed on a smaller scale and lined with ash, for refining silver, just like the cupellation hearths found at Porco. The larger version had a square platform in which a circular hearth was constructed and then lined with *carbonilla*, which is a mixture of earth and charcoal. A domed roof with a circular opening large enough for a person to enter was placed on top of this. To one side of the hearth was a rectangular firebox provided with a grate on which wood was burned to fire the furnace. A narrow opening or rectangular chimney was constructed on the opposite side of the hearth to allow smoke to escape. Triangular windows were left on the two remaining sides for the use of a bellows, if needed, and so that ore could be added and stirred or slag could be removed. Although the superstructures of UR10 to 12 were not intact, what remains of the bases conform to the reverberatories described by Alonso Barba. In the best-preserved example, UR11, a small rectangular extension opposite the firebox may indicate the presence of a chimney, and this also seems to be the case with UR10; UR 12 is too badly damaged to be able to detect this feature.

The similarities between the cupellation hearths found in the archaeological record at Porco and the small reverberatory furnaces used for refining silver that are described by Alonso Barba seem clear. However, our understanding of the origins of this technology is further confounded by a linguistic discrepancy. Alonso Barba states that a muffle furnace—a type that was used extensively in Europe—was employed by Native miners to refine silver ore after it had been smelted in a huayrachina, and he called this furnace a "tocochimbo." Carlos Cuiza never used this term, instead referring to his reverberatory furnace simply as an "horno." However, Eloy Mamani, a resident of Porco who is familiar with traditional silver production, does associate the word *tocoj* or tocochimbo with these cupellation hearths. Thus, two different types of furnace—a muffle furnace and a cupellation hearth—are identified by the same name and associated with Indigenous use.

No matter what the ultimate origin of the reverberatory furnace might be, it is clear that small-scale silver-processing technology remained important after the widespread adoption of amalgamation and that it was the subject of innovation by Indigenous metallurgists. The diversity of the technology deployed by producers during the colonial period, specifically in the southern Andes, reflects the interaction of miners and metallurgists from different technological traditions as well as different scales of production. Some of this technology, such as the patio system and, perhaps, reverberatory furnaces, were introduced under state auspices in a conscious attempt to increase productivity. In other cases, such as quimbaletes and maybe cupellation hearths technologies were reconfigured to meet the needs of small-scale producers.

Some relationship between casta, class, and technology existed; ingenios were owned almost exclusively by Spaniards, huayrachinas and cupellation hearths appear to have been used primarily by Indigenous people, and there was a strong association between trapiches and an emergent urban class of kajchas composed of various castas.

Conclusion

The implementation of the Toledan reforms in the 1570s marked the beginning of a colonial system that functioned—with modifications—to extract mineral wealth from the Andes for the benefit of Spain for the next two and a half centuries. Two reforms were especially critical for augmenting silver production: the introduction of the patio process, a technology that could process large quantities of lower grade ores, and the institution of the mita, which provided forced labor to azogueros. A less direct subsidy came in the form of an Indigenous head tax that pushed free laborers, or mingas, into the mines and mills to earn the silver they needed to pay their tribute. The mita, in particular, had a transformative, and largely negative effect on Native communities, causing demographic decline as well as massive movements of people who were either complying with or fleeing the labor requirement. Despite Toledo's totalizing vision for the reorganization of silver production, the colonial government did not succeed in completely controlling it and lost much of the associated tax revenue because of ore-sharing and the numerous types of theft that occurred throughout the production process. Like another of the Toledan reforms, the imposition of nucleated settlements, or *reducciones*, described by Mumford (2012), regulation of the silver industry was only partial and strongly resisted.

Much of the resistance came from kajchas and the small mills that served them, which together formed a parallel economy that produced a substantial amount of the silver that flowed into the global economy (Barragán 2017a). During the height of silver production in the late sixteenth and early seventeenth centuries, these workers, many of whom were Indigenous, developed an array of technologies for the processing of ore. The drive for silver combined with the interaction of people with different kinds of knowledge about the productive process resulted in a diverse set of technologies that are reflected in the documentary and archaeological records.

The colonial regime was thus characterized by a variety of metallurgical practices conducted by a wide range of practitioners working at different scales. An interdependent and often fractious relationship developed between

EXTRACTION UNDER THE COLONIAL REGIME (1573–1825)   125

large- and small-scale producers, with the level of conflict determined in large part by whether mineowners regarded ore-sharing as a necessary means of attracting labor or as theft. The state, on the other hand, treated all untaxed silver production as illicit, a position that received support from the church. Despite operating within a mercantile system that relied on both forced and free labor, the relationship between large- and small-scale production was similar to that which prevailed during the liberal economy of the nineteenth century; large-scale producers required labor, independent miners needed access to mines, and workers, both mitayos and mingas, often sought to augment their incomes by directly appropriating ore. The latter practice emerged early in the colonial period when Spaniards with little knowledge of mining gained control of exceptionally rich deposits that were worked by Indigenous people using native technologies.

4

Spanish Conquistadors and Indigenous Control of Mineral Production (1539–1572)

IN 1533 THE CONQUISTADORS, led by Francisco Pizarro, executed Atahualpa, the last sovereign Inka emperor, after acquiring an enormous ransom in gold and silver from his followers. The following four decades were characterized by a plunder economy (Spalding 1984) in which outright looting was accompanied by the extraction of surplus from Andean communities without investing in them. The key institution for accomplishing this was the *encomienda*, a system by which conquistadors were rewarded for their service to the Crown with assignments of Indigenous ethnic groups. The recipients of these grants, called *encomenderos*, could demand goods and services from Natives under their control. Many, like the Pizarros, articulated their encomienda holdings with other properties such as mines in order to create vertically integrated enterprises in which agricultural holdings generated products that were either sold in regional markets or used to sustain workers (Varón Gabai 1996). This state-authorized tribute system was wedded to the emergence of a market economy; food, fabric, and other items were accumulated and sold by encomenderos in emerging population centers, services sometimes included activities such as mine labor, and tribute in silver required Indigenous people to engage in wage labor or sell their own products.

This tumultuous period was also characterized by political conflict between Spaniards and the neo-Inka state established in the jungle at Vilcabamba as well as competition between the Pizarros and fellow conquistador Diego de Almagro and his followers (MacQuarrie 2007). Almagro arrived in Peru too late to participate in the distribution of Atahualpa's ransom, and armed conflict soon erupted as the two factions each attempted to gain

126

control over Cuzco. These internecine struggles were followed by outright insurrection against the king. In 1544 Charles V sent Viceroy Blasco Núñez Vela to Peru with orders to enforce the New Laws, which were an attempt to regulate the encomenderos and their treatment of Natives. Gonzalo Pizarro, half-brother of Francisco, opposed these regulations and organized a rebel army that killed the viceroy in 1546. Two years later Gonzalo himself was defeated and executed on the battlefield.

Spanish control over Porco was imposed during these turbulent times, and the archaeological and documentary records reflect the abrupt change from centralized state control over production by the Inkas to decentralized profit or tribute seeking by individuals. Despite the radical shift in the political economy, however, historians of early colonial Potosí have emphasized the continuity exhibited in mining technology and its control by Native people during this period (Bakewell 1984a; Lane 2019; Mangan 2005). Production became more extensive; in other words, the means of production changed very little, but overall volume was substantially increased as numerous individuals and institutions attempted to acquire mineral wealth.

While these processes clearly occurred in Porco, historical documents, particularly accounts rendered to Gonzalo Pizarro and his brother, Hernando, by their *mayordomos*, or representatives, in the mining center, suggest that during the very first years after the imposition of Spanish control European techniques were attempted but met with relatively little success. For the most part, however, the mines of Porco were exploited by Indigenous people using Native technology but functioning in different capacities—as encomienda Indians working their turn, as mingas or yanaconas. Varied arrangements akin to sharecropping developed, and rights to ore beyond that which was required by the Spaniards were recognized. It was in this hybrid economic system that illicit silver production developed.

From Inka to Spanish Control

Ana María Presta (2008) provides an account of the early history of Porco beginning with Spanish exploitation that started in 1539, seven years after the initial conquest of Peru. Almagro had passed through the area on an expedition to Chile between 1535 and 1537 but failed to find the mine, most likely because it had been hidden by the Inkas. It was only after Europeans had displayed their military prowess during the campaign of Cochabamba that the leader of the Charka federation, Kuysara, and his Qaraqara counterpart, Muruq'u, agreed to submit to the Crown and reveal the location of the mine to Hernando and Gonzalo Pizarro (Espinoza Soriano 1969). The Indigenous politics motivating this transaction can only be glimpsed in the documentary record, but Porco may have been a red herring of sorts, a gift to deflect Spanish attention away from the much larger silver deposit in nearby Potosí (Platt and Quisbert 2007); from the perspective of the Pizarros, it may have been intended as a gift to the king that could help mitigate the royal response to their execution of Almagro in 1538 (Platt, Bouysse Cassagne, and Harris 2006, 127).

An early drawing of the initial division of the mine shows that lengths of vein were allotted to Hernando, Gonzalo, and Francisca Pizarro, as well as two conquistadors, Juan Vendrel and Garci Michel. In addition, Hernando assigned a length of vein adjacent to his to the king. Additional divisions and allotments were made over the decades, and reassignments occurred after the death of Gonzalo in 1548, but the exact locations of these different holdings are unknown (Presta 2008). The drawing also depicts a small Spanish settlement with a plaza and church at the foot of Huayna Porco. Hernando returned to Spain in 1539 to defend his family against accusations made by the *almagristas* and was imprisoned in the castle of La Mota de Medina del Campo for the next 20 years. He was allowed to keep his holdings in Peru and, after Gonzalo's death in 1548, exploited them with the help of a mayordomo who supervised work in Porco as well as some of his encomiendas. Before his death Gonzalo, who had a large encomienda consisting of the Qaraqaras and most of the Charkas, was also an absentee mineowner, relying on his business partner, Antonio Álvarez, to manage the holdings in Porco (Presta 2008).

No documents have been located that systematically report mine productivity during the first decade of exploitation under the Spaniards, probably because of the lack of a fiscal system for tracking this information and also because Gonzalo's earnings, in particular, were most likely used to fund the rebellion (Presta 2008). The documents that do exist, however, provide intriguing information about the earliest years of mining at Porco, data that suggest that rather than relying completely on Indigenous labor and technology, the Pizarros and their partners initially attempted to reproduce at least some aspects of European mining and metallurgical techniques. Three documents are particularly informative regarding the technology and labor deployed to extract silver: a letter from Hernando Pizarro to the king of Spain that probably dates to after 1551, a 1563 report of income and expenditures made by Cristóbal Alvarez to Antonio Álvarez, Gonzalo's former partner, and the accounts of Gabriel Velázquez, Hernando's mayordomo, covering the period between 1548 and 1551. The latter are held in the Pizarro family's private library and have been analyzed by Miranda Díaz (2014).

FIGURE 20 Sixteenth-century drawing of Porco showing the village and initial division of the mines. Courtesy of Archivo General de Simancas.

Based on what can be gleaned from Velázquez's account, Hernando Pizarro supported a household in Porco composed of a detachment of Spaniards, some soldiers under the command of Captain Martín Monje, and a chaplain. Alongside the house were small buildings for Indians, yanaconas, and enslaved Africans, both men and women (Miranda Díaz 2014). This complex could possibly correspond to the foundation of a large building situated on the southeastern edge of Santiago hill, just to the west of the Hundimiento mine. This site, also called Santiago, was one of the few Spanish-style buildings identified during fieldwork. Mapping and excavations conducted in 1999 revealed a compound composed of a series of rectangular rooms surrounding a central patio; the walls were thick, with stone footings and whitewash on the interior, and the two rooms tested were largely devoid of remains except for a few concentrations of tin-bearing ore, likely the gangue that remained after the silver ore was removed. Three or four small rectangular foundations were located to the southwest of this building on the other side of an arroyo. Two of these were tested, but preservation was poor due to damp, acidic conditions, as well as disturbance by mining activities. In the mid-twentieth century locals referred to this compound as "Pizarro's house," an attribution that is impossible to verify. While it may have belonged to one of the Pizarro brothers or to another conquistador, the paucity of artifacts does not suggest a residential occupation. The building was probably used to store minerals and equipment, rather than as a residence which would most likely have been in the village of Porco itself.

Hernando's missive to the king, in conjunction with the other two documents, provides some information about the organization of production. His letter consists of a long complaint about his mine's lack of productivity and the possible reasons for this, including the theft of silver by one of Almagro's associates, mismanagement by his mayordomos, the time and resources needed to remove debris from the mine, and, perhaps most important, the high cost of maintaining both the mine and workforce relative to the yield in silver. Unlike Inka mines, which were comprised of open trenches and short shafts (Cruz and Absi 2008), the mine Hernando described was a long gallery driven into bedrock that was choked by fallen debris due to the poor way in which it had been constructed. Lighting was a constant concern, as reflected by the list of goods that Alvarez purchased between 1560 and May 1563. Aside from miscellaneous small items, which were not enumerated, these included candles, tallow, steel, hides, tin, cotton, "magueyes" (probably rope), and bellows, with the first four items being listed repeatedly.

As early as 1539, wooden cranes were included in a list of materials that would be supplied by one partner in a company that was established to mine silver in Porco (Presta 2008). In 1548, Hernando's administrator, Velázquez, oversaw the construction of a wooden crane to clear the mines of debris and, presumably, to aid in mineral extraction. Spaniards, enslaved people, and Indians were sent to cut the wood for the machine that was constructed by a carpenter and ironworker and had to be maintained on a regular basis by making repairs to the structure and greasing the ropes (Miranda Díaz 2014). This technology was unknown in the pre-Hispanic Andes and represents the introduction of a European technology that was not subsequently adopted by miners in the region.

On the other hand, bellows, a European tool for supplying oxygen to furnaces, were employed and saw continuous use through the colonial period. Hernando noted that during the early years in Porco, smelting was not possible because of the lack of bellows, and as a result there was so much raw ore that there were insufficient pack animals to transport it to the port. While no information is provided about the specific type of smelting furnace employed, Hernando clearly states that enslaved Africans worked the bellows when they became available. He purchased 120 enslaved people on two different occasions, but because of the high death rate due to maltreatment during the journey and the loss of others who escaped in ports, only thirty or so individuals reached Porco. According to reports from associates in Peru, these people did not fare well in the cold environment and became crippled due to exposure to the fumes emitted during smelting. As a result, Hernando told his mayordomo to purchase slaves in Peru, because even though they cost more, they would not be subject to the kind of losses that overseas shipment entailed. Hernando's account thus suggests that huayrachinas were not initially used in Porco, and that rather than employing encomienda Indians to work the bellows of European furnaces, he footed the expense of importing costly slaves to perform that job.

Indigenous people were, though, employed to extract, process, and transport ore. Lope de Mendieta, a conquistador, was assigned a mine in Porco as well as a large encomienda in Carangas, located a few hundred kilometers to the northwest; his brother, Juan Ortiz de Zárate, inherited his holdings at Mendieta's death in 1553. As Presta (2000) recounts, the extended Zárate family controlled a web of holdings in what is now southern Bolivia that ultimately included mines, urban real estate, a textile factory, and haciendas that produced a variety of products. In addition to labor, encomienda workers provided food, clothing, tallow, and other items as tribute; these were used to support the yanaconas and enslaved workers at Porco and Potosí and were also sold in urban markets.

In both the Alvarez and Velazquez accounts, a distinction was made between "indios" who worked in the mines and "yanaconas" who washed the extracted ore to rid it of salts and clay prior to smelting. Alvarez also differentiates between renting Indians to work the mines—probably a reference to a system by which an encomendero was paid to allow Natives under his control to work for another—and providing a daily wage, or *jornal*, to these workers. He purchased maize specifically for the yanaconas, and when he failed to provide them with food, he gave them money to buy it, a reflection of their role as personal retainers or servants; no mention is made of supplying Indians with food, most likely because they were expected to purchase it with their jornales. The provisioning of food by encomenderos or via the market is reflected in the macrobotanical remains associated with excavated structures. These include introduced foods such as lentils, wheat, and oats, as well as native plants such as chili peppers, maize, and squash, none of which could have been grown nearby (Muñoz Rojas 2019).

The way in which silver extraction was organized by the Pizarros during the first decade of Spanish mining in Porco differed substantially from the strong reliance on Native labor and technology that characterized the following twenty years of production prior to the Toledan reforms (Bakewell 1984a; Lane 2019; Salazar-Soler 1997b). Most significantly, Indigenous smelting technologies, specifically huayrachinas, do not appear to have been used, and yanaconas, rather than taking charge of the smelting as they did in subsequent decades, engaged in washing and sorting ore. Instead, enslaved Africans were employed to work the bellows of European-style smelters, a technology that was noted as characteristic of Porco by a Spanish observer, although it was not successful in Potosí (Cieza de León 2005 [c. 1549–1553], 271–72). Finally, the long, apparently poorly built, underground galleries required massive numbers of candles to illuminate and, more importantly, the use of a mechanical crane to clear them of debris and extract the ore. Rather than the rapid adoption of Native practices for producing silver that can be seen in Potosí, the Pizarros, instead, relied primarily on European techniques that proved only somewhat successful. Despite early accounts of the riches of Porco (Presta 2008), between 1548 and 1551, Hernando Pizarro invested more than he earned from his mines, although they did become profitable in subsequent years (Miranda Díaz 2014). The initial poor return on his investment was probably due, at least in part, to the chaotic conditions under which the mines operated during the Civil War and the fact that Hernando was an absentee mineowner attempting to administer his holdings from Spain. However, the imbalance between expenditures and yields may also have resulted from the attempt to replicate European practices, rather than adopting appropriate Indigenous techniques. This scenario is similar to what Deagan (1996) documented at La Isabella, Columbus's first settlement on Hispaniola. There colonists attempted to directly transfer Spanish lifeways without incorporating local dietary and other practices, a strategy that ended in the failure of the colony. Subsequent integration of Native and European material culture resulted in long-lived communities in Hispaniola and, later, other parts of the Caribbean. Unsurprisingly, the successful (from a Spanish perspective) hybridization of European and American practices necessitated familiarity with Native organization and technology that required a period of sustained interaction between colonizers and the colonized.

Indigenous Production in Potosí and Porco

The circumstances under which the "discovery" of Potosí was made have recently been called into question. One version of the traditional narrative is that Diego Guallpa, a yanacona from Porco, discovered the enormous silver deposit after being ordered by his master to ascend the mountain to look for

SPANISH CONQUISTADORS AND INDIGENOUS CONTROL   133

a shrine which he did, indeed, find. After sending the offerings that he recovered down the mountain with a companion, he descended and was blown over by a gust of wind. While righting himself, he grabbed a handful of sediment that he recognized as silver ore. He returned to Porco where he smelted the ore, which turned out to be incredibly rich. Word of the discovery reached a Spaniard named Villaroel who staked a claim, thus initiating a silver rush that included many of the yanaconas who had been working at Porco. While these events may have occurred, Platt and Quisbert (2007, 2010) have questioned the notion that the Spaniards were the first to discover Potosí, arguing, instead, that the Inkas suppressed information about the silver mine until they decided to reveal it as a gift to the Crown—rather than to the Pizarros—in 1545. Cruz and Absi (2008) suggest that Guallpa, who was an Indigenous nobleman and had been keeper of the Inka's royal featherwork, purposefully visited a *huaca*, or ceremonial precinct, on the peak of Cerro Rico to engage in some sort of ritual prior to revealing the location of the mines to the Spaniards. In any case, 1545, the year Gonzalo rebelled against the king, was marked by an influx of Indigenous workers and Spanish mineowners into the newly formed mining town that was surrounded by encomiendas controlled by the Pizarro brothers.

Peter Bakewell's 1984 analysis of the organization of production in Potosí during the first century after the conquest describes the nexus of participants in this activity. Bakewell identified two key forms of Indigenous labor in Potosí that were also present in Porco: yanaconas and *hatunruna*, the latter being the Quechua term for community members who were assigned in encomienda to Spaniards. As Bakewell notes, the precise nature of yanaconas, who had their origins in Inka times, is difficult to determine, but as early as the late 1530s the term had come to refer to personal servants who had abandoned their Indigenous masters and attached themselves to individual conquerors. Unlike hatunruna, they were not affiliated with ayllus, were not subject to the labor tax, and prior to 1572 did not pay tribute. For these reasons, many regular encomienda Indians most likely joined the ranks of yanaconas in order to escape those obligations (Salazar-Soler 1997b). Yanaconas engaged in a wide variety of tasks, including craft production in urban centers and agricultural work. However, during these early years they were primarily known for their use of huayrachinas to smelt silver ore. While some of them arrived from Porco with this expertise, others, like Diego Guallpa himself, must have learned the skill from fellow Indians.

Huayrachinas were so abundant in Potosí during this time that one observer described them as looking like luminarias arrayed against the night sky (Cieza de León 2005 [c. 1549–53], 375) and another counted 6,497 of them in 1585, most derelict and unused after the widespread adoption of mercury amalgamation in the 1570s (Capoche 1959 [1585]). Owing to their construction on ridges and hillslopes surrounding the city, they were easily seen, and a number of observers wrote descriptions of them (Oehm 1984; Van Buren 2003), accounts that generally accord with what is known from later historical (Alonso Barba 1992 [1640]; Peele 1893) and ethnoarchaeological (Van Buren and Mills 2005) information. A summary of these descriptions (Oehm 1984) indicates that huayrachinas were flower-pot shaped furnaces with flaring sides that were perforated with holes. They were constructed of clay on small stone pedestals and were approximately 1 m in height. Two authors (Garcilaso de la Vega 1941 [1609]; Ramírez 1965 [1836], 119) noted that they were portable. Almost all reported that charcoal was used as fuel, although a few mentioned that llama dung and firewood were also employed (Acosta 1954 [1590]; Capoche 1959 [1585]; Zárate 1965 [1555]). Refining furnaces, in contrast, were poorly described, probably because they were used in Indigenous homes rather than in public spaces. As mentioned in the previous chapter, Alonso Barba, who wrote a century later, called these furnaces tocochimbos, and others noted that they were used with *sopladores* and *fuelles*, blow tubes and bellows, the latter, a European introduction.

A sixteenth-century watercolor titled *Estos yns. estan guayrando*, or "these Indians are smelting with huayrachinas," depicts two Indigenous men operating three huayrachinas that correspond in all details except for height to the descriptions found in colonial documents. Interestingly, the Indians wear Andean ponchos and European-style hats, suggesting an affinity with Spanish culture that would have been characteristic of yanaconas. Remnants of huayrachinas have been found in the vicinity of Potosí as well as Porco. In the case of Potosí, Pablo Cruz has identified the remains of huayrachinas on some of the hills surrounding the city, particularly Juku Huachana where they are arrayed near sixty round and rectangular structures associated with the storage of fuel and food (Cruz and Absi 2008). In Porco, the remains of huayrachinas occur on most of the lower hills surrounding the village but form a palimpsest representing multiple uses over a long period of time. No intact examples have been found, nor have any foundations been identified, because as described and depicted in the documents these small furnaces were either portable or constructed on flat rocks and thus have been eroded away by rain and wind. Instead, the ridgetops and slopes immediately below them are littered with huayrachina fragments, fire-reddened and vitrified rocks, small pieces of slag and charcoal, and ceramics dating from Inka to recent times (Van Buren and Mills 2005). Fragments of stationary versions with

FIGURE 21 *Estos yns. estan guayrando.* Sixteenth-century watercolor of Natives smelting ore in huayrachinas. Courtesy of the Hispanic Society of America.

thick walls and large holes as well as thin-walled portable types with small apertures have been recovered.

The yanaconas who operated the huayrachinas may have been the same people who were called "indios de vara" by colonial writers (Bakewell 1984a, 49–51). These were skilled Indigenous men who were assigned to work lengths of mine by the encomenderos who owned the claim. The indios de vara operated as supervisors of Native work but were themselves usually supervised by European or even Indigenous administrators (Lane 2019, 52). According to one source quoted at length by Bakewell, indios de vara would give the richest ore, called *cacilla*, to the mineowner who would then sell it back to him or to some other Indian who would smelt it; the indio de vara could keep the *llampu*, which was lower grade, for himself. Interestingly, the author of this observation noted that cacilla means something given for free, in this way acknowledging that the mineowner profited from ore that he had done nothing to extract. The llampu, however, and the profit made from the smelted cacilla were sufficient to cover the Native's costs and occasionally made some of them wealthy. This sharecropping arrangement could be implemented in a variety of ways, but the essential aspect of the relationship entailed ore-sharing between the legal owner and the individual who actually worked the mine and smelted the ore.

The distinction between ore-sharing and theft is not always clear, although it probably turned on whether or not the miner removing the ore had an agreement with the owner or was a hatunruna who was simply expected to work for a daily wage. From early on, observers noted that Indians enriched themselves in the silver mines (Cieza de León 2005 [c. 1549–53], 375–76) often "stealing" ore during their regular work assignments. Women were specifically implicated in this activity and appear to have smelted the silver obtained in this manner. Diego de Ocaña, a traveler who visited Potosí in 1600, described the process in the following way: "These metals that the Indian women smelt are pieces of ore very rich in silver, that the Indian who is a pick man working in the mine, when he finds a rich piece of ore and that has a lot of silver, hides, and when he goes to the mine mouth to receive food that his wife brings on Wednesdays, takes out the ore that he has hidden and gives it to the woman; although the miners watch them carefully, in this way they all hide what they can" (Ocaña 1969 [c. 1599–1608], 184). Raquel Gil Montero (2014, 83) found that women engaged in the same activities in Lípez. After smelting and refining the ore, the women in Potosí then took it to the *khatu*, or Indigenous market, where they sold it; smelters could purchase raw ore and other supplies there as well (Mangan 2005). As Allison Bigelow's (2016) and Rossana Barragán's (2020) work demonstrates, women were involved in more than processing and selling ore that their husbands appropriated. Many Indigenous women were discoverers and owners of mines, operated trapiches, and also did hands-on work in the mines and mills.

One way in which surveillance of mine workers was carried out can be seen at Site 24 in Porco (Van Buren and Mills 2005). This site is situated on a ridge called Zodillos whose spine is formed by a mineral bearing deposit radiating from Huayna Porco to the north (Cunningham et al. 1994). Three mine shafts are located on the eastern edge of the site, and to the west of these are concentrations of huayrachina fragments, sherds, and small pieces of slag and charcoal as well as a series of small boulders that were probably used for windbreaks and as pedestals for the huayrachinas. A large quantity of ground stone fragments, used primarily for crushing rather than grinding, was found on the surface, but these were not intermixed with the furnace fragments. The presence of sherds from Spanish botijas in association with decorated Indigenous ceramics indicates an early colonial date. A rectangular foundation, Structure 23, is located on a rise to the northwest with a clear view of the mines and huayrachinas. Excavations in this structure revealed the remains of what seem to be refining furnaces as well as cooking and serving vessels indicative of domestic activity. The location of Structure 23 on a barren ridgetop without access to water, but with a clear view of the mines and huayrachinas, suggests that it played a role in the surveillance of miners and smelters. Site 24 is unusual in two ways. First, no other mines or

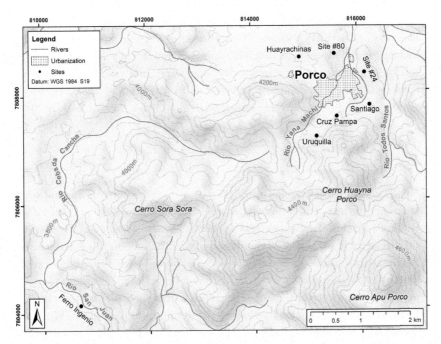

MAP 7 Location of sites mentioned in text. Map by Brendan Weaver.

smelting locales are associated with structures from which work could have been supervised. Second, a number of stages of production can be found at Site 24: mineral extraction, comminution of the ore, smelting, and, most likely, refining. As will be seen below, in most sites at Porco extraction and refining were usually spatially distinct.

Decentralized Mineral Production in Porco

There is abundant archaeological evidence at Porco for the decentralized nature of mineral production conducted by small teams of people during the sixteenth century. Under the Inka, distinct facilities for accommodating the different stages of the *chaîne opératoire*, or productive chain, were constructed at some distance from one another. Under the Spaniards, most of these structures were reused by small groups of people engaged in the same activities, namely silver processing and basic domestic activities such as food preparation and consumption. These sites include Site 80, the early component of Ferro Ingenio, Uruquilla (not to be confused with the ethnic group of the same name), Cruz Pampa, and Huayrachinas. The contemporaneity of these sites is indicated by similarities in the artifact assemblages, particularly ceramics; the sixteenth- to early seventeenth-century date rests on the presence of small quantities of Panamanian blue-on-white and Polychrome A majolica, the relative abundance of decorated Indigenous wares, and rarer finds such as a hawksbell from Cruz Pampa, glass beads, and a silver coin produced between 1596 and 1612 from Ferro Ingenio.

Site 80

Site 80 was constructed in an unusual location on the eastern, downwind side of a ridge to the north of the village of Porco, just to the west and above the Río Yana Machi. The entire extent of the site, as defined by a light scatter of surface artifacts consisting of sherds, slag, crucible and portable huayrachina fragments, and pieces of burned clay, is now covered with a small dune field that makes walking difficult. Excavations revealed that the dunes existed prior to the site's establishment. The choice of this particular location is difficult to explain, except for its proximity to huayrachinas (the site of Huayrachinas Altas) on the ridge crest to the west and the fact that it is sheltered from the wind and close to a source of water.

FIGURE 22 Ceramic huayrachina and crucible fragments from Site 80, Porco. Photograph by the author.

Excavations in three rectangular stone structures (the only foundations that were visible on the surface of the site) and two small test units in extramural areas revealed an assemblage that consists almost entirely of Indigenous material culture with the exception of the rim of a Spanish-style soup bowl made with Indigenous technology and a single fragment of iron. The scarcity of European artifacts, such as botija sherds, at Site 80 suggests a very early occupation, and the presence of crucibles and fragments of what were either portable huayrachinas or muffles indicate it was used to process silver. This pattern of limited domestic activities associated with mineral processing and refining is found throughout Porco.

Early Colonial Ferro Ingenio

An early Indigenous component of Ferro Ingenio is represented by a dozen or so rectangular foundations located in the southeastern sector of the site, just to the east of a battery of reverberatory furnaces. The latter were in a rectangular depression that was dug into the hillside at a later date and cut through this residential area. Four structures and two extramural areas were tested in 2007 as part of Brendan Weaver's (2008) thesis project. Slag and

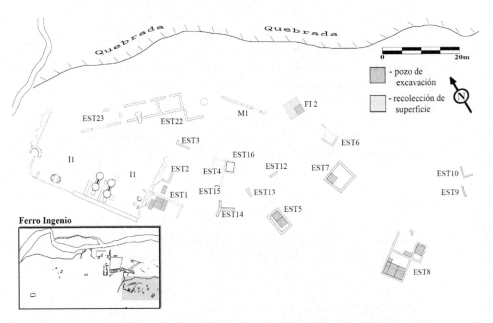

FIGURE 23 Southeastern sector of Ferro Ingenio. Map by Brendan Weaver.

 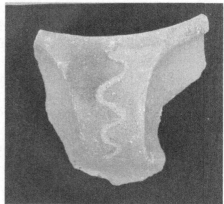

FIGURE 24 Ceramics from Ferro Ingenio. The three sherds in the center are Panamanian majolicas; the rest appear to have been produced in the Andes as they are visually similar to Group 4 ceramics identified by Smit and VanValkenburgh (2023). The sherd on the right is an unglazed earthenware with a serpentine appliqué. Photograph by Brendan Weaver.

gangue, as well as domestic refuse, particularly cooking and serving vessels, were ubiquitous.

Structure 8 contained a metallurgical feature of unknown function that bears some similarities to the hearth found in Structure 7 at Site 35 and to the features uncovered in Structure 1 at Huayrachinas and Structure 14 at Uruquilla, which are described below. In the case of Ferro Ingenio, the feature consisted of an elliptical adobe trough with a small clay-lined tongue perched 6 cm above it. Small pieces of lead were found in this structure as well as the others at Ferro Ingenio. These features apparently employed gravity, perhaps to separate liquid metal from waste material, and the process involved the production or use of lead, maybe in cupellation. The precise function of these hearths, however, is far from clear.

Uruquilla

Uruquilla is located upstream and to the southwest of the village of Porco and is sometimes referred to as Porco Viejo, or old Porco. It consists of a series of one-room rectangular structures arrayed in irregular northwest–southeast-oriented rows on a relatively flat area overlooking the Yana Machi River, which is entrenched below. The original disposition of buildings is difficult to discern because the site has been reworked in the recent past to create a few

FIGURE 25 Uruquilla (Porco Viejo) looking east. Most of the structures have been reused as corrals. Photograph by the author.

small houses and continues to be used for sheep and llama corrals today. Structure 10, which contains the well-preserved reverberatory furnace described in chapter 3, is located on the eastern edge of this part of the site.

The main cluster of buildings is bounded on the north by the Yana Machi, to the east and west by smaller dry arroyos, and to the south by two large rock outcrops. To the southeast of these rocks is an open area that appears to be a plaza, delineated by a low stone wall. To the west, east, and south of the core of the site are the poorly preserved remains of rectangular and circular foundations and quimbaletes on stone platforms; the line of three reverberatory furnace foundations described in chapter 3 is located upslope and at the base of Huayna Porco.

Excavations in Uruquilla took place during two seasons. The goal of the first, in 1998, was to determine whether the subsurface remains in the core of the site had been preserved and, if so, what they represented; four rectangular foundations, three circular foundations, and nine extramural contexts were tested. The second season, in 2005, focused on the industrial facilities, especially the previously described reverberatory furnaces. The 1998 excavations revealed that many of the subsurface deposits were still intact. All but two extramural contexts yielded pieces of gangue, or waste rock left over from ore selection, as well as lumps of fire-hardened and sometimes vitrified clay, some of which appear to have been parts of metallurgical facilities. Charcoal and carbonized llama dung were also recovered from many contexts, as was evidence of food preparation and consumption. While all the structures and most of the outside areas that were tested yielded artifacts indicative of metallurgical activities, no intact refining features were found. The only exception to this was the 2005 excavation of what at first appeared to be an extramural area (designated UR14) but that turned out to be a rectangular foundation with a small feature that was quite similar to the one found in Structure 7 at Site 35, which was described in chapter 3. This crudely made structure was located to the south of the core of the site, adjacent to the arroyo that runs along its east side. The feature was built into the east wall and had external dimensions of 1.5 m by 1 m. The part extending into the wall was slightly tongue-shaped and sloped downward toward a small rectangular basin 10 cm below. Found nearby were fragments of burned, ceramic cigar-shaped artifacts as well as a provincial Inka plate. As is the case with the feature located at Site 35, the purpose of this hearth is unknown, although it undoubtedly was related to metallurgical production.

Cruz Pampa

Cruz Pampa is located on a steep slope and is divided into two parts by a quebrada, with five or six rectangular stone foundations situated on both sides. Poor preservation, due to erosion as well as reuse of the site for corrals and small fields, make it difficult to determine the total number of original buildings at the site, or the overall layout. The location and material culture, however, are similar to Uruquilla, which is just 200 m to the southwest and separated from Cruz Pampa by a low ridge with a scatter of huayrachina remains on its surface. Excavations took place at Cruz Pampa during two seasons, 2002 and 2005, with a total of three structures and ten extramural test pits excavated.

As was the case in Uruquilla, debris associated with processing and refining silver was ubiquitous; pieces of gangue and burned clay were found in the three structures and all extramural units, and a clay huayrachina fragment was recovered from CP8—an excavation in what appeared, at first, to be an extramural unit but that turned out to be within a rectangular building. Tools indicative of earlier steps in the process of mineral extraction were also found in CP8, including an iron bar used to pick ore, although it was above the living surface and thus probably not associated with the occupation of that

SPANISH CONQUISTADORS AND INDIGENOUS CONTROL   143

structure. Excavations outside Structure 3 yielded two stones with dimples on multiple surfaces that were used to crush ore.

CP2, one of the extramural units near the center of the site, also revealed a well-preserved reverberatory furnace. This was similar in plan to UR10, with a round hearth, rectangular firebox with stone slats, and a possible chimney. This furnace was smaller, though, than the reverberatories uncovered at Uruquilla, and parts of the dome and the vitrified furnace floor were intact.

Huayrachinas

The site of Huayrachinas is located 500 m to the north of Porco, on the western side of the ridge on which Site 80 is also located. A cluster of huayrachinas, called Huayrachinas Altas, is situated on the ridge top immediately to the northeast, which is how the site received its name; however, the site of Huayrachinas itself consists of forty-five circular and rectangular stone foundations arrayed around the head of a dry arroyo. Two rectangular buildings, one circular one, and two extramural areas were tested during the 1999 season. Metallurgical debris consisting of burnt and vitrified clay and pieces of gangue were ubiquitous, occurring in all excavated contexts, as did animal bone and domestic ceramics. A number of small, shallow mortars, made from sandstone that outcrops near Agua de Castilla, were found on the surface of the site. Unlike the dimpled crushing stones recovered from Cruz Pampa, these were used for grinding. No reverberatory furnaces were identified at Huayrachinas, but an intact metallurgical feature, most likely used for refining, was uncovered in Structure 1. Although distinct in form, it had two heavily burned small hearths or chambers, one located about 10 cm above the other so that liquid could flow from the upper to lower hearth.

Excavations in a wide variety of contexts in Porco have thus revealed a redundant archaeological record that clearly reflects the focus on mineral processing and refining within structures where people prepared and ate food, slept, and engaged in a limited number of other activities, such as spinning. Overall, artifact diversity was low, and other than a few spindle whorls and an occasional projectile point, artifacts reflect the production of metal and the maintenance of workers but little else. That women were members of these groups is reflected most directly by the inadvertent discovery of the lower part of an adult female skeleton that was eroding out of a path adjacent to Huayrachinas. Spindle whorls (sometimes used by men in the Andes but more commonly associated with women) and fragments of tupus, or women's pins, were found at all sites except Site 80, and *laurakes*, women's bronze hair

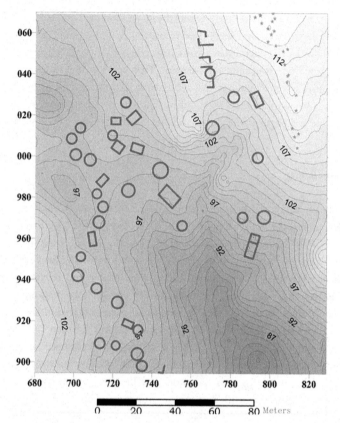

FIGURE 26 The site of Huayrachinas. Rectangles and circles are stone foundations; huayrachina remains on the ridgetop are represented as stars. The entire area is referred to locally as "Huayrachinas." Plan by the author.

ornaments, were recovered from Huayrachinas, Cruz Pampa, and Ferro Ingenio. Laurakes are most commonly found in the far southern Titicaca Basin in the area occupied in pre-Inka and Inka times by the Pacajes but have been recovered from a small number of Inka sites as well, perhaps because of the presence of Pacajes women at them (Sagárnaga Meneses 2021).

Three excavated contexts are also suggestive of the presence of yanaconas, specialized workers most likely engaged in smelting and refining at the behest of their Spanish masters. Structure 1 at Huayrachinas is the largest of all the foundations at the site and yielded European-style artifacts that are otherwise rare in Porco. These include a small quantity of glass, glass beads, and, most notably, the firing mechanism from a matchlock. Guns were extremely expensive during the late sixteenth century, and Indigenous people were discouraged from owning them. Whether this artifact represents an actual firearm or was scavenged for its scrap metal is unknown, but in either case it suggests a level of engagement with European material culture that probably would not be typical of mitayos. Similarly, a hawksbell, silver coins, and glass were recovered from CP8 at Cruz Pampa. Finally, Structure 8 at Ferro Ingenio yielded a silver tupu, a leather shoe sole, and a silver-wrapped tassel, items that are indicative of modest wealth but, perhaps more importantly, the use of European footwear and bodily adornment in the case of the tassel.

Like many late pre-Hispanic and early colonial sites in the Qaraqara region of southern Bolivia, the ceramic assemblage from Porco is characterized by a wide variety of types (Cruz 2007). Provincial Inka ceramics, consisting of decorated jars and shallow bowls, sometimes with nubs in the shape of animal heads, comprise a substantial component of the decorated sherds from the sites. This style persisted for decades after the Spanish conquest as its presence at Ferro Ingenio as well as at Torata Alta, a Peruvian site dated precisely to 1600 by a volcanic ash fall, attests (Van Buren and Weaver 2014). It may have functioned as a symbol of affiliation with the Inka Empire for yanaconas, like Diego Guallpa, who had served the empire in the past, or others who wished to enhance their status. Chillpe-Carangas ceramics are another Indigenous decorated ware that occurs at Porco. This style is represented primarily by slightly deeper bowl forms with black undulating lines or spirals on a slightly burnished reddish slip. This type of decoration is widespread in the Carangas region to west of Lake Poopó and may be associated with that ethnic group (Michel 2000). However, Cruz has located a workshop producing this pottery close to Potosí and refers to it as Qolla Tardío I and II (Cruz and Téreygeol 2014); it occurs in association with Inka wares at that site. At Porco, this style is also found in conjunction with a loosely defined group of ceramics referred to as Late Altiplano wares that consist primarily of black-on-red bowls as well as small quantities of Pacajes (also called Saxamar) pottery that is sometimes attributed to the ethnic group of the same name located to the south of Lake Titicaca. While it is tempting to infer the presence of members of specific ethnic groups at Porco from the occurrence of certain ceramic types, Cruz and Téreygeol (2014) make the point that this complex of types is commonly found at mining sites throughout the region; decorated ceramics appear to reference the presence of "Qolla" people from the circum-Titicaca region but cannot be used as markers of specific groups. This is particularly true because pottery vessels may have been brought by mitayos from home, but they could also have been purchased in Potosí, where large contingents of Carangas, Lupaqa, and other Qolla groups (Nicolas 2018) could have made a variety of wares available.

FIGURE 27 Provincial Inka jar fragments from Site 80; provincial Inka bowl fragments from Huayrachinas. Photograph by the author.

FIGURE 28 Carangas and Chillpe bowl fragments from Cruz Pampa. Photograph by the author.

The archaeological record at Porco, then, indicates the presence of multiple, small groups of workers, probably from the Qolla region. These squads, which included both men and women, appear to have been supervised by people who sometimes deployed European material culture, possibly yanaconas. Teams processed ore and engaged in silver refining within spaces that were also used for residential purposes. Direct evidence for mineral extraction in the mines of Huayna Porco, however, has been destroyed by subsequent mining activities.

Ideological Violence

Mines, mountains, chunks of pure ore, even the smelters used to refine it—were considered *huacas* by Andeans, nonhuman beings with whom people attempted to establish reciprocal relationships; typically, offerings and care were given in exchange for health, fertility, resources, or some other aspect of well-being (Bray 2015). Huacas were the manifestation of animistic worldviews that were prevalent in Andean societies (Sillar 2009) and distinct from the perspectives of early Modern European ones, even if a mechanistic view of the universe had not yet become dominant in the latter.

The imposition of forced labor on the Native population of the southern Andes had its ideological counterpart in the campaign against religious practices that ran counter to Catholic dogma. The extirpation of idolatry, as it was known, reached its organizational peak in the early seventeenth century with the full force of the inquisition behind it (Spalding 1984). In the decades immediately following the conquest, however, such activities were more closely associated with the plunder economy as Spaniards despoiled huacas, as much for their treasure as for ideological purposes. The Spaniards seem to have quickly recognized the relationship between mines and huacas in the Andes, which may have been a factor in the "discovery" of Cerro Rico (Salazar-Soler 1997a). In any case, huacas were often associated with offerings, some of which were made of silver or gold.

Information about the Porco huaca comes primarily from a document composed at some point between 1591 and 1606 that has been extensively analyzed by Platt, Bouysse Cassagne, and Harris (2006). It consists of a *probanza de méritos y servicios* in which Hernán González de la Casa, a Spanish priest, recounted his service to the king in an attempt to receive special favors, namely a higher position in the Charkas diocese. One of the key events in the account occurred early in his career: the discovery and destruction of a huaca located in the valley of Caltama, 50 km to the south of Porco. González described the huaca as consisting of five idols, one of which, "Porco," was made of three stones and a piece of rich silver ore called *tacana* and was dedicated to the eponymous mines and mountain. The other four were named after unidentified mountains with silver and lead mines: Cuycoma, Chapoti, Suricaba, and Aricaba. The huaca was served by a religious practitioner named Diego Yquisi, who heard the confessions of people who came on pilgrimages from the districts of Charkas and Qaraqara and as far away as Cochabamba to make offerings to cure their infirmities, receive rain, and predict their futures. Yquisi said mass, performed communion with maize beer, offered novenas to the huacas, heard confessions, and assigned penance.

The religious activities described by González de la Casa appear to reflect the interpenetration of Indigenous and Spanish practices (Abercrombie 1998, 266–70), although distinguishing between the exact nature of these behaviors and the Catholic lens through which he understood them is difficult. It seems likely that Diego Yquisi had adopted some Catholic practices but that the meaning to Native participants would have been shaped by both cultural tradition and historical experience; confessions, for example, were a common part of ritual practice even in pre-Hispanic times. However, given the changes that were wrought by the Inka as well as the Spanish conquest, the degree to which González de la Casa's account can be used to infer ritual activity in the distant past—specifically, the early centuries of the Late Intermediate Period—is debatable. What seems certain, though, is that under the Inka there had been a huaca at Porco that was the focus of a regional pilgrimage cult and that it was subsequently hidden in Caltama to avoid the notice of Spanish priests.

González made off with the idols as well as objects associated with its veneration, including silver vessels, musical instruments, and cloth. One hundred armed Indians chased him down the river, but he managed to escape with his loot, numerous children, and "infidel" Natives, as well as Yquisi whom he ultimately enslaved in a hospital (Platt, Bouysse Cassagne, and Harris 2006, 186). His actions clearly had both religious and pecuniary motives. The latter are revealed by the fact that he took a scribe and other officials with him precisely so that he could record the anticipated treasure and pay the appropriate portion to the state.

One of the few other descriptions of a huaca located within a colonial mine comes from a seventeenth-century author who encountered a figure found by Spaniards in 1575 within one of the most important mines in Cerro Rico. He described it as a "statue made of different metals" about the size of a medium man with a beautiful face made of white silver, a chest of ruby silver, arms of mixed ore, and ill-formed legs of black silver ore. When the Spaniards tried to remove it, they found that its head was attached to the mine shaft, and they had to hack it out much to the consternation of the Natives, who likened this desecration to the dismemberment of Tupac Amaru, the last Inka. Apparently, the figure was replaced two days later with one of "almost monstrous form," with a head resembling a frog, one human and one cow leg, and a torso like the shell of a tortoise (Arzans de Orsua y Vela Tomo I, 1965 [c. 1705–35], 160, quoted in Nicolas 2018, 111–13). Like the huaca at Porco, these were made of rich ore, but in contrast the figures had the inchoate forms of animate beings probably because they evoked them in their natural state and were, perhaps, only partially worked by humans. They are very similar to illas,

SPANISH CONQUISTADORS AND INDIGENOUS CONTROL 149

spiritually powerful representations of mineral or agricultural productivity (Bouysse Cassagne 2005).

González's *probanza* will be discussed further in the following chapter as it relates to the pre-Hispanic situation. However, the case is relevant to the early colonial period because it speaks to both the continuation of Native rituals as well as the success that the conquerors had in dismantling regional forms of religious practice such as pilgrimages to Porco. While religious activity at the community and regional levels was crushed, individuals and households continued to practice Indigenous rituals, including those associated with metallurgy and mining. Bartolomé Alvarez, who worked for the Inquisition, described such practices in 1588:

> There are in Potosí a large number of smelters called huayradores. These smelt—or huayran—for themselves one week what they hid in another; and the week that they decide to smelt they confess to their confessors— that they call *ichuiris*—in order that the silver metal is produced in abundance. When they are smelting, they offer coca to the fire in the *huayra-china*, the burning of which they think brings better earnings after the smelt. They have little furnaces in their houses in which they refine silver; in lighting the furnace and putting the silver in to refine, they begin to offer cocoa in the fire and an aborted llama or a guinea pig, and hair from their eyebrows and eyelashes. (Alvarez 1588, quoted in Nicolas 2018)

Such rituals are similar to one practiced recently by Carlos Cuiza when he was initiating a smelt. At root they embody the reciprocal nature of human interaction with nature; making offerings to the huayrachina ensures that the yield of smelted metal will be high, just as offerings to the huaca of Porco were expected to heal illness or bring rain. The Andean sacralization of the natural world, including the mines and the ore they produced, was attacked by the Spaniards who succeeded in destroying the most overt religious activities performed at the community and regional levels.

Conclusion

Historical documents attest that ore-sharing was commonly practiced in Potosí during the early decades of exploitation when Spaniards left most of the productive process in Indigenous hands. While they demanded a specific quantity of silver per week, workers, specifically the yanaconas, were allowed to retain the rest for themselves or to buy it back to smelt in their huayrachinas. Two factors could have shifted this system from ore-sharing to ore theft. First, hatunruna—most of whom probably did not have this kind of agreement with mineowners—also appropriated high-quality ore that they obtained during their shifts. Second, as ore quality declined, owners were less likely to allow the retention of ore by workers of any type.

No such documentation exists for Porco where production was initially organized according to a traditional Iberian model. Nevertheless, the archaeological record clearly indicates that small crews of workers of the type described by Bakewell (1984a) in Potosí, quickly came to engage in metal production. Diverse technologies are present in the archaeological record including crucibles, shallow bowls used to refine silver, huayrachinas, reverberatory furnaces, and small, inclined hearths of unknown function. Many of the traces of metallurgical activity occur in spaces that were also used for domestic purposes, so there would have been ample opportunity to appropriate or "steal" ore at these points in the chaîne opératoire as well as in the mines as was commonly described. Ore-sharing—or theft—was thus an integral aspect of early colonial mining and one that fueled the creation of a parallel mining sector that was dominated by Indigenous actors.

5

Inka Silver Mining and Its Antecedents in the Southern Andes

THE INKAS BEGAN THEIR EXPANSION into the southern Andes in the fourteenth or early fifteenth century, a process that entailed various types of engagement with local societies prior to imperial consolidation. This occurred in the late fifteenth century, perhaps under the regime of Pachakuti (Platt, Bouysse Cassagne, and Harris 2006, 27). Archaeologists have long maintained that the primary factor driving the conquest was the availability of rich ore deposits as well as the labor of skilled artisans to work them (Earle 1994; Raffino 1983; Raffino et al. 2013). Recent research, however, emphasizes the Inkas' relationship with regionally important huacas (Hayashida et al. 2022), as well as their interest in procuring metals from spiritually significant mineral deposits (Cruz 2022). Inka beliefs about mountains, mines, and metallurgy were part of a broader cosmovision that was tightly imbricated with the imperial political economy and shaped the exploitation of mineral deposits throughout southern Bolivia, northern Chile, and northwestern Argentina.

Earle and D'Altroy (D'Altroy and Earle 1985; Earle 1994) posit that the Inka employed two means of financing the government: staples, which were the food, clothing, and tools produced for the state, and wealth, which consisted of valuable objects that were distributed to leaders in return for their political allegiance. The latter allowed the decentralization of the extraction of resources such that local rulers were responsible for providing them to the Inka as part of the asymmetrical reciprocity that characterized the empire's relationship with its subjects (Earle 1994). Metal objects, which were produced by a process most people never witnessed and often came from distant lands, connotated high status and were imbued by the specific meanings associated with their origins as well as their form, color, and reflectivity. These were

151

particularly important components of wealth finance, and their production may have been one of the primary goals of Inka expansion to the south. The use of such metal objects in the establishment and maintenance of political relationships does not stand in contradiction to the complex webs of meaning in which their production was embedded.

Pre-Hispanic and European silver production thus occurred in profoundly different contexts. Markets and money did not exist in the Andes prior to the Spanish conquest. Silver was used for religious objects and was also associated with high social status, but the metal was not regarded as economic wealth in the way it was by Spaniards who participated in a mercantile system that was shaped by market forces. Despite radical differences between the political economies of the Inka and Spanish Empires, however, there is some evidence that competition over mineral resources occurred in both. This resulted in the physical and ideological control of the richest (and for the Inkas most symbolically potent) deposits by powerful outsiders and the exploitation of lower yielding, less important mines by locals working for themselves or their ethnic leaders.

This chapter first describes pre-Inka mining and metallurgy in the southern Andes, then examines the organization of production at Porco, and finally considers the imposition of Inka control over mineral extraction in the southern Andes. Prior to Inka domination, metal production was associated with increased social differentiation, but thus far little evidence exists for elite control of the process. The Inkas, however, regulated the production of metal in conquered provinces; many metallurgical facilities were reorganized, and new centers were constructed. Copper minerals and finished objects may have been gifted to local elites or offered to huacas (Salazar et al. 2022), but silver appears to have been siphoned off from the local economy and transferred to Cusco or other imperial centers. In Porco the Inkas created an entirely new system of exploitation in which different tasks—probably conducted by different social groups—were coordinated by the state. At the same time, the empire co-opted an earlier cult associated with the veneration of Apu Porco and the mines in its vicinity. These strategies of control are also reflected at other metal-producing sites in the region.

Pre-Inka Metallurgy in the Southern Andes

The mineral-rich southern Andes was one of a number of regions in which Indigenous metallurgy emerged, the best known being the north coast of Peru. Artisans in these areas developed different technological styles (Lechtman

MAP 8 Location of sites mentioned in text. Map by Brendan Weaver.

1988; González 2007), as well as distinct finished products. In all areas, objects of copper, gold, and silver were used primarily in ritual and political contexts, but the different historical trajectories of these regions shaped the scale of production and the ways in which metal items were understood and displayed. The ostentatious use of precious metals and their alloys to sheath leaders in elaborately worked headdresses, back flaps, and earspools made of hammered metal was practiced by the Moche, Sicán, and Chimú (Lechtman 1993), Peruvian North Coast societies that had clear ruling and commoner classes. Even there, however, variation existed in the ways that metallurgical practices were organized and the meaning associated with the productive process as well as finished items (Swenson and Warner 2012).

In the southern Andes, metal objects were made primarily of copper or copper alloys, tended to be cast (Zori 2019), and were used in smaller quantities than in the north. As elsewhere in the Andes, finished objects included small tools such as tweezers, chisels, and needles but were dominated by sumptuary and ritual items. The development of metallurgy in the region prior to the Inkas, while tied to an emergent elite particularly during later periods, did not occur under conditions of political domination, nor did it exist in relation to larger, centrally organized productive enterprises. Although modest in scale, these metallurgical practices cannot be understood in the same terms as the kinds of small-scale production that emerged in relation to large-scale enterprises and that are the focus of this book. Knowing something about the development of metallurgy in the region is important, however, to more fully understand the changes that were introduced by the Inkas.

Metallurgy developed in two areas of the southern Andes, the circum-Titicaca region and northwestern Argentina, with a possible third center somewhat later in northern Chile (Salazar et al. 2011). The earliest dated metal objects in the region consist of gold beads found in the burial of an elderly individual from an early horticultural society in the Titicaca Basin; the burial dates to approximately 4,000 years before present (Aldenderfer et al. 2008). The beads were made by cold-hammering native gold, so their manufacture did not entail ore processing. Indirect evidence for actual metallurgy comes from the Bolivian Illimani ice core, which preserves a record of atmospheric pollution extending back thousands of years. The data indicate that the earliest copper emissions occurred between 700 and 50 BCE while later maxima correspond with Tiwanaku and then the Inkas, followed by large spikes associated with the colonial period and Industrial Revolution (Eichler et al. 2018). The ice core data are roughly compatible with the dating of the earliest copper artifacts discovered in the Andes, a mask and a pendant found in the graves of individuals buried 3,000 years ago in Catamarca, Argentina (Scattolin et al. 2010).

Catamarca appears to have been a center of early metal production, yielding evidence for systematic experimentation with copper and its alloys beginning in the middle of the first millennium BCE and the extensive use of copper-tin alloys to fabricate elaborate items by the Middle Period (450–900 CE). Metal objects were largely ornamental in nature and included ceremonial axes, bells, and richly decorated plaques and disks. The number and elaboration of items produced increased markedly in the Late Period (900–1430 CE) just prior to the Inka conquest, a trend that González (2004, 140–50; 2007) believes was intimately related to population agglomeration, increased ceremonial complexity, and the emergence of local elites. A handful of production locales have been excavated in the area, with the most extensively reported being Site 15 at Rincón Chico (González 2010). Site 15 is located 1 km from the residential core of Rincón Chico, a settlement consisting of 360 structures in the Yocavil Valley of the province of Catamarca. It is composed

INKA SILVER MINING AND ITS ANTECEDENTS   155

of a rectangular compound surrounded by open-air workspaces and was occupied from approximately 900 CE until the Spanish conquest. The full range of metallurgical tasks was performed at Site 15, as evidenced by fragments of copper mineral, different types of slag, hearths and crucibles for smelting and alloying, refractory containers for distributing the molten metal to molds, and molds for producing disks, bells, axes, and chisels. Excavations also yielded domestic debris. However, no finished metal items were recovered. A similar pattern exists at Pucará de Tilcara, where excavation revealed a compound with rooms dedicated to living spaces as well as to different craft activities, including the production of ceramics, pigments, and metal objects. In the latter case, a mold used to make ornamental copper items was recovered, but only utilitarian objects were found at the site. The complex productive chain uncovered during excavation and the absence of finished ornamental items in residential contexts associated with these workshops suggest to the excavators that production was directed by an outside authority that commandeered the finished goods (González 2007; Tarragó and González 1996).

Angiorama (2005) takes a somewhat different view based on his analysis of metallurgical finds at the Late Period site of Los Amarillos in the province of Jujuy. In Unit 400, on the periphery of a residential area, excavators uncovered evidence of metallurgical activities including small stone hammers and anvils, two hearths, and some finished items. There were few traces of smelting or refining other than stone containers with copper residue, but some evidence (two large hammers, Andean deer antlers that could have been used for digging, and a few pieces of ore) suggests that the same people may also have engaged in mining. Angiorama argues that rather than being an activity directed by elites, metallurgy was just one task among many accomplished by occupants of the site. He also cites the widespread distribution of copper artifacts in the graves of both wealthy and poor residents of the area as further evidence that metal objects were not monopolized by elites.

These contrasting interpretations of the role of elites in metal production appear to be shaped by local variation as well as differing theoretical perspectives regarding the development of complexity in the region, particularly the degree to which evolutionary models are embraced. They also result from the relative paucity of research on mining and metalworking locales or of analyses of the ubiquity of metal objects within sites. All would agree that the manufacture of copper artifacts took place in workshops associated with non-elite households. The question of whether the residents consumed the items they produced is more difficult to answer because ornamental or ritual objects would probably not be discarded in household refuse, but in burials or other ceremonial contexts. Similarly, without more information about the relationship of metallurgical workshops and mines to social groups within residential communities, it is difficult to determine the overall organization of production. The metal objects were integral to local ideological systems associated with social differentiation, at least in some communities, but the degree to which elites controlled raw materials, finished objects, or caravan trade involving these products is unknown.

Metallurgy may also have developed in northern Chile during the Formative Period when small numbers of plaques, diadems, and pendants were interred in burials. The quantity of such objects increased dramatically in the Middle Horizon, particularly in the oasis of San Pedro de Atacama, where T-shaped axes, discs, tweezers, chisels, and other items have been recovered from cemeteries. Although traces of local production are limited, slag, metal droplets, and bars have been recovered from a few tombs providing unequivocal evidence that some level of metallurgical activity occurred in the vicinity (Salazar et al. 2011). San Pedro de Atacama is relatively close to the large copper deposit at Chuquicamata, which Núñez and his colleagues (Núñez et al. 2003) have posited was the source of ore for that site as well as for Tiwanaku, an expansive polity centered in the Titicaca Basin. However, Lechtman and Macfarlane's (2005) comparison of the isotopic signatures of bronze artifacts with those of copper ore bodies in the region suggests that the source was elsewhere, most likely in the highlands.

Chuquicamata is the location of the famous "copper man," the naturally mummified body of a young male miner who died in a narrow tunnel in the sixth century CE. This mummy, in addition to the remains of five additional individuals—one of whom was a woman—provide the most direct evidence for pre-Hispanic mining in the Andes. These mummies were found in conjunction with mining tools, isolated examples of which have also been recovered from mines and other contexts. The standard set of tools consisted of hafted lithic hammers, unhafted hammerstones, wooden and hafted lithic shovels, baskets, and bags made of rawhide or textiles (Figueroa et al. 2013). Whether individuals engaged in the full range of mining tasks or if these were accomplished by different people is not known.

Tiwanaku metallurgy has been less well studied than the traditions to the south, with only one production locale in the Tititcaca Basin that is tenuously associated with the Middle Horizon state investigated thus far. Early evidence for silver metallurgy dating to approximately 100 CE was uncovered at the site of Huajje, a U-shaped mound on the Peruvian shore of Lake Titicaca (Schultze et al. 2009). The excavation was placed between the arms of the monumental structure and revealed evidence of a 1,900-year long sequence of silver manufacture that included crucibles, slag, matte, and vitrified ceramics, which together suggest that scorification (a process intermediate between smelting and refining) and cupellation took place there. In addition to metallurgical debris, deposits yielded domestic refuse and ritual paraphernalia. Unlike the manufacturing locales in northwestern Argentina, silver production at Huajje clearly took place within a ritual compound, one that was incorporated into the Tiwanaku state between 600 and 700 CE. Indirect evidence for silver production comes from lead pollution recorded in a sediment core from Lake Taypi Chaka, which is located approximately 40 km to the northeast of the site of Tiwanaku (Cooke et al. 2008). The first traces of lead, which is used in the production of silver, occur at 400 CE, which corresponds to the rise of the Tiwanaku state.

The site of Pulaco50 in Pulacayo provides some tantalizing evidence of Tiwanaku's involvement in copper mining to the north of San Pedro de Atacama (Cruz 2009b). Pulacayo is located in Bolivia just to the east of the Salar de Uyuni and would have been an important node in the network of camelid caravans that connected the Bolivian highlands with communities to the south. Pulacayo is also just 100 km to the southwest of Porco and is the only pre-Inka metallurgical site identified in the region thus far. The site consists of two sectors with evidence of mineral processing and metallurgy. The excavator has recovered evidence of the full range of tasks required to manufacture metal objects. These consist of copper ore interspersed with large grinding stones for comminution, a series of combustion structures including the reverberatory furnace discussed in chapter 5 as well as what may be very early huayrachinas, slag and droplets of copper metal, and an area with blocks of pumice and tools for polishing finished items. Radiocarbon samples have yielded dates from the Middle Horizon and the Late Intermediate Period, and associated ceramics suggest occupation during the same time frame (Cruz et al. 2022; Macfarlane and Lechtman 2016).

Pulaco50 appears to represent metallurgical production that was in some way connected to the Tiwanaku polity. One of the primary lines of evidence for this interpretation is a funerary cave near Pulacayo that was looted by a local resident of the area in the early 1990s. It contained the partially mummified remains of three adults and two children and a spectacular array of finely made artifacts with strong affiliations with Tiwanaku and San Pedro de Atacama, in particular a man's shirt that was probably produced in Tiwanaku, and an elaborate, four-cornered hat (Cruz 2009b). The isotopic signature of a bronze arm band that was also found in the tomb corresponds to the Pulacayo ore body as well as a sample of the ore fragments recovered from Pulaco50 (Macfarlane and Lechtman 2016). Cruz (2009b) argues that while the tomb as well as specialized metal production suggest social differentiation, the data do not indicate that there were elites in charge of copper production. The precise nature of the relationship between the copper-producing community and the altiplano polity is unclear, but no evidence exists for direct control by Tiwanaku.

The development of metallurgical traditions in the southern Andes was linked to the expansion of exchange networks, elaboration of ritual practices, and the emergence of social differentiation (Zori 2019). Unlike the North Coast, however, it does not appear to have developed in the context of stratified societies in which elites controlled the production and distribution of metal objects. This changes, however, under Inka control.

The Inka Regime in Porco

No evidence for mining prior to the Inka conquest has been found in the immediate vicinity of Porco, but a sediment core from Laguna Lobato, a small lake perched above Potosí, suggests earlier metallurgy in the area (Abbott and Wolfe 2003). Concentrations of metal particulates created by smelting rose abruptly shortly after 1000 CE, reaching a first peak at about 1140 CE. The authors inaccurately attribute this to Tiwanaku metallurgical activities, but Tiwanaku had collapsed by the end of the first millennium. It coincides, instead, with the first centuries of the Late Intermediate Period. Subsequent peaks are associated with early colonial times and the Industrial Revolution. Interestingly, while there is a slight increase in air pollution under the Inka regime, this peak is much lower than the previous one, suggesting that smelting was more intense three centuries prior to the Inka conquest. These data are provocative but have not yet been confirmed by archaeological findings that indicate intensive metal working in the vicinity of Potosí during the Late Intermediate Period.

At the time of the Inka conquest of the region, Porco was located in Qaraqara lands, which extended across southern Potosí as well as parts of the departments of Chuquisaca and Tarija. The core territory of the Qaraqara was in the cold highlands, but like other groups in the region they had colonists in the warmer valleys where maize and other low elevation crops could be grown (Bouysse Cassagne 1987, fig. 13). This was the case under the Inka, but whether a similar arrangement existed prior to their rule is unclear. The Qaraqara were composed of a number of ethnic groups including the Macha, which included Puqutu, Aymaya, and Macha, and the Chaqui, which included Chaqui, Colo Caquina, Picachuri, Tacobamba, Moromoro, Qaraqara, and Visijsa; Porco was situated in the territory of the latter. These, in turn,

INKA SILVER MINING AND ITS ANTECEDENTS

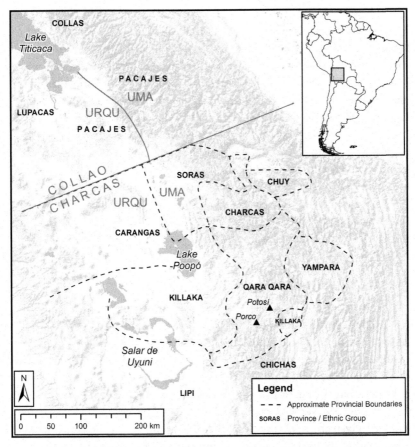

MAP 9 Qaraqara-Charka federation. Map by Brendan Weaver (redrawn from Platt, Bouysse Cassagne, and Harris 2006, 45).

formed a loose political alliance with the Charka who were similarly organized and occupied the area to the north of the Qaraqara in what is now south-central Bolivia. These social formations have typically been regarded as chiefdoms (*señoríos*)—internally ranked, with control over the production and distribution of goods by a centralized leader.

Nielsen (2006), however, has questioned the applicability of the chiefdom model to the Late Intermediate Period societies of the region which appear to have undergone an increase in the scale of political integration with a simultaneous decrease in the level of social differentiation. He proposes, instead, that we view them as corporate societies in which power, and particularly the mobilization of resources, was a matter of negotiation rather than a simple prerogative. Organizationally, they can probably be best understood as a type of segmentary social formation based on Andean kinship groups called ayllus. Smaller ayllus were grouped into larger ones, which in turn formed moieties that composed the ethnic groups. Leaders existed at all levels, and while maximal leaders were of higher status and wielded more power than lower ones, they could not necessarily intervene in the affairs of their constituent members. When the Charka federation formed is uncertain; it existed at the time of the Inka conquest and resisted that invasion (Bouysse Cassagne 1975; del Río 1995b). In fact, the federation may have emerged as a defensive response to the challenge posed by the Inkas as well as the frequent incursions of lowland peoples called Chiriguanos into the eastern flanks of the Andes. The Charka and Qaraqara were renowned for being soldiers of the Inka, warriors who were deployed by the empire to conquer and quell dissent even in distant parts of the empire.

The *Huaca* of Porco

As recounted in the previous chapter, according to Platt, Bouysse Cassagne, and Harris (2006), Porco was a mine and pilgrimage center, the site of a sacred huaca that was destroyed by the Spanish priest González de la Casa after it had been hidden in Caltama. Offerings made to Porco brought health and prosperity, but the huaca also had another aspect. As González de la Casa fled Caltama, the Natives who pursued him lamented his theft of "Father Porco" who had given them victory over an ethnic group called the Chichas. This suggests that the god of rain and lightning was also a god of war, the very attributes that are characteristic of the Indigenous deity Illapa.

As Platt and his colleagues (2006) suggest, it is likely that the huaca of Porco was kept inside the mine of Huayna Porco and attended by a *punku camayoc*, a keeper or guardian of the portal like Diego Yquisi. The three stones mentioned in the probanza may have been akin to three stones that were described in the mine of Chaquí, also in Qaraqara territory. In that case, one of the stones was said to have been split by lightning. These subterranean huacas were usually associated with separate manifestations of the cult on the surface (Platt, Bouysse Cassagne, and Harris 2006, 149–50).

In fact, the summit of Apu Porco is crowned by an ovoid platform constructed of unmortered stone which encircles an area in which a number of smaller platforms and two vertical mining shafts are found (Cruz 2009a). Four sub-rectangular platforms are located outside the primary platform. Surface inspection of the summit yielded a small assemblage of ceramics, none of

INKA SILVER MINING AND ITS ANTECEDENTS

which were diagnostic other than a few fragments of Spanish olive jars. The peak continues to be venerated today, as is evidenced by empty alcohol bottles and coca leaves placed within the pits and in other rocky crevices. The crowning platform could be considered a rudimentary type of Inka *usnu*. These are usually thought of as "sacred platforms for ritual performance" but more specifically were associated with basins in which libations of maize beer were poured (Coben 2015, 275). Rituals on such a platform with an imposing view of the surrounding landscape—including a series of locally important sacred peaks—would have projected imperial authority not just over the mines but also over the entire region subject to Inka rule (Meddens 2015).

The Inkas, like other Andean groups, venerated mountains that were often associated with ancestors and regarded as sources of water and fertility (Besom 2013). In the southern reaches of their realm, however, mountaintop shrines appear to have been more specifically linked to mining. Cruz and colleagues (2013) argue that even Inka *capacocha* ceremonies, during which specially selected young people from the provinces were brought to Cuzco, where they participated in elaborate rituals and then returned to their homelands to be sacrificed, sometimes on mountain peaks, were more common in the southern reaches of the empire precisely because this area was also the richest in mineral resources. A specific example of this practice is the mummy of a young boy found near Salinas Grandes in northwestern Argentina, whom Besom (2010) maintains was sacrificed during a capacocha ceremony that was intended to establish a reciprocal relationship between the Inka and the local huaca; by conducting the ritual the Inkas hoped to enhance salt production as well as assert their dominance over the resource. While there is no evidence that Porco hosted a capacocha ceremony, the conjunction of stone platforms on its summit is similar to other high-altitude shrines constructed by the Inka on important peaks in the region. Cruz (2009a; see also Cruz et al. 2013), for instance, discovered an adoratory on the summit of Cerro Cusco, 75 km to the west of Porco, consisting of a sub-rectangular enclosure with three circular structures on the interior, a rectangular platform 60 m to the northeast, and at least eight mining pits. Few artifacts were found on the surface, but firewood, perhaps deposited as offerings, was abundant at the site. Radiocarbon assays on the latter yielded one very early date between 1295 and 1404 CE, which the investigators attribute to old wood being collected, and another date of 1400–1465 CE that coincides with the expansion of the Inka into this region. One of the most interesting aspects of the site is a series of boulders along the pathway to the peak with rock art that looks like lightning bolts, providing a strong indication that like Apu Porco, Cerro Cusco was associated with Illapa, the god of lightening and warfare.

The shrine on the summit of Apu Porco thus appears to have been just one of an array of peaks in the region associated with the cult of lightning as well as mining, part of what Platt and colleagues call a regional religious-economic complex (Platt, Bouysse Cassagne, and Harris 2006, 151). Porco was known for the very high quality of its ore, which often formed potato-like lumps of pure silver that the Inkas understood as being generated by Illapa, the deity of lightning. These occurred in pockets that were concentrated toward the surface of the mine but continued to be found at greater depths and were regarded as illas. Distinctive in their shape, size, and brilliance, they embodied the light that was generated by the sun and associated with the Inka, the son of the sun. Bouysee Cassagne (2004) argues that the silver from Porco was valued not just as a precious metal, but because it was imbued with the same powers of martial success and fecundity as the Inka himself. This contrasts with the usual characterization of Inka conceptions of silver as being associated with the moon and royal women and reflects the multivalent nature of this prized substance.

The Inka's tendency to reconfigure conquered landscapes and co-opt local sacred places has been documented throughout the Andes (Acuto and Leibo-weicz 2018; Bauer and Stanish 2001; Chase 2018; Moyano 2009), and most likely played a role in expanding the influence of the huaca of Porco. This process, which Chase refers to as the creation of local-imperial landscapes, in-volved negotiation between the state and conquered peoples over sacred places and their meanings and often resulted in the "internalization" of the recon-figured histories by locals to the extent that they were represented as autoch-thonous beliefs even after the Spanish conquest (Chase 2018). Huacas from the Charka region were taken by the Inkas to Cusco where they were subject to a ritual of reinvestiture; huacas who answered the Inka when questioned were returned to their original locations and continued to be venerated, while those that did not were rejected by the state (Platt, Bouysse Cassagne, and Harris 2006, 152–53). In the case of Porco, the enhancement of the huaca's importance would have been beneficial to both the empire and the Charka federation, particularly with regard to defending against Chiriguano incur-sions. On the other hand, gathering the huacas of outlying mines in Porco would have fortified the Inka's claim to all mineral resources in the area as well as emphasized the significance of Porco itself.

Archaeological Evidence for Late Intermediate and Inka Occupation at Porco

To date, little evidence for the use of Porco during the Late Intermediate Period—the centuries immediately prior to Inka occupation—has been identified archaeologically. Lecoq briefly investigated the area as part of a larger reconnaissance project that had as its objective the identification of pre-Inka sites and their relationship to the development of the Charka confederation (Lecoq 2003; Lecoq and Cespedes 1996, 1997). He found only two sites with Late Intermediate Period ceramics near Porco: a tomb and an isolated domestic structure. No settlements or mineral extraction locales of that date were identified in the immediate vicinity, but a number of Late Intermediate Period and Inka sites were found near Yura, a warmer valley 30 km to the south of Porco, confirming that the area sustained modest agricultural populations in late pre-Hispanic times.

Pedestrian survey conducted by the Proyecto Arqueológico Porco-Potosí in the area around the town of Porco has similarly yielded scant evidence for occupation there prior to the Inka conquest. An intensive survey conducted in a 2.5-km^2 block surrounding the village using 5-m intervals between transects resulted in the identification of eighty-two sites. On the basis of surface ceramics and architecture, over half can be dated to the Late Horizon, the early Colonial Period, or most frequently both, and almost all were related to mining and metallurgy or to the support of workers and administrators engaged in this activity; none were dated to the Late Intermediate Period. Survey of an additional 12 km^2 surrounding the original survey block using 20-m intervals between transects located an additional seventy-two sites. None were clearly Inka or colonial in date, but eight Late Intermediate Period sites were found. These consist of ceramic and lithic scatters sometimes associated with rectangular stone foundations that were most likely the remains of single-family residences. No evidence of mineral extraction or processing was found at these sites, all of which are located 2 km or more to the north of the mines in Huayna Porco. This pattern suggests that prior to the Inka conquest, human occupation in the vicinity of Porco consisted of isolated agro-pastoral households and did not focus on mineral exploitation or associated ritual activities.

The closest substantial Late Intermediate Period population near Porco was clustered near the bofedal of Condoriri, 14 km to the northeast of Porco. Located initially by Lecoq and Cespedes (1996, 1997), two large sites, CS1 and CS50, were mapped during a survey of the area conducted by the Proyecto Arqueológico Porco-Potosí in 2003. They are situated on the tops of steep mesas about 2 km apart on opposite sides of a small water course that drains the marsh. Both consist of rectangular stone foundations with entrances that open onto irregular patios that sometimes include bedrock mortars; CS1 has over one hundred foundations, while CS50 includes about seventy-five. Pedestrian survey using 30 m intervals in a 15-km^2 area centered on the bofedal identified thirteen additional Late Intermediate Period sites all of which are associated with Condoriri-Chaqui ceramics, a type that has not yet been precisely dated. However, a variety of styles, including Hedionda and Chillpe as well as yet-unidentified wares, are present at the larger sites, reflecting the broader web of relations in which the population was embedded. The lack of Inka or colonial ceramics suggests that these settlements might have been occupied early in the Late Intermediate Period and abandoned before the Inka arrived in the area; absolute dating would help confirm that hypothesis. No evidence for mineral processing or metal production was found in association with CS1 or CS50, nor, indeed, with any of the other Late Intermediate Period sites located during the Condoriri survey.

The reconnaissance and survey data thus suggest that the area immediately surrounding Porco was sparsely populated prior to the Inka conquest, and that denser populations resided near Yura and, to a lesser extent, in the oases created by bofedales such as Condoriri. This can be explained by the low agricultural potential of the area which receives approximately 200 mm in precipitation annually and experiences only two frost-free months per year (Montes de Oca 1989, Fig. 4.4, Table 4.5). The absence of evidence for a Late Intermediate Period occupation of Porco could, of course, be due to the continued exploitation of the mines and the construction of modern infrastructure, particularly the current administrative offices and flotation plant at the foot of Apu Porco, which would have been a suitable staging area for processions to the summit. The overall paucity of traces of use during the period prior to Inka control, though, does suggest that if mining and ritual activity occurred it was not intensive. The archaeological evidence of mining and metallurgy at Porco reflects an entirely Inka project with no direct antecedents during the Late Intermediate Period, at least that can be detected today. This does not mean, however, that Apu Porco was not venerated by the local population prior to the arrival of the Inkas, just that activities on and near the mountain were probably limited as they have left no detectable traces.

Berthelot's (1986) historical study of Inka gold mining suggests that although the state claimed rights to all mineral deposits, conquered communities were allowed to work smaller mines. He argues that in many ways agriculture and mining were organized in a similar fashion, and that just as agricultural land was controlled by either the state or the community, there were also distinct state and community mines. Berthelot focused on the Carabaya and Chuquiabo regions to the east of Lake Titicaca and found that imperial gold mines were centralized in zones with the most productive deposits, employed relatively sophisticated technology such as subterranean galleries, and were closely supervised by state personnel. With regard to the latter, an early chronicler, Cieza de León (2005 [c. 1549–53], 372), stated that silver was mined in Charka territory under the Inkas and that for this they posted Indians who gave the metal they mined to imperial inspectors and their delegates, which suggests a high level of supervision. Native informants interviewed in Huánuco, in what is now central Peru, in 1559 explicitly stated that the Inkas recruited couples, rather than individual adult men, to work in mining centers. In contrast, community mines in the Carabaya and Chuquiabo regions were small, dispersed, located in alluvial deposits, and worked with simple technology by local populations under the control of their own leaders. A final distinctive feature of state mines, according to Berthelot, is that because they tended to be located in mountains, rather than alluvial deposits—and here he is referring specifically to gold deposits—they were highly sacralized. As he expresses the relationship between the mines, the mountains that contained them, and particularly notable pieces of ore, "On the one hand they are a symbolic link between the world on high (hanaqpacha), the special domain of the sun god; on the other, the world within (ukhupacha), revealed in the gallery mines but also in the domain of seeds, the ancestors, and—according to ancient Andean cosmogony—the primordial beings as well" (Berthelot 1986, 84). Under the Inka, then, mining entailed both large- and small-scale enterprises that paralleled, in some ways, the multiple scales of production that are seen in later periods. The primary difference, of course, is that in the Inka case the objective of mining at both scales was the production of objects of ritual or sumptuary value rather than the enrichment of individuals in a market economy. However, in both instances, large-scale production was dominated by outsiders who employed cutting-edge technology, were intertwined with state interests, and set the terms of use for small-scale miners.

Porco clearly falls into the category of a state mine that was constructed entirely de novo by the empire rather than embedded in a previously established settlement, as Lecoq's reconnaissance data from the region suggests was common in the region (Lecoq 2003; Lecoq and Cespedes 1996). Early colonial writers noted that the silver from Porco was used to decorate the Inka's litter, adorn the Temple of the Sun in Cusco, and produce serving ware used by the royal household (Cieza de León 2005 [c. 1549–53], 372; Ocaña 1969 [c. 1599–1608], 182). The probanza composed by González de la Casa as well as the physical evidence of the shrine on the peak of Apu Porco indicate the existence of a state cult, most likely associated with Illapa, the deity of lightning.

In addition to the ritual significance of Porco, the nature of state control over the mine is also reflected in the way economic space was organized under the Inkas. As described in the previous chapter, mining took place on the slopes of Huayna Porco, and smelting was carried out on the ridges surrounding the village. Since pre-Hispanic and colonial remains are mixed and superficial, however, it is impossible to differentiate between occupations. Of the seven sites with substantial architecture (more than five buildings or connected rooms) that were located during survey, five appear to have been constructed under the Inka regime based on their architectural layout; a sixth site, located under the high school, may also have been Late Horizon in origin but was destroyed before it could be tested. These five sites are spatially as well as functionally distinct.

Jalantaña is located on the west side of the Todos Santos River directly downstream from the company mines and is unusual in that it includes buildings that were constructed entirely of stone: at all other sites, except Site 80, adobe walls were built on top of stone foundations. The best-preserved building at Jalantaña, and indeed in all of Porco, is a gabled structure with interior trapezoidal niches that is clearly of Inka origin. This building is located in the central portion of the site and appears to have been part of a *kancha*, an architectural unit employed by the Inkas that consisted of single-room rectangular buildings arranged around a courtyard. Occasional segments of straight, stone walls are visible elsewhere at the site, but the overall pattern is difficult to discern because of the disturbance caused by subsequent agricultural activities. Provincial Inka and European ceramics occur on the surface, and three furnaces are situated at the east edge of the site, which is delimited by a large stone wall to the west and south. Test excavations conducted in the kancha yielded few artifacts, but the majority of decorated sherds were from provincial Inka vessels. Jalantaña appears to have been a modest administrative complex or, perhaps as Lecoq (2003) suggests, a small tambo, or waystation, on a spur of the Inka highway.

As described in the previous chapter, the site of Huayrachinas consists of the stone foundations of circular and rectangular structures that are located just to the west of a ridgetop on which huayrachina remains are clustered. The architectural remains at Huayrachinas are similar to those found at other Inka storage centers in the southern Andes (e.g., Raffino 1983, 201) where circular and rectangular storage buildings, called *qollqas*, are interspersed. The nature of the architecture at Huayrachina strongly suggests that the site was constructed by the Inkas to store provisions for mining personnel. This would have included fuel for the furnaces as well as food and supplies for the workers and administration, almost all of which would have been imported from lower elevations. However, all excavated structures contained early colonial components that reflect reuse for housing and refining activities as discussed in chapter 4.

The two sites closest to the mines, Uruquilla and Cruz Pampa, are residential complexes that may have housed workers. Both are located on the flanks of Huayna Porco, to the south of the modern village. The architectural layout of Uruquilla and its association with provincial Inka ceramics, including a subfloor offering of an undecorated aryballos, or Inka-style jar, suggest that it had been constructed under the Inkas, perhaps to house mining personnel. Indigenous-style bowls that had been repurposed for open-vessel refining were also found. These are similar to specimens recovered at Tarapacá Viejo in Chile (Zori and Tropper 2013) and were probably used during the Inka occupation until they were replaced, perhaps, by the small cupellation hearths employed for refining in later times. A smaller complex that is less well preserved, called Cruz Pampa, is located on the other side of the ridge to the northeast of Uruquilla and may have served a similar purpose.

Site 80 is situated approximately 1 km downstream and to the north of the village of Porco, on the west side of the Yana Machi River. Crucibles and Late Horizon ceramics including provincial Inka and Carangas wares are scattered across the surface. One of the three rectangular buildings that were tested contained a burned clay feature measuring 95 by 55 cm and 23 cm high, slightly larger and deeper than a traditional cooking hearth or k'oncha. The presence of crucible fragments and the paucity of domestic debris recovered from this structure suggest that the feature was used to process small quantities of metal.

The simplicity of the architecture present at the Inka sites in Porco, the absence of elaborate features such as a large plaza, and the relatively thin cultural deposits all evoke a rather brief, or perhaps seasonal, occupation with silver production being the one overriding goal. This impression is supported by the evidence recovered during excavation that reflects an extremely limited range of activities. While artifacts and features associated with mineral extraction are nearly ubiquitous, as are ceramics used in the preparation and consumption of food, few other activities appear to have occurred at these sites on a regular basis. Evidence of lithic production was recovered only from Site 80, and spinning and weaving tools occurred in very limited numbers. The range of activities associated with metallurgical production is also limited. There is abundant evidence for mineral extraction and the crushing and separation of ore, as well as smelting and refining. However, the manufacture of finished products appears to have been accomplished elsewhere; no molds, scrap metal, or stone tools used in the final production stages of metal objects have been recovered. Silver appears to have been exported to Cusco or provincial centers in raw form where it was transformed into prestige and ritual objects that conformed to state ideology and imperial aesthetic norms.

Labor Organization at Porco

The Inkas had a number of organizational strategies for mobilizing labor in support of state projects of various types. The most ubiquitous was the *mit'a*, a rotating labor draft that inspired the Spanish colonial tax instituted by Viceroy Toledo. Under the Inkas local leaders, or kurakas, were responsible for assigning a specific number of individuals, or couples, to provide labor for tasks as diverse as mining, textile production, harvesting, transporting goods, and construction. Mit'a workers relied on skills that were commonly held by members of conquered populations. Another frequent strategy with broader geopolitical implications was the deployment of *mitmaqkuna*, communities that were permanently resettled in new locations often far from their places of origin. These people retained ties to their original kurakas and tended not to become integrated into local societies. They were thus used to stabilize restive parts of the empire as well as to provide labor of various types, including agricultural production and the garrisoning of forts. These tasks often required generalized skills, but sometimes colonies specialized in craft production such as ceramic manufacture. A third, and less well-understood, labor category was the yanakuna. These were personal retainers who were cut off from their communities of origin and thus dependent on the elites whom they served. Their positions were hereditary, and their status may have varied according to the tasks in which they specialized, but many were highly regarded. This Inka institution persisted under the Spaniards, although it was greatly altered by the late sixteenth century. Finally, there were state administrators, either ethnic Inka or people who were designated as "Inkas by privilege" who directly represented imperial authority in the provinces.

No historical documents indicate how labor was organized at Porco, but a combination of archaeological and ethnographic data as well as comparisons with Inka projects in other parts of the empire allow some inferences to be made. A reconstruction of the way in which silver production was organized suggests that most, but not all, of the tasks could have been accomplished by mit'a laborers with relatively little training. Today, the silver minerals present in the deposits at Porco are sulfide and mixed ores that include pyragyrite, acanthite, and stephanite, but in the past oxide ores, native silver and argentiferous galena were probably the most important sources. These minerals are associated with a series of narrow veins radiating from the Huayna Porco stock, many of which outcrop at the surface (Cunningham et al. 1994). Both open-cast and subterranean mines have been identified in these areas but are difficult to date because of the lack of diagnostic artifacts. The ore would have been crushed to remove the metallic mineral from the rocky matrix, or

INKA SILVER MINING AND ITS ANTECEDENTS

gangue. A number of small (approximately 12- by 12-cm) blocks of igneous rock that are dimpled on three or four surfaces have been recovered near mines and were probably used for this purpose. Huayrachinas were then employed to smelt the silver ore or to generate the lead used in cupellation. Metal produced by this process would then be refined in shallow ceramic vessels or, perhaps, in small cupellation hearths located in protected locations, most likely within structures at lower elevations.

The relatively unskilled tasks of mineral extraction, crushing and sorting ores, and transporting materials within and between sites were probably accomplished by mit'a laborers who were recruited on a seasonal basis, perhaps during the winter months when there was a lull in the agricultural cycle. As noted in the previous chapter, determining the ethnicity of these workers on the basis of ceramic style is problematic; ceramic types may not be associated with bounded territorial groups (Villanueva Criales 2015), and in most late pre-Hispanic and early colonial mining sites a mix of styles from the Titicaca Basin and Carangas region is present. Another potentially confounding factor is that the Inkas sometimes supplied workers with vessels made by other groups, and these could be provincial Inka ceramics or in the style of the manufacturing community (Hayashida 1999). Fortunately, colonial documents do contain definitive information about the ethnic affiliation of some workers at Porco, and this accords with the archaeological record; the Lupaqa, who resided on the west shore of Lake Titicaca, provided mit'a labor to the mines. Witnesses interviewed during the 1567 census of the Lupaqa stated that the Inka had occasionally required them to go to Porco to extract silver (Diez de San Miguel 1964 [1567], 39, 81, 92, 99, 106), and one elderly man specified that they sent 100 to 200 men and women there to mine.

In addition to mit'a workers, the labor force at Porco would also have included yanakuna. Observations of traditional smelting and refining practices suggest that while these activities do not require full-time specialization, they do demand a high level of skill that would not have been available among the general tributary population. Early colonial chroniclers noted that yanakuna from Porco who specialized in smelting quickly moved to Potosí after rich silver deposits were discovered there (Bakewell 1984a, 14). These workers may have also been considered *kamayoc*, individuals or groups who practiced a specialized craft or skill (Julien n.d.). Unlike the term *yanakuna*, which refers only to some sort of servile status, *kamayoc* implies specialized, guarded knowledge as well as an obligation to work for the state. It derives from the word *kamay*, which means "to animate" or "to give form and force," in other words to create something and imbue it with a life force (DeLeonardis 2011). The term was applied to a wide variety of specialists including some who provided services rather than material goods: religious practitioners, palace guards, weavers, salt producers, and rope makers, among them. While smelters were not mentioned in the list of kamayoc produced by a Spanish observer in 1567 (Falcón 2018), gold workers were. Whether these individuals smelted gold in addition to crafting or mining it is not clear, but in general, the transformative process of creating precious metal from ore seems like it would be encompassed by the verb *kamay*.

The Inkas scaffolded different types of labor in support of specialized production (Julien n.d.). There is no evidence that a mitmaqkuna settlement was established at Porco. The harsh environment would have made it difficult to sustain more than a few households based on agropastoral production in the immediate vicinity of the mines, and the restricted variety of artifacts recovered points to an exclusive focus on mining and metallurgy rather than the full range of tasks associated with a self-sustaining community. Mit'a and other workers would have required food and supplies brought in from other areas. Colonial documents do not indicate where these settlements were located, but one possibility is known archaeologically. Visijsa, an Inka site located some 70 km to the southwest of Porco, is situated at a lower elevation with greater agricultural potential. This site may have employed mit'a workers to produce food, and, in the case of Visijsa, charcoal, for use in Porco (Lecoq 2003). Another possibility is the site of Paria, the primary Inka administrative center in the region (Gyarmati 2015). It is located 200 km to the northwest of Porco on the Bolivian altiplano within Soras territory. Paria is over 100 ha in size and is associated with 1,539 storage structures. It sits at the juncture of the Inka highway and roads extending to lowland valleys to the east and the Pacific Ocean to the west, which facilitated access to various ecological zones from which different types of products could be obtained. A key resource was maize which was cultivated by Sora mitmaqkuna on the imperial farm project in the Cochabamba Valley to the east. Most of the maize produced was shipped to Paria, and then distributed to other centers, perhaps including Porco. The administrative connection between the Charka federation, which claimed Porco as a pilgrimage center and mine, and Paria is suggested by a statement in an early colonial document indicating that when Charka warriors were called up by the Inka Empire they assembled at Paria before moving on to Cusco (Gyarmati 2015).

Two or three tiers of scaffolding would thus have been required to supply workers at Porco with food as well as the materials necessary to perform their jobs, and depending on the nature of the required goods, a number of different communities may have been involved (e.g., fuel from Visijsa, maize from Paria, perhaps baskets, hide containers, and hammers from elsewhere).

The mining center thus represents a node in a network of state facilities that provided a variety of goods, and through which the silver from Porco was disbursed to Cusco and, perhaps, provincial centers where it was used to manufacture ritual and sumptuary items. While this configuration of labor and supplies was specific to Porco, it is similar in many respects to the organization of metal production in other areas of the southern Andes (Julien n.d.), as the following section will demonstrate.

Inka Mining Centers in the Southern Andes

Known Inka mining and metallurgical sites are concentrated in the south-central Andes, although two—Curamba (Vetter Parodi et al. 2008) and Cerro Huaringa (Epstein 1993)—have been identified in Peru. While diverse, the complete productive chain ranging from mineral extraction to the manufacture of finished products never occurs in one place, but, instead, is extended in space with different social groups responsible for distinct tasks. This spatial segregation of activities occurs within sites as well as between them (Zori 2019) and was one of the key imperial strategies for organizing and controlling the production of highly valued objects. In general, three types of sites can be identified, although they sometimes overlap: metallurgical workshops, smelting facilities, and mines. The intensification of metal production under the Inkas resulted from the harnessing of local expertise to the imperial project (González 2016), the reorganization of labor, and the scaffolding of support for mine workers. On the technological level, though, little changed other than the introduction of huayrachinas and a few new products such as *tumis* (ceremonial knives) and tupus (Angiorama and Becerra 2021; González and Gluzman 2007).

A number of important metallurgical workshops have been identified in the Quebrada de Humahuaca and Calchaquí Valleys in northwestern Argentina and in northern Chile, including Los Amarillos (Angiorama 2004, 2005), Pucará de Tilcara (Otero and Cremonte 2014), Potrero de Payogasta (Earle 1994), Rincón Chico 15 (González 2010, 2016) and Tarapacá Viejo (Zori 2016; Zori and Tropper 2013; Zori, Tropper, and Scott 2013). All these sites were occupied by permanent communities whose members engaged in subsistence as well as craft activities. With the exception of Potrero de Payogasta, these settlements were also inhabited prior to the Inka conquest, so there was continuity in the population as well as in metallurgical practices. For instance, at Rincón Chico 15 metal objects were produced for centuries before a workshop was established there under the Inkas (González 2010). At that time, production was augmented by an expansion and reorganization of the workspace that entailed spatially separating steps in the productive process, which were discontinuous and interspersed with areas for the manufacture of pottery. In addition, a battery of five huayrachinas was constructed for smelting larger quantities of mineral, while open hearths continued to be employed along with crucibles during the later stages of the process. Copper was the principal metal worked. Copper mining probably took place at deposits 30 to 80 km to the south, but the tin used to produce bronze was imported from much farther away.

Most steps in the productive chain are represented at Rincón Chico 15: smelting, refining, alloying, and the manufacture of ingots and finished objects. The latter, however, are not found at the site, suggesting that the final product was exported by the Inkas. While the workspace was reorganized and huayrachinas introduced, project personnel noted few other technological changes. The use of the lost wax process and the production of tin bronze continued under the Inkas, as did the manufacture of large disks and bells that conformed to long-standing local tradition. Refractory ceramics, such as crucibles and molds, were lined with bone ash, a practice that was common in northwestern Argentina prior to imperial control as was the use of perforated crucibles. These techniques continued under the Inka and may have been introduced by them to other metallurgical centers. Other than the use of huayrachinas, the only other technological shift was the production of copper ingots of various sizes, either for use on site or for export. The manufacture of traditional sumptuary and ritual items as well as their distribution outside Rincón Chico, suggest that the Inkas sustained the prestige and authority of Native elites and manipulated the expression of local ideology by controlling the production and supply of these goods (González 2010).

Rincón Chico 15 is similar to other metal-producing sites in a number of respects. Like Los Amarillos, Pucará de Tilcara, and Potrero de Payogasta, the manufacture of finished objects took place within households, although at Potrero de Payogasta metallurgical production occurred in Inka domestic spaces rather than indigenous ones (Earle 1994). Residents also engaged in other craft activities in addition to metallurgy. The Inka tactic of relying on local expertise with only minor modifications of the productive process (González 2016) is clearly visible at Tarapacá Viejo where Zori (2016, 2019; Zori et al. 2013) has documented the reorganization of metal production under imperial auspices. During the Late Intermediate Period very small-scale copper production using huayrachinas took place at sites dispersed throughout the valley. The Inkas increased the scale of production and centralized it at Tarapacá Viejo, where the full range of tasks associated with the manufacture of metal objects took place, from ore processing to the use of molds to produce

INKA SILVER MINING AND ITS ANTECEDENTS   173

finished pieces such as traditional hatchets. With regard to new technology, they appear to have introduced perforated crucibles that were lined with bone ash, adopted, most likely, from the workshops of northwestern Argentina. The Inkas also initiated the production of silver, using huayrachinas for smelting and open-vessel cupellation for refining (Zori and Tropper 2013). Metallurgical practices at Tarapacá Viejo spanned the full gamut with the exception of mining, and like most workshops the manufacture of copper objects was probably part of the tribute exacted from groups with prior experience in metallurgy.

The site of Quillay in Catamarca is one of two known Inka sites in the southern Andes that were dedicated exclusively to copper smelting, the other being Viñas del Cerro in Chile. Quillay consists of two sectors without architecture that were inhabited prior to imperial expansion, a small Inka compound for habitation and storage, and thirty-two huayrachina-like furnaces for smelting copper that are dispersed on the sides and tops of nearby gullies (Spina and Giovannetti 2014). Raffino and his colleagues (1996) believe that the presence of Belen and Inka-influenced Belen ceramics in the compound indicates that mit'a workers from Belen resided at the site and conducted smelting operations there. While the compound appears to have housed workers and perhaps their supervisors, smelting would have required a level of expertise not usually found among subsistence farmers; either the workers from Belen had some previous experience with smelting or the laborers in Quillay just used ceramics produced in Belen. The lack of grinding stones and presence of only one perforated crucible suggest that smelting was the primary task accomplished at the site; the ore was extracted and comminuted at the mine, and the raw metal produced at Quillay was sent elsewhere to be manufactured into finished objects.

Viña del Cerro is a more formal site that is situated in a landscape that was reconfigured by the Inkas within the Copiapó Valley (Moyano 2009). The site is composed of three sectors, the largest of which is a walled plaza with a possible ceremonial platform, or usnu. Attached to the northwestern side of the plaza are three symmetrical walled spaces, each with two rectangular habitations. To the northwest of this compound is a smaller walled space with a single building that includes a sleeping platform. On the highest point of the ridge on which Viña del Cerro is situated there is a battery of twenty-six circular furnaces arranged in three rows. These are much larger than the huayrachinas at Porco with a diameter of 2 to 3 m, but their location on a windswept ridgetop suggests to the excavators that they may have functioned in a similar way (Niemeyer et al. 1983). Recent analyses by Garrido and Plaza (2020) have demonstrated that the furnaces were used to produce copper; no evidence for tin bronze exists at the site, although tin bronze artifacts are commonly found at Late Horizon settlements in the valley. This finding as well as the scarcity of mold and crucible fragments suggest that comminuted copper ore was brought to the site where it was smelted to produce pure copper, which was then exported to a workshop where it was alloyed with tin to make finished objects. Garrido and Plaza (2020) argue that the tin bronze artifacts recovered from settlements in the area were distributed as gifts by the Inka as part of a system of prestations that structured the asymmetrical reciprocity characteristic of imperial relations with provincial populations. Similarly to Quillay, then, Viña del Cerro was focused on copper smelting, and also like Quillay, a residential sector probably housed the supervisors and specialized laborers who worked at the site, perhaps on a seasonal basis given the relatively scant remains they left behind.

None of the sites discussed so far were located adjacent to mines. The latter tend to be in isolated areas without permanent populations. The best-preserved Inka mining complexes are in the Chuquicamata district in northern Chile and have been investigated by Núñez (1999) and Salazar (2008; Salazar et al. 2013; Soto Rodriguez and Salazar 2016), with the mining complex of El Abra being particularly well reported. El Abra is located in a desolate part of the Atacama Desert that has little vegetation or water. Prior to the Inka conquest households from nearby communities in the middle and upper Loa River valley exploited the deposits for turquoise and copper minerals. They extracted and comminuted the ore with hammers that litter the area around the mines and in small camps where mineral processing also took place (Núñez 1999). Under the Inka the same technologies were employed, but the scale of operations increased, and site function became more specialized, including locales dedicated to each of the links in the productive chain. This entailed extraction, the initial crushing and selection of ore near the mine, further processing in camps, storage of the product, and its transportation out of the mining district. Facilities were also established for housing, food preparation, and ceremonial purposes (Salazar 2008). The workforce at El Abra appears to have been composed of mit'a laborers drawn from the same communities that had worked the deposits prior to the arrival of the Inkas, thus providing continuity in the workforce and the technology for mineral extraction. As was the case with Porco, communities that supported mining operations by providing food, animals, and other supplies played a key role in their success. This kind of scaffolding, along with the transportation routes that were established or consolidated by the empire, were critical for maintaining workers in areas that were devoid of necessary resources.

There is little evidence for smelting at El Abra, and Núñez (1999) has interpreted the small amount of slag that is present as the result of assaying rather than full-scale metal production. Given the paucity of vegetation in the vicinity, the ore was probably transported to communities with access to fuel. It is important to note, however, that ground copper mineral was a significant component of ritual practice in the region from before Inka times and so was valuable even without further processing. Salazar (2008; Salazar et al. 2022) makes the interesting argument that the semiprecious stones and copper minerals produced at the mines did not directly benefit the Cusco elite but instead were distributed among the local population that had already come to rely on these items for ritual and sumptuary use. This was part of the system of asymmetrical reciprocity established by the empire but calls into question the notion that Inka expansion into the region was motived primarily by the presence of mineral resources that could be used as a means of imperial wealth finance (Earle 1994). This issue cannot be resolved until more information becomes available regarding the origins and distribution of such items within the local population in order to determine precisely where the mineral products from El Abra ended up.

The sites discussed so far were all under imperial control and can be considered "large scale" in the sense that they were affiliated with the state and reflect an augmentation of production compared to pre-Inka times. Not surprisingly, evidence for small-scale mining is scant as these sites are more difficult to detect and would attract less attention from investigators. The best evidence for small-scale mining under the Inka comes from the Cachiyuyo de Llampos mountains in the Atacama Desert of northern Chile, where Garrido (2016; Garrido and Salazar 2017) has identified a series of small mining camps near the Inka road. These sites were occupied by people from the Copiapó Valley who had engaged in lapidary and pigment production prior to the Late Horizon but, with the arrival of the Inkas, increased the scale of their operations and moved them close to the road. The camps were comprised of clusters of circular structures that accommodated households or small kin groups. These are located near sources of cupriferous minerals that were used to make greenstone beads and iron oxide that was ground to produce red pigment. Multicrafting increased during the Late Horizon, with evidence for the continued production of lithics and the modification of marine shell at most sites. Garrido argues that these camps housed independent craft workers who were organized similarly to contemporary artisanal miners; they were egalitarian producers with direct access to resources and without imperial oversight. These workers leveraged state infrastructure—in this case the Inka road—to intensify craft production. Despite imperial attempts to restrict traffic to people on official business, the road provided the potential for exchange with local travelers and also facilitated the movement of supplies to the isolated camps.

A second example of small-scale metallurgical production is Campo de Carrizal in Catamarca (Zagorodny et al. 2015). This site consists of a set of residential compounds surrounded by terraced fields and was occupied from the tenth to the end of the fifteenth century. A small but diverse set of artifacts related to metallurgy was recovered from Campo de Carrizal including fragments of copper sheet, drops of pure copper and of tin bronze, slag, crucible fragments, and molds, including one for making traditional circular plaques. Late Horizon ceramics occur at the site in small quantities, but there is no suggestion of state control. Production was domestic and small in scale, continuing a metallurgical tradition that had been established prior to Inka presence in the region.

The continued production of arsenical bronze and pure copper in northern and central Chile also hints at the existence of dual scales of production. Inka expansion was associated with the adoption of tin bronze throughout the empire (Lechtman 1996), but in the Copiapó Valley Garrido and Li (2017) found that while tin bronze artifacts predominated in Late Horizon contexts, a substantial number of arsenical bronze objects, particularly locally traditional types such as fish hooks, continued to be manufactured. This suggests that some production existed outside imperial purview. A somewhat similar case was identified in the Aconcagua Valley of central Chile where Plaza and Martinón-Torres (2015) found two Late Horizon sites with different technological practices. At one, Cerro La Cruz, both the style of metal artifacts and the absence of tin bronze indicated the continuation of local technology, while at the other, Los Nogales, a tin bronze artifact was recovered as well as perforated crucibles lined with bone ash, techniques closely associated with the Inka Empire. This is a perplexing case, however, because Cerro La Cruz was established by the Inka and is characterized by provincial Inka ceramics and architecture, while Los Nogales is a local site that had been occupied prior to Inka presence in the region. The authors attribute these differences to distinctive relationships with and attitudes toward the Inka on the part of local populations, but the sample of analyzed artifacts, particularly from Los Nogales, is so small that perhaps the difference between the two sites is not as salient as the current analysis suggests. In any case, the manufacture of copper and arsenical bronze objects does indicate that some subject populations continued local metallurgical practices, perhaps because the Inkas allowed provincial leaders access to less productive deposits.

Small-scale production by conquered communities, either "legal" or illicit, is challenging for archaeologists to identify, particularly near gold and silver mines that would have attracted the attention of conquistadors and been reworked by their successors. In addition, the spatial separation of different links in the productive chain makes it difficult to trace the overall organization of production and to identify the nature of state control—if any—over the process. Small-scale production under the Inka is probably best investigated in regions where small deposits of copper or other non-precious metals would have escaped the notice of subsequent miners. In addition to examining such locales and being generally alert to independent mining and metallurgical activities, the use of isotopic techniques similar to those employed by Macfarlane and Lechtman (2016) might in the future enable scholars to trace the products from specific mines to smelting and manufacturing facilities, and then to their point of consumption. In conjunction with archaeological evidence, such data would enable investigators to assess the labor conditions under which metal objects were produced.

Porco obviously shares more in common with the state-controlled mining complex of El Abra than with the small-scale camps in the Cachiyuyo de Llampos Mountains or the smelting facilities and metallurgical workshops described above. Both sites consist of facilities constructed under Inka auspices, and clear similarities exist with regard to the types of tasks performed and their spatial segregation. This is the result not only of the nature of mining, but the fact that mineral extraction was accomplished by mit'a laborers who were working in inhospitable environments that did not sustain permanent populations. In the case of Porco, those workers were joined by yanakuna who specialized in smelting. Salient differences between Porco and El Abra are due to differential preservation (with El Abra being exceptionally well preserved), environmental conditions, and the nature of the mineral extracted. Smelting was performed at Porco because the transportation of raw metal was more efficient than moving loads of ore long distances, and local stands of queñua trees as well as thola bushes, yareta, and llama dung provided fuel for the furnaces (Goldstein 2006). Unlike the cupriferous minerals that were extracted at El Abra, which the Inkas regarded as suitable for provincial subjects, silver and gold were officially reserved for the Cusco elite and those recipients deemed worthy of gifts of precious metals from the state. The refined silver was thus transported from Porco to Cusco or administrative centers such as Paria for manufacture and distribution of the finished products. A similar process appears to have occurred at Tarapacá Viejo where Zori (Zori and Tropper 2013; Zori 2016) has found evidence of the manufacture of finished copper objects but not of silver ones. In the Mantaro Valley in central Peru the ubiquity of silver artifacts declines from the Late Intermediate Period to the Late Horizon, a trend that the excavators also attribute to their requisition by the state (D'Altroy and Earle 1985).

Regulation of the production and distribution of silver—a substance associated with the life-giving and life-taking force of the Inka royalty—was an ideological tactic for controlling the relationship between the empire and provincial elites as much as it was a financial one. A more comprehensive strategy, though, entailed the creation of ritual spaces within production centers and the reconfiguration of the sacred landscapes in which metallurgical and other types of settlements were embedded. As Acuto and Leibowicz (2018, 2) argue, "Through the politics of space . . . the Incas pursued the construction of a new socio-spatial order with clear-cut differences in status, roles, and power between the Inca representatives and the indigenous people." They constructed ceremonial platforms at many metal-producing sites, such as El Abra (Soto Rodriguez and Salazar 2016), Viña del Cerro, Potrero de Payogasta, and Cerro Verde in northern Chile (Adán and Uribe 2005), and at others such as Los Amarillos, they reconfigured preexisting ritual spaces. At a regional level, the empire transformed entire landscapes, intensively in places like the Humahuaca Valley (Acuto and Leiboweicz 2018), and with less investment in more lightly populated areas such as southern Bolivia (Cruz et al. 2013). The platform on top of Cerro Apu Porco, then, was related to the specific meanings associated with the lightning cult and silver mining, but its construction was part of a larger program of socio-spatial transformation that the Inka promulgated to varying degrees throughout the southern reaches of the empire.

Conclusion

Inka exploitation of Porco was clearly an imperial project, a large-scale enterprise organized by the state. Like the El Abra copper mining complex in northern Chile the operation at Porco was organized by task, with distinct locales devoted to different activities that were accomplished by distinct social groups. Unlike El Abra and some other sites that produced cupriferous materials that were distributed locally, the silver from Porco was exported and manufactured into finished items that were distributed by the state, a reflection of the meanings this particular metal held for the Inka as well as its role in wealth finance. The maximization of production to enhance individual or corporate gain, as occurred in the colonial and Republican periods, was not a motivating factor under the Inka.

No archaeological evidence of small-scale mining in or near Porco has been uncovered. However, the mention by González de la Casa (Platt, Bouysse Cassagne, and Harris 2006, 185) of four nearby mountains that had lead and silver mines suggests that these may have been smaller deposits, perhaps worked by local groups with imperial permission. Whether production at such mines was oriented toward local consumption and exchange, or intended for the manufacture of items that were then gifted to the Inkas, is unknown. In the first case, small-scale production would have operated parallel to state enterprises as it did in Cachiyuyo de Llampos, while in the second it would have been imbricated with the imperial political economy. Theft, of course, would be another way by which subjugated peoples could have gained access to ore and finished metal objects, but this possibility is difficult to verify archaeologically. The evidence that it did occur comes only from reports that the Inkas had regulations and practices in place meant to inhibit such activity (Berthelot 1986).

Although archaeological traces of small-scale production under the Inkas are still scant, the evidence that does exist indicates that conquered groups sometimes had direct access to the means for producing ritual and sumptuary objects outside imperial control. While individual desire to own such items may have motivated this activity, the role played by metals in the empire suggests that such practices would have been political in nature. By directly controlling the production or distribution of metal objects, subjugated leaders would have been asserting their independence from the Inka state, not just in the sense of abrogating imperial regulations but by acquiring the products necessary to maintain their own political or religious hierarchies without Inka oversight.

6

A Return to the Present

KAJCHEO IN GLOBAL PERSPECTIVE

THE HISTORICAL TRAJECTORY OF kajcheo is unique; it was shaped by two colonial incursions into the southern Andes, both of which were motivated by the potential for extracting mineral wealth, followed by two centuries of exploitation by primarily foreign companies that sought first silver and then industrial ores. Kajcheo emerged as a concomitant of large-scale mining almost immediately after the Spaniards gained control of the mines, perhaps even under the Inkas. Informed by notions of reciprocity as well as sacrifice, and often reliant on Indigenous technologies for the extraction and processing of ore, kajcheo is a culturally distinct activity characteristic of the Andes. A consideration of global data on mining practices, however, demonstrates that it is also a regionally specific variant of the much broader phenomenon of artisanal and small-scale mining (ASM) that can be found in most, if not all, poor countries with a mining sector.

This chapter returns to the present and examines Bolivian kajcheo in comparative perspective. The goal is twofold: to investigate the relationship between small- and large-scale mining in countries other than Bolivia, and to elucidate the aspects of kajcheo that are similar to those of ASM in general and thus identify the global factors responsible for the commonalities. After first reviewing contemporary ASM in Bolivia, three cases from other parts of the world, India, Nigeria, and Ghana, will be described and then compared with Bolivia. The chapter closes with a reflection on how the comparison of these cases might help us understand the factors that shape ASM globally.

180

Contemporary Small-Scale Mining in Bolivia

As described in chapter 2, the practice historically known as kajcheo gave rise to the first mining cooperatives. In the 1930s the number of cooperatives multiplied when many mines closed, and unemployed miners sought to make a living from the abandoned workings. This pattern was repeated after subsequent crises in the industry, most notably with the implementation of the Triangular Plan in 1961 and then in 1985 after the global tin market collapsed. The Triangular Plan was an attempt to improve the performance of COMIBOL and undermine the militant unions by instituting massive layoffs (Burke 1987). This resulted in unemployment and rampant ore theft, which the government countered by creating more mining cooperatives; in 1968 cooperative miners established FENCOMIN, the umbrella organization that represents their interests at the national level (Marston and Kennemore 2018). In 1985 a more severe crisis occurred. The global price of tin plunged, and over 20,000 salaried miners were let go; as in previous crises, many of them became cooperative members.

The growth in cooperatives is spurred not only by economic downturns, though. Cooperative membership also rose steeply during the first decade of the twenty-first century as global demand for commodities, particularly by China, drove increases in the price of metals. Between 2006 and 2017 the number of cooperatives rose by 50 percent (Mamani 2018); in this case many people were attracted to the industry in the hope of earning a living and, perhaps, striking it rich. Much of the recent growth has been in alluvial gold mining in the eastern lowlands (Mamani 2018), but a mining boom also occurred in the traditional tin belt in the south-central region of the country. In Porco the rapid increase in mining activity was reflected by a doubling of the village's size.

The organization of mining cooperatives in Bolivia is variable. In general, though, they consist of ten or more members (socios) who are recognized by FENCOMIN. Oftentimes cooperatives are dominated by members of the same family, and many divide their time between agriculture and mining. Cooperatives sometimes include a small percentage of women, but since they are largely prohibited from working underground, most of these are pailliris, pickers who sort through waste dumps on the exterior. In addition to being barred from the more lucrative jobs within the mine, women face discrimination on a variety of fronts, including sexual harassment and exclusion from administrative posts.

To gain access to mineral deposits, the cooperative leases a mine from the state or a private enterprise, and an individual socio then locates an ore face within it; if it is productive, a team, or *cuadrilla*, of socios might share in its exploitation. In general, however, profits from the mineral produced by the cooperative are not redistributed. Instead, socios and cuadrillas are compensated based on what they alone have produced. The mineral, either unprocessed or concentrated, is sold to private businesses that are notorious for cheating socios. A percentage of the earnings is earmarked for the rental of the mine, contributions to the National Health Service, dues to the national and regional cooperative federations as well as the cost of electricity and equipment (Michard 2008).

Most cooperatives are at least partially mechanized and use small compressors, pneumatic drills, pumps to drain water, and winches to remove ore (Michard 2008). Much of the work, however, is still manual, with miners using picks and hammers to make holes for dynamite, hauling ore out on their backs or by pushing small trolleys, and using quimbaletes—large rocker stones—to grind it. Labor conditions are physically punishing and dangerous. Mines are poorly maintained because each socio is concerned primarily with his or her immediate profits, earnings are usually low, and there is no overall coordination by the cooperative to ensure the safety of its workers. Accidents are caused by explosives, the accumulation of gases, and cave-ins, but more dangerous in the long-term is the inhalation of pulverized rock, which leads to silicosis. The average life expectancy of miners is forty to fifty years, less if a person starts working underground at a young age.

Bolivian mining cooperatives are democratic in that all socios have the right to participate in general assemblies during which decisions are made by voting. The director and other officers are elected by the general assembly and serve one-year terms. However, they only partially adhere to the internationally accepted definition of a cooperative as "an autonomous association of persons united voluntarily to meet their common economic, social, and cultural needs and aspirations through a jointly-owned and democratically-controlled enterprise" (International Co-operative Alliance 2021). The internal differentiation of the workforce is often exploitative; in many cooperatives socios hire *peones*, workers who perform much of the labor and are compensated by the day or engage in short-term contracts. Peones receive low wages, no benefits, and are excluded from general assemblies; the conditions of their employment are no different than they would be in a commercial enterprise. Likewise, the goal of most socios is individual profit; there appears to be little interest in the broader values that are typically espoused by cooperatives such as "equality, equity and solidarity" or "social responsibility and caring for others" (International Co-operative Alliance 2015). This discrepancy between international and commonsense definitions of a cooperative, and how these entities actually operate has exacerbated the hostility that has been expressed by many who argue that they are identical to private businesses but demand special treatment by the state.

The mining boom in the first decade of the twenty-first century was accompanied by an increase in conflicts between cooperative and salaried miners over access to productive mineral deposits. Cooperative miners claim that mining companies, and thus the miners employed by them, monopolize rights to the most lucrative mines, while cooperatives are relegated to poor, depleted deposits. This tension erupted into one of the worst conflicts in Bolivian mining history in October 2006 when cooperative and salaried workers battled over access to the most productive mine levels in Huanuni, an important tin producing center in the Department of Oruro. This conflict—during which miners on both sides lobbed dynamite at each other—left seventeen people dead and dozens injured; over one hundred houses were also destroyed when a store that sold explosives was accidentally hit (Howard and Dangl 2006). Conflicts in Porco have been much less lethal, although disputes have occasionally culminated in acts of aggression. For instance, in 2010 company miners accused two engineers of allowing members of Cooperativa Huayna Porco to access a vein of silver that was off-limits to cooperatives. They took more than ten technicians and administrative staff hostage to force the company, at that time Sinchi Wayra, to fire the engineers (Redacción Central 2010).

The expansion of mining activity overlapped with the presidency of Evo Morales (2006–19) whose government benefited from the revenue generated by the increase in commodity prices. More importantly, mining cooperatives were initially some of his strongest supporters and have been privileged by the government. Article 369 of the 2009 Bolivian constitution formally recognizes cooperatives as economic actors equivalent to private and state entities, and the subsequent article states that "The State shall promote and strengthen cooperative mines so that they contribute to the social and economic development of the country" (Constitute 2009). Cooperatives pay only 2.5 to 5 percent in royalties, compared to the 8 percent paid by private companies, and they remain exempt from taxes as well as environmental and labor regulations. In addition, between 2006 and 2016, mineral concessions to cooperatives increased over 500 percent. The sector was also integrated into MAS (Movement Towards Socialism), Morales's party, and has become an important player on the national stage, owing largely to its capacity for political mobilization (Achtenberg 2014). This primarily takes the form of demonstrations and road blockades that can paralyze regional economies for months.

Despite the close ties between the cooperative mining sector and the Morales government, there were also serious rifts, particularly regarding provisions in the new mining code that was enacted in 2014. These exposed multiple tensions within and between Bolivian society and the state. Most notably, the government's platform, which declares that mineral resources belong to the state and claims to honor the earth, is in direct contradiction with its dependence on a neo-extractivist economy (Gudynas 2009; Perreault 2017) as well as the political support of the cooperatives. Indigenous peoples and the agricultural sector are also opposed to the privileges accorded the mining sector, which threatens Native lands as well as irrigation water, but were excluded from negotiations over the new laws (Achtenberg 2014) and generally marginalized by the government (Andreucci and Radhuber 2015). In August 2016, the cooperatives responded to a change in the Cooperative Laws that would have allowed unionization within their ranks with a massive protest and road blockade as well as a counterproposal rejecting the change and calling for access to more mineral deposits, exemption from environmental regulations, and, most importantly, the possibility of contracting directly with private domestic or transnational companies. In the midst of this upheaval, Rodolfo Illanes, the deputy minister of internal affairs, was sent to negotiate with the miners, but was instead taken hostage, beaten, and killed. Three miners also died during the incident (Redacción BBC Mundo 2016). Morales's immediate response to this tragedy was to arrest a dozen cooperative leaders and issue a series of decrees intended to exert more government control over the sector. These included the reversion of cooperative leases that were idle or subcontracted to private entities to the state, the extension of labor protections, including unionization, to cooperative workers other than socios, annual audits of all cooperatives, and a prohibition on the use of dynamite during demonstrations (Achtenberg 2016).

The assassination of Illanes intensified negative coverage of mining cooperatives by the Bolivian press. The depiction of cooperative miners as savage capitalists in the clothing of communitarian social entities (Redacción BBC Mundo 2016) is specific to the twenty-first century, but the characterization of them as violent, unruly, and focused only on quick profits rather than the sustained and rational exploitation of mineral deposits is reminiscent of earlier descriptions of kajchas. Their outsider status is paradoxically even more pronounced now that they have access to legitimate political representation in the form of cooperatives, the federations that represent them, and seats in congress. Even prior to the 2016 incident, a mining analyst for a major newspaper stated that "They are a plague, the worst that could have happened to this country, but they have political power. They are engaged in depredations against nature and men, first because they irrationally and selectively exploit the richest deposits, and second because they brutally exploit workers; they don't comply even minimally with labor laws" (Jordán 2012 in Carrillo et al. 2013, 251).

Interestingly, cooperatives that extract alluvial gold in the eastern lowlands of Bolivia are much less militant than the hard rock miners of the highlands despite being members of FENCOMIN. Carrillo and his colleagues (2013) attribute this to the different histories of the two groups. Alluvial gold cooperatives are relatively recent phenomena without a history of militant opposition to the state. The historical memory, identity, and collective action of highland miners are predicated on their long and contentious entanglement with state and corporate actors. Furthermore, they have a long-standing connection to place, and many are the children and grandchildren of miners. Alluvial gold miners, in contrast, have no such historical connections, nor are they seeking to expand access to rich ore deposits the way that hard-rock miners are. In fact, the very materiality of the different types of ore—alluvial gold and tin, silver, lead, and zinc found in underground veins—conditions the relations between miners, large companies, and the state. In the latter case, the large amount of capital needed to create an underground mine often precludes small-scale miners from establishing their own operations, but the persistence of this infrastructure over time provides the opportunity for further exploitation. Struggles over access to rich deposits occur between cooperatives and large-scale operations that have been run by both the state and private corporations. Such competition generates the kind of violence that has been described above.

The foregoing sketch of highland Bolivian cooperatives underlines both the political power that this sector enjoyed under the Morales government as well as the contentious politics in which it was—and continues to be—engaged. However, despite their recent political gains, most cooperative miners barely eke out a living, even when mineral prices are high. During the Morales presidency monthly incomes ranged from $40 to $400, with the lower end being well below the government mandated minimum wage of $300 per month, which is at a subsistence level (Díaz Cuellar 2017). This range reflects both the variable productivity of cooperatives as well as the income inequality within them; a socio can make ten times or more than the monthly salary of a peon, although even socios can go for long periods of time earning little to nothing if the ore face they work is poor.

In addition to the dangerous working conditions and precarious livelihoods associated with cooperative mining, small-scale mineral extraction in Bolivia generates other problems that have been at the center of considerable debate. Chief among these are the use of child labor and environmental degradation. Bolivian labor law has recently changed twice, first lowering the minimum working age to ten in 2014 and then raising it again in 2018 to fourteen under international pressure (Agencia DPA 2018). The reality, though, is that hundreds of thousands of children, many of whom are below the age of fourteen, work in Bolivia, and approximately 7,000 work in cooperative mines (Izagirre 2010), including in Porco. Some are as young as nine. Poverty is the driving force behind child labor; children work to support themselves and their families, many of which are headed by the widows of miners. Children often start working with their mothers as pailliris, selecting and grinding ore from waste heaps. When they are a bit older they work underground transporting ore to the surface, and when they reach about eighteen can advance to operating rock drills (Quispe Condori 2021). While most children working underground are boys, girls—sometimes disguised as boys—form a small component of the workforce (Izagirre 2010).

Globally, the environmental degradation associated with small-scale mining has received a great deal of attention, with much of it focused on the contamination of watersheds with mercury (Jacka 2018). The toxic metal is used to process gold ore, and approximately 100 tons are released into waterways every year, causing fish populations to plummet and endangering ecosystem and human health (Franco Berton 2016). However, hard-rock mining in the Bolivian highlands has also resulted in severely contaminated land and water. Five hundred years of mining have left a toxic legacy of mercury-impregnated soils, particularly in Potosí and the mercury mining center of Huancavelica (Robins 2011; Robins and Hagan 2012). Environmental problems caused by contemporary cooperative mining in the highlands include acid mine drainage, the accumulation of solid residues such as tailing heaps, and the disturbance of ground cover (Bocángel Jerez and Leyton Michovich 2009). Nevertheless, the large scale of industrial mining sometimes results in large-scale environmental disasters. The 1996 rupture of the COMSUR tailings dam in Porco released approximately 235,000 m³ of mining effluent into the Río Pilaya, a tributary of the Río Pilcomayo, the largest river system in southern Bolivia. Heavy metals contaminated the water from its source in Porco all the way to the border between Paraguay and Argentina, killing fish and making the water undrinkable for hundreds of kilometers downstream. A more persistent problem, though, is that the mills to which cooperative miners sell their ore allow the effluent to drain into local waterways on a daily basis (Hudson-Edwards et al. 2001), creating some of the same hazards as the breach in the Porco dam but at a smaller scale.

Bolivian mining cooperatives are situated at the tense intersection of two sets of contradictory relations. Their political value to the Morales government resulted in their formal recognition within the 2009 constitution as well as favorable fiscal treatment and exemption from environmental and labor regulations. The neo-extractivist policies of the state, however, are in direct opposition to the government's professed respect for the earth, the rights of Native people, and collective ownership of Bolivia's natural resources (Perreault 2017). These contradictions are embedded in the constitution and were regularly expressed in the Morales government's treatment of cooperatives, international mining companies, small farmers, and Native populations, among other societal entities. In addition to conflicts with the state, the privileged position of cooperatives generated ill will within the Bolivian population, many of whom view cooperatives not as collective social entities but as private businesses. The problems of poverty, child labor, and environmental degradation that are typically associated with ASM thus persist in Bolivia despite government recognition of the mining cooperatives and their transformation into a potent political force over the last two decades. In fact, their ability to thwart state regulations is predicated, in part, on their political value to the government.

A second contradiction stems from the relationship between cooperatives and large-scale private and state mining enterprises, which are ostensibly equal economic players according to the constitution. Cooperatives depend on these large companies for access to ore, but also compete with them for the most productive mineral deposits, a situation that generates conflict between socios and salaried workers. This type of competition is frequent in other parts of the world, as well, since in many cases ASM is closely bound to large-scale mining.

A Global Perspective on ASM

The rapid increase in commodity prices over the last two decades has resulted in the explosive growth of ASM worldwide. As of 2017, approximately 40.5 million people in eighty countries were directly involved in the industry (IGF 2018). ASM is most prevalent in the extraction of precious metals and stones such as gold, diamonds, and sapphires because of their high value relative to volume. However, oil, coal, tin and more recently, metals such as coltan and cobalt that are used in the manufacture of lithium batteries (Smith 2021; Sovacool 2021) have also been extracted or processed by small-scale producers.

The fact that poverty—rather than fortune-seeking—is the primary factor that pushes people into ASM is now quite clear. This is particularly true for the rural poor who turn to mining as an alternative or supplement to agricultural activities. Lahiri-Dutt (2018b), who has worked extensively throughout

Asia, even proposes that we conceptualize artisanal and small-scale miners as "extractive peasants" a term that recognizes the long history of income diversification by agrarian households as well as their more recent participation in the mining sector at unprecedented levels. In the case of sub-Saharan Africa, for instance, structural adjustments imposed by the World Bank in the 1990s perpetuated widespread rural poverty and resulted in a desperate scramble to find new sources of income (Hilson et al. 2018; Hilson and Garforth 2013; Hilson and Potter 2005). In India, artisanal coal mining is often accomplished by people from agricultural or foraging communities whose land has been encroached upon and polluted by large state and private mining companies (Oskarsson et al. 2019). Most of the women sapphire miners studied by Lawson (2018) in Madagascar come from rice-producing households that were devastated by drought; many hope to purchase cattle with their earnings. Throughout the Global South, people are drawn to mining because agriculture can no longer sustain them. In many cases this is because states have withdrawn agricultural subsidies and generally implemented policies that disadvantage rural populations. Households often send some of their members to work in mining or participate on a seasonal or occasional basis; income from ASM complements what is earned from agriculture. In other cases, the reverse is true, with farming being a source of food for a family that is devoted full-time to mining. Finally, some households sever their ties with agriculture completely, becoming, in the process, members of a working class that is poor, dependent on global commodity prices, and unfairly compensated by employers large and small (Lahiri-Dutt 2018b). Rural populations are not the only ones who participate in ASM. In Ghana, for instance, the lack of employment in cities and towns has driven recent graduates, public servants, and professionals into the gold fields (Hilson and Potter 2005), and opportunistic entrepreneurship also plays a role. However, the majority of artisanal and small-scale miners do come from impoverished agrarian backgrounds (Banchirigah and Hilson 2010).

Globally, the link between ASM and large-scale mining (LSM) is variable. Kemp and Owen (2019) are among the few scholars who have focused explicitly on the relationship between the two. They argue that the nature of the mineral being extracted and, especially, the degree to which activities physically overlap are key to understanding this relationship. They use these two variables to characterize the "interface" between different sectors, conceptualized as the operation of the two types of mining in the same physical environment. Kemp and Owen (2019) describe scenarios in which LSM and ASM are in competition for the same space and then provide a typology of interfaces. While such interfaces are at the crux of conflicts between LSM and ASM, they

A RETURN TO THE PRESENT 189

do not adequately encompass the full range of relationships in which LSM and ASM are entangled. The authors, in fact, note this when they state that

> further types can be discerned based on other factors, including: the mining method applied; stage in the mine lifecycle; cross-over in labour force between the sectors; whether the two sectors use common natural or built amenity, such as rivers or towns. In addition, these interfaces can form irrespective of whether or not LSM and ASM are working within a single concession area, noting that multiple "types" may be present in and around a single LSM project. (Kemp and Owen 2019, 1096)

This suggests that while geographic overlap is a key component in conflicts between ASM and LSM, assessments of the relationship between the two must consider a broader range of factors that should be identified through empirical analysis of different cases. However, even the addition of more variables fails to reveal a crucial fact about the relationship between the two forms of mining: LSM often engenders ASM and frequently benefits from it; in almost all instances they are both shaped by trans-local economic relations. This is, perhaps, most clearly seen in cases where direct appropriation of a commodity that is produced by LSM companies has resulted in a multi-tiered system of production. Two of these cases, coal mining in India and oil refining in Nigeria, are described below, followed by a third, gold mining in Ghana, which is one of the best-studied instances of ASM globally.

Coal in India

The outside world discovered coal in eastern India in 1774 when two British administrators observed locals using it to heat their homes (Deb et al. 2008). It was not until after rail transport had been established during the second half of the nineteenth century, though, that mining became a lucrative industry, as railways were both consumers of coal as well as an efficient way to move it for export to other locations in Asia. Coal extraction was based, in part, on a colonial reconfiguration of traditional "zamindari" land tenure by which British capitalists gained rights to coal deposits by purchasing agrarian land titles. The zamindari system, which was feudal in nature, allowed companies to access not only mineral resources but also labor.

Companies sometimes did this by purchasing entire villages and then forcing peasants to work in the mines in return for allowing them to continue to occupy agricultural land. In other cases, they contracted with labor recruiters, or "*sirdars*" who gave advance payment to a village headman; villagers under his jurisdiction were then compelled to work in the mines. Sirdars also acted as foremen who managed the underground mining crews. This system led to haphazard extraction of ore and extreme exploitation of workers because sirdars attempted to maximize profits over the short term. Environmental devastation ensued as land subsidence resulted in the destruction of topsoil, upending of irrigation systems, and collapse of mines and adjacent housing. Slow-burning coal fires, some of which have lasted until the present, led to more subsidence as well as grossly polluted air (Pai and Carr-Wilson 2018). These environmental effects often made farming impossible, pushing peasants to find work in the very mines that had destroyed their livelihoods (Shutzer 2021).

With independence, coal mining became part of a nationalist endeavor to modernize India. This project culminated in the nationalization of the mines between 1971 and 1973 and the creation of the state-run company, Coal India Limited in 1975. Lahiri-Dutt (2016) identified four types of coal mining that coexisted between the 1990s and 2015 when the mines were de-nationalized: state-run; neo-liberal; the special "non-legal" case of Indigenous communities in the remote northeast that were awarded the right to exploit natural resources on their land; and subsistence mining, which is conducted by peasants displaced by large-scale coal operations. Despite the formalization of the state-run and neo-liberal sectors, both employed contractors who hired substantial numbers of laborers to do most of the production-related tasks. These workers, often displaced peasants, were paid extremely low wages on a daily or weekly basis and constituted an informal "shadow economy" within the formal sector (Lahiri-Dutt 2016).

The history and organization of subsistence coal mining—or ASM—in eastern India is not well studied, but according to Lahiri-Dutt (2007) takes at least three different forms, all of which are illegal. In some cases, mining is conducted in small village collieries, usually adjacent to large mines. These are run by local leaders on private or community lands. Coal is extracted using pickaxes from open mines or shallow underground workings, and then packed into containers and removed by loaders who carry the ore on their heads; many of the consumers are small brickworks that are located nearby. Extraction from abandoned state mines is a second type of subsistence mining, while scavenging from active state or private mines is a third. As is the case for state mines, these forms of small-scale mining are often conducted by villagers whose own land has been consumed by the large mining companies, and the work is frequently seasonal, with the miners employed in the agricultural sector during the rainy season. In India, as in the two cases that will be described below, artisanal miners are regarded as uncivilized thieves who engage in criminal activity that destroys property and creates social havoc (Lahiri-Dutt 2016).

The growth of illegal mining has followed the expansion of formal coal operations in eastern India. The mafia controls much of the purchase and distribution of ore, although the degree to which artisanal producers are intertwined with them is unclear (Lahiri-Dutt 2007). Daniel and Williams (2013), for instance, claim that subsistence miners, many of whom are women, sell their product to organized crime syndicates, which prior to denationalization provided coal to state-run electrical plants. In the same region "coal cycle wallahs" illicitly appropriate ore, take it to rudimentary coking facilities to burn away excess impurities, and then transport the coal by bicycle to households and small businesses throughout the region (Lahiri-Dutt and Williams 2005; Singh 2013). Lahiri-Dutt (2016) estimates that in the states of Jharkhand and West Bengal 15 million tons of subsistence coal were moved in this fashion in 2014.

Large-scale coal extraction in India, then, began under British colonial rule and was initially intended largely for export in an expanding global market. Although the history of small-scale and artisanal mining has not yet been well documented, it likely developed in the wake of formal mining operations. Currently, the same pool of disenfranchised peasants labor in both types of mining. Scavenging, working abandoned mines, and ore theft are the most obvious ways in which small-scale subsistence mining is shaped by large-scale operations, but the relations between the two can be understood on a deeper level, one in which the latter engenders the former. This takes place through the dispossession and impoverishment of the peasant population resulting from the growth of large collieries, as well as the formation of state policies that privilege large operations and render ASM illegal. Similar processes can be seen in the following two cases.

Oil in Nigeria

Nigeria offers a rare instance in which oil is produced at an artisanal level. In this case, it is primarily the processing and distribution, rather than the extraction of the commodity, that are conducted illegally. Oil prospecting was first attempted in 1903 by the Nigerian Bitumen Corporation and was continued in the 1930s by the Shell D'Arcy Petroleum Corporation in the interior of Nigeria. Only small quantities were discovered, although the poor treatment of local communities and the environment presaged the problems that occurred when large-scale production began in the Niger Delta in 1956

(Umejesi and Akpan 2013). Commercial production rapidly became a crucial source of revenue for the Nigerian state after independence in 1960, and multinational companies like Shell, ExxonMobil, Equinor, and Chevron are among the top producers today.

Artisanal refining of oil began during the Nigerian Civil War, which took place between 1967 and 1970 (Stakeholder Democracy Network 2018). Today small-scale artisans as well as "big boys" tap into pipelines and sometimes well-heads to steal, or bunker, crude oil and then distill it in homemade refineries. The big boys include capitalists and government officials, as well as members of the security apparatus (Watts 2004). Local "youth" (very broadly defined) have engaged in bunkering because of extreme poverty and a lack of employment in other sectors; more recently militant groups have turned to illegal production as well. Oil bunkered by larger producers is destined for foreign markets and often leaves Nigeria by the tankerful. Much like Indian coal wallahs, small-scale operators refine crude oil to produce kerosene, gasoline, and, most importantly, diesel, for sale to local consumers. This business is profitable because, ironically, Nigeria suffers from a lack of refinery capacity and so must import relatively high-priced petroleum products. Although exact figures are lacking, approximately 10 to 30 percent of all the oil produced in Nigeria is "stolen" (Barnett 2023). On the other hand, the entire bunkering sector generates at least $9 billion per year in economic activity and employs upwards of 26,000 people (Naanen 2019).

Bunkering begins with the tapping of pipelines, a dangerous procedure that requires skilled welders, many of whom learn their trade as employees of large oil companies (Adunbi 2017). After the pipeline is tapped, the crude oil is transported by boat to a small refinery, hundreds of which dot the creeks and wetlands of the Niger Delta. Many of the refineries are owned by investors who do not directly participate in production (Stakeholder Democracy Network 2018). The refineries themselves, however, as well as the boats that service them, are constructed using local materials and knowledge gained, in part, from long experience with distilling moonshine (Adunbi 2017). Illicit refining, locally called *kpo fire*, is associated both ideologically and practically with resistance to the Nigerian state and multinational businesses. In fact, locally bunkering is not considered theft because residents believe that international oil companies—and the central government—are stealing resources that belong to them. As one recently interviewed small operator stated: "We call it drinking from your well. It's not theft. It's our resources" (Barnett 2023).

Violence in the delta has resulted from a complex mix of political movements that oppose both international oil companies and the government, infiltration by criminal bands, rampant corruption, ethnic conflicts over the control of petroleum resources, and oppressive military tactics (Watts 2004). Organized opposition to foreign oil corporations began in the 1980s. At first communities used the legal system and peaceful protests to demand that these enterprises pay compensation for environmental damages, employ local people, and fulfill their promises to create basic amenities in the region. The military violently intervened on behalf of the oil companies, razing villages and refineries, and, in 1995, executing Ken Saro-Wiwa along with eight other activists, an incident that drew global attention. As a result of this and other military actions, the movements became more militant, shutting down flow stations, blowing up pipelines, confiscating company vessels, and kidnapping personnel (Ibaba 2008). Violence is not directed only at corporations and the state; a wide range of stakeholders, including recently created "cults" or militant gangs, are vying for economic advantage and frequently target each other (Barnett 2023). Artisanal production plays only a small role in this complicated "oil complex" that political economist Michael Watts (2004, 201) attributes to a "miserable, undisciplined, decrepit, and corrupt form of 'petro-capitalism.'" Small-scale refining does, though, constitute a regionally significant activity that supports thousands of households and contributes to the violence associated with the industry.

Oil production in the Niger Delta has generated an enormous amount of pollution, devastating fisheries and farmland, fouling drinking water, and contaminating the air. Like other types of ASM, bunkering has contributed to these problems. Illegally tapped pipelines often result in oil spills, and air is polluted by the distilling process itself. The considerable amount of waste produced during refining is usually buried in shallow pits or discharged into waterways that run black with oil. However, the degree to which small-scale producers are responsible for the tragic state of the delta's environment is open to debate as determining the source of contamination after the event is difficult. International companies like Shell regularly blame ASM for these problems in an attempt to avoid liability (Oil Spill Intelligence Report 2011). On the other hand, small-scale producers downplay their role by blaming large corporations (Barnett 2023). The little research that has been done on the topic, though, suggests that large corporations and the federal government that has formed joint venture agreements with them are the primary culprits (Chukwu and Oladejo 2020).

Small-scale oil production in Nigeria is thus clearly shaped by—and is influencing–large-scale enterprises. Because extraction requires large amounts of capital, small producers are excluded, but they benefit by literally tapping into the infrastructure created by international companies. The conflict over resources between local residents, many of whom are involved in small-scale production, and large enterprises supported by the state is explicit and has become increasingly violent over time. Militants who represent the interests of delta communities are becoming important participants in the national discourse about the disposition of oil and the question of regional sovereignty.

Gold in Ghana

Unlike the two cases described thus far, gold mining in Ghana has a long history, and the recent trajectory of ASM is well documented. Dumett (1999) and Hilson (2002) provide the most comprehensive accounts of the history of this industry. Little is known about the earliest mining that began perhaps 2,500 years ago (Jackson 1992), but Ghana was first mentioned by Arabic sources in the late eighth century CE when North African Muslim populations began trading with West Africa for gold. By that time gold was used to adorn the king and his court, and gold dust was employed as a form of currency. Subsequent kingdoms continued these practices (Hilson 2002). The Portuguese, Dutch, and British successively attempted to control the gold trade but rarely interfered in its production.

Dumett (1999) describes mining among the Wassa of southwestern Ghana prior to European colonization. The Wassa economy was based on farming, foraging, and gold mining. The latter was carried out by residents or by itinerant miners from a neighboring group who would obtain permission from the local authority to mine. Gold was extracted from alluvial (placer) deposits, shallow pits, and, occasionally, underground shafts. Placer mining was often a family affair in which women, adolescent girls, and young boys participated. Shallow pit mining was the most common; trenches or circular pits eight to ten feet in diameter and up to ten feet deep were excavated into valley bottoms or the sides and crests of hills using garden hoes. Such work was conducted by households and sometimes by entire villages. Hard-rock, underground mining was the least common because the host rock was very hard, and flooding was common. However, shafts up to 200 feet in length were occasionally excavated (Dumett 1999, 47–59).

As is the case in many ASM operations today, women played a key role in aboveground activities. Ore from shallow pits and shafts was first separated from gangue using a hammer and a granite slab. Women then ground the ore into a powder and washed and panned it to separate out the gold. Gold dust was used as currency, and it was also fashioned into jewelry; gold symbolized godly and royal power and was associated with Mankouma, an earth deity linked to farming and the forest as well as mining (Dumett 1999, 60–66).

Access to mines was structured by a three-tiered political hierarchy that determined rights to land. At the apex was the paramount ruler, or king, and under him were a set of stools, or chiefs. Chiefs had authority over multiple villages, each of which was led by a headman. Individuals or groups could mine in lineage or stool lands, but they, as well as outsiders, had to gain permission from the paramount leader to access royal land. In exchange for this right, they paid a portion of the gold they recovered to the king. Exact proportions varied, but usually this was a third, or *abusa*, with another third sometimes going to chiefs, and the last third retained by the miner. Oral traditions suggest that commoners often evaded these levies by hiding what they had found. Gold was obtained by chiefs and kings using the abusa system as well as via direct taxation and compulsory labor. In the latter case, leaders would require their subjects to extract gold on their behalf just as they demanded labor for building roads and other projects. The involvement of slaves in mining is a matter of debate, with some scholars arguing that they participated primarily as members of household units and others contending that kings organized large squads of slaves to mine rich deposits (Dumett 1999, 68–76). If the latter is correct, then there was some precedent for the coexistence of large and small-scale mining in precolonial times.

The British Gold Coast Colony was established in 1874, and a series of gold rushes ensued in the early 1880s; all the mines worked by foreigners had been previously identified by local residents. At this time international companies faced a series of obstacles, particularly a lack of technical expertise and insufficient capital (Hilson 2002). Also problematic, from their perspective, was the unwillingness of the local workforce to engage in low-paid industrial labor in underground mines. Companies were forced to take a flexible approach to employment, allowing workers to return to their farms on a seasonal basis and relying on the abusa system, in which miners provided two thirds of their ore to the company. Sometimes the companies even relied on local chiefs and headmen to organize labor, thus completely circumventing investment in recruitment, housing, or management. In other instances, they combined the employment of Europeans to blast, stope, and manage the mines with the use of African teams supervised by local headmen to extract the gold. In this case, half the ore was given to the company to process using industrial techniques, and the other half was retained by the local workers who processed it with traditional methods (Dumett 1999, 207–22).

The explosive growth in mining concessions undermined traditional land rights as well as Indigenous authority. Encroachment on Native mines as well as farming and hunting lands was common. Local miners were usually pushed to the edge of large mining concessions or sought out new deposits that were not under company control. In some cases, miners continued to exploit mines within newly acquired concessions, and companies responded by demanding tribute comparable to the abusa (Dumett 1999, 220–21). These arrangements reflect the emergence of a dual system of mining in which LSM and ASM were cocreated.

Gold production boomed in Ghana between 1892 and 1901 and then again after World War I; it then fluctuated until World War II when it collapsed. After independence in 1957, the national government claimed rights to all minerals, and the mines were nationalized, but the industry continued to decline (Jackson 1992). It was only in the 1980s that the government made a concerted effort to revitalize the mining industry. It launched an economic recovery plan in 1983 that was part of a larger structural adjustment program overseen by the World Bank/IMF (Ofosu-Mensah 2017). A key component was a new mining law that reversed previous nationalist policies and facilitated foreign investment. Gold production increased by 700 percent in the following two decades, and the precious metal is now Ghana's most important export (Hilson 2002). Rather than returning to the underground operations that characterized mining in the early twentieth century, most gold extraction now takes place in large, open-pit mines; new technology allows the processing of low-grade deposits, fewer workers are employed, and correspondingly less community infrastructure, such as schools and roads, is constructed by international companies. Open-pit mining also leads to substantially more surface disturbance and encroachment on farmland (Jackson 1992).

The history of illegal ASM, called *galamsey* in Ghana, is much less clear. It appears to have emerged alongside the development of industrial mining in the late nineteenth century as mentioned above but took a more modern form when traditional mining techniques were combined with tools like buckets and picks as well as the use of mercury, which was introduced in the late nineteenth century (Ofosu-Mensah 2011). The passage of the Mercury Ordinance of 1932 is a clear indication that this form of ASM was already widespread at that time. The law prohibited the use of mercury by Native miners in the hope that by criminalizing ASM, its practitioners would seek employment in "legitimate" industrial mines (Yankson and Gough 2019).

Since the turn of the last century, commodity prices have soared, agriculture has stagnated, and industrial mining has dispossessed farmers without creating new jobs. Consequently, galamsey has become a crucial part of Ghana's economy; approximately one million people are directly engaged in both legal and illicit forms of small-scale mining, an activity that produces 34 percent of the nation's gold (Antwi-Boateng and Akudugu 2020).

Contemporary ASM in Ghana involves a complex group of stakeholders who operate at different scales. Ferring and colleagues (2016) have captured its fluid, variable nature by documenting active sites within a kilometer of their study community. While all seven operations involved digging open-cast pits and then using water to wash the sediment, different configurations of technology were employed, from simple hand tools to mechanical excavators, bulldozers, wash plants, crushing machines, and pumps. Similarly, the number of miners, their origins—local or from other regions of Ghana—and the ways in which the enterprises were organized, by local bosses, gold buyers, or foreign operators, varied.

The widespread mechanization of galamsey has occurred quite recently with an influx of migrants from Shanglin, an important gold-mining county in China, who entered the sector in large numbers with the upturn in gold prices in 2005. In contrast to state-sponsored investments elsewhere in Africa, the miners from Shanglin act as private individuals and usually pool funds from home to gain access to productive concessions and to purchase heavy equipment. This has resulted in the rapid mechanization of small-scale operations (Antwi-Boateng and Akudugu 2020).

The types of problems that are associated with ASM in India, Nigeria, and much of the rest of world are common in Ghana as well—environmental degradation, poor working conditions, poverty, and social conflict—most of which are attributed by policymakers to economic informality. Galamsey is, by definition, illegal. In 1989, the Small-Scale Gold Mining Act was passed in an attempt to eliminate illegal mining by providing licenses to small-scale operations. The hope was that the formalization of the sector would result in payment of taxes and fees as well as state regulation of environmental impacts, child labor, health and safety practices, and other issues. However, the expense of obtaining a license, bureaucratic hurdles, weak state enforcement, and rampant corruption have impeded widespread legalization (Yankson and Gough 2019). There is some evidence that formalization does result in safer working conditions (Calys-Tagoe et al. 2017), but in many respects illegal and legal small-scale mining are indistinguishable, and workers frequently move from one to the other.

Conflict between ASM and LSM is frequent in Ghana, due largely to the fact that miners are competing for the same near-surface resources (Patel et al. 2016). Enormous concessions are awarded to large-scale operations, which then exclude artisanal and small-scale miners from the land or provide them with unproductive sites. When small-scale miners encroach on LSM concessions, violence often ensues. This has occurred repeatedly, for instance, at Ghana's largest mine, Obuasi, which is operated by Anglogold Ashanti.

Small-scale miners, many of whom joined this sector when the shift to aboveground mining left them unemployed, have established surface operations on the Anglogold Ashanti concession and have used old mine shafts to access underground deposits. The company has responded by calling in the police and the military who violently evict the intruders (Yankson and Gough 2019). Similar problems have arisen at another large mine, Prestea. In that case, the company refused to relinquish unused or abandoned portions of its concession to small-scale miners, many of whom had received permission from local leaders (but not the central government) to access the land. In 2005, the army fired on a protest by *galamseyers* against the company, wounding seven (Hilson and Yakovleva 2007). More recently, the Ghanaian government has moved against Chinese miners. As Tschakert (2016) argues, the stereotypes deployed to demonize galamseyers were quickly and effectively turned against immigrant miners who were portrayed as criminal outsiders who caused social disruption and grave environmental damage. This vilification paved the way for the aggressive expulsion of over 4,500 Chinese miners by the Ghanaian military and police in 2013.

The organization and technology of traditional gold mining in Ghana shaped the industrial mining operations that were established shortly after the inception of colonial rule. Independent small-scale mining, though, was rapidly criminalized and, as was the case in Bolivia, India, and Nigeria, these miners are now maligned for operating outside the law. ASM is associated with the pollution of waterways with mercury that is used to amalgamate gold and with the destruction of riverine landscapes by thousands of small-scale operators who employ both hand tools and heavy equipment to excavate large pits along streams and rivers. While large-scale underground operations and small-scale surface mining were often physically separated in the past, the shift to international investment in open-pit mining has brought large- and small-scale miners into direct conflict. State violence has recently been directed toward the 50,000 or so Chinese miners who have established enterprises. The historical interpenetration of ASM and LSM combined with the criminalization of the former has resulted in the same litany of problems associated with small-scale mining that can be recited for Bolivia, India, and Nigeria.

Conclusion

The four cases of ASM presented here vary in terms of the resource being mined, the specific historical trajectory that resulted in the current relations of production, the knowledge and technology involved in its extraction, and many other local factors. However, the similarities among them are also striking. In all cases, LSM began under colonial rule, and it quickly engendered small-scale production, many times by peasants who sought to diversify or replace income generated by agricultural activities. The economic vulnerability of these households resulted from a variety of factors, including the appropriation of their land by large companies, environmental destruction, structural adjustment programs, and generalized conditions of poverty and unemployment that characterize the Global South. Commodity prices also shaped participation in ASM; low prices often resulted in the closure of industrial mines and the dismissal of large numbers of workers who continued mining on parcels leased from the company or in abandoned works. Spikes in mineral prices could also lead to an increase in ASM as high prices attracted farmers as well as unemployed urban dwellers to the sector. Until very recently, the cost of entry was low as the technology employed consisted primarily of hand tools.

In most cases, ASM has been illegal, relegated to the marginalized informal sector that is, by definition, unregulated by the state. Policymakers, the media, and the public often vilify artisanal and small-scale workers as unruly criminals who pose a threat to social stability. While this discourse serves to promote state and corporate interests and deflect responsibility away from LSM, it is derived from real problems associated with ASM. Over the last two decades, scholars and NGOs have promoted formalization as a solution to this suite of problems (Hilson and Maconachie 2017). Ghana and Tanzania were among the first to do so, although many others have since implemented similar programs. Unfortunately, such projects have failed to resolve the challenges faced by the sector. While some observers blame the cost, bureaucratic hurdles, and corruption encountered by small-scale miners who want to legalize their claims, others emphasize the continued privileging of LSM as well as wealthier small-scale miners even in countries with governments that claim to promote ASM (Tschakert 2016). In some cases, including Bolivia and Ghana, small-scale operations have recently become medium-scale businesses that require substantial investments in heavy machinery and that exploit wage laborers who come from the most disadvantaged stratum of the population.

In all four cases examined here large-scale mineral extraction was initiated by colonial entrepreneurs who were supported by the state, which sought to augment taxes, royalties, bribes, and other types of income that would benefit the government as a whole, individuals employed by it, and components of the national elite. The creation of ASM, or the local variants it encompasses, was part of the same colonial project, a means of divorcing Indigenous people from resources by declaring their attempts to gain access to minerals illegal. In this sense, what Tschakert (2016), Fisher (2007), and Verbrugge (2015) describe as exclusion was central to the creation and maintenance of colonial economies that funneled resources to privileged Europeans while simultaneously disenfranchising "natives" who were not considered worthy subjects. This division was along racial lines and reiterated the Western binary of "modern," technologically "advanced" projects associated with substantial capital outlays in contrast to "primitive," "rustic" operations conducted by families or kin groups. The privileging of revenue-generating capitalist enterprises over employment-generating subsistence practices continues today even in countries that encourage the formalization of ASM (Banchirigah 2008; Fisher 2007; Tschakert 2016).

Kajcheo, coal theft, bunkering, and galamsey are complex, internally differentiated phenomena with historical roots in specific cultures. When examined comparatively from a global vantage point and a high level of abstraction, however, these cases exhibit similarities in the nexus of relations in which they are embedded. Most of these were generated by their practical connections with and legal separation from large extractive enterprises. The mutually constitutive ways in which ASM and LSM have formed suggest that policies meant to improve conditions in the small-scale mining sector by either divorcing the two entirely on an institutional level or relying on large enterprises to voluntarily provide small mining operations with productive sub-leases will not be successful. Similarly, formalization without a commitment to the economic well-being of the general populace will also fail, as recent attempts have made clear. What appears to be an intractable development problem can only be resolved if governments value the right of impoverished households to sustain themselves with publicly held resources over the revenue-producing activities of large companies that benefit the state as well as local and foreign elites.

Conclusion

TO THOSE WHO ARE FAMILIAR with Andean history, huayrachinas—small, wind-oxygenated furnaces used to smelt metallic ores—evoke the crucial role played by Indigenous people in the production of silver immediately after the Spanish conquest and even earlier under the Inkas. Today, these furnaces appear to be vestiges of a traditional way of life, one that has faded with the passage of time and the incursion of "modern" practices into the Andean countryside. A deeper look into the history of the technology, though, reveals that it is intimately tied to the trajectory of both small- and large-scale mining, and specifically to kajcheo, which can be broadly defined as the direct appropriation of ore by miners, either legally or illicitly. To determine why this technology and the mining activities with which it is associated have persisted for five hundred years, one must examine the history of these practices and explore the social relations that engendered them. Doing history backward allows us to understand kajcheo at specific points along its trajectory without simply ascribing it to the passive persistence of "lo andino," a concept that dehistoricizes the Andean world by attributing to it certain permanent and essential characteristics.

Kajcheo is a uniquely Bolivian instantiation of the broader phenomenon referred to as artisanal and small-scale mining (ASM), and its analysis is enhanced by investigating it in relationship to large-scale mining as well as the political economy in which both are embedded. The analytical treatment of mining as large- or small-scale is an abstraction in that it ignores some of the variability within those categories as well as the overlap between them. It does, though, capture many of the key differences in class, access to resources, technology, and legal status that distinguish these types of extraction.

201

202 CONCLUSION

However, rather than treating these different scales of production as separate "things," a relational approach focuses on the mutual constitution of the two, highlighting the conditions that engendered them as well as changes in the relationship over time.

The careful examination of kajcheo from different vantage points reveals four key aspects of its development: (1) it has been tightly imbricated with the evolution of large-scale mining over the course of the last five centuries; (2) the relationship between the two is marked by interdependence as well as tension and conflict; (3) it has played a critical role in household subsistence strategies despite radical changes in the overall political economy; and (4) kajcheo, like other forms of artisanal and small-scale mining throughout the world, was a product of ongoing colonial relations that continue today in somewhat attenuated form.

The Long-Term History of Small-Scale Mining and Metallurgy in Bolivia

A brief summary of the trajectory of kajcheo in Bolivia, presented chronologically, underscores shifts in the nature of independent mining and metallurgy as well as continuities in practice.

Inka Mining

The degree of elite involvement in the development of metallurgy in the far southern Andes is debated, but by Inka times state control over this craft is clear. According to historical sources (Berthelot 1986), the empire had a legal monopoly on mining, although it ceded the right to work smaller deposits to conquered elites who did so using simpler technology. The Inkas reorganized existing production in the hinterlands or installed new complexes as seen in Porco. Theoretically, at least, this created a dual system somewhat comparable to the coexistence of small- and large-scale mining enterprises commonly found in the region after the Spanish conquest. Unlike later periods, though, silver was not used as currency but rather to fashion sumptuary and ritual objects that reinforced elite status and expressed the sacred nature of state authority. The gifting of silver objects was also a component of the political economy; these were given by imperial actors to elite subjects who, in return, were expected to mobilize labor for the empire. Rules prohibiting the theft of ore suggest that commoners who were assigned to work in the

CONCLUSION 203

mines occasionally smuggled it out for their own use. What they may have done with the ore is an open question; perhaps it was used to make ornaments, offered to huacas, or bartered for other products. With the exception of a few sites in northwestern Argentina, no evidence for the use of huayrachinas has been reported for local domestic contexts. Instead, these furnaces appear to have been deployed under state auspices and constituted the cutting-edge technology of the time.

Like the Spaniards, the Inkas imposed a colonial system in which they monopolized access to high-quality ore deposits and prohibited their exploitation by conquered communities. Provincial elites could, though, legally mine less productive deposits. The tension in this arrangement was reflected, in part, by ore theft at state production sites. However, much more investigation of small-scale mining under the Inka needs to be done to illuminate the relations among imperial authorities, regional huacas, provincial elites, and commoners with regard to these practices.

The Early Colonial Plunder Economy

Except for a brief period immediately following the transfer of Porco from Inka to European control, the means of production remained largely the same for the first few decades after the Spanish conquest. Productive relations, however, changed dramatically with the ownership of mines claimed by individual Spaniards who worked them primarily with encomienda labor under the direction of indios de vara or yanaconas whose technical expertise had been acquired under the Inkas. Initially, the deposits in Porco and Potosí were exceptionally rich, and the Spaniards, who had little if any mining experience, relied on share-cropping arrangements. Indigenous teams of workers using mostly Native technology would remove the ore; part was given to the mineowner and the remainder was retained by the miners (or at least the indios de vara), who smelted it and sometimes sold the refined product in the Indigenous mineral market in Potosí. The Spaniards thus profited without intervening in the productive process, an aspect of the plunder economy that characterized the first forty or so years of Spanish rule. The individuals who actually did the mining, mostly encomienda Indians, but probably some wage workers as well, sometimes engaged in "ore theft," which provided them with access to minerals that could be processed in huayrachinas and cupellation hearths. Some Indigenous households thus engaged in the production of metal as one strategy for adapting to the new economic environment. Mineowners relied on ore-sharing because they lacked the capacity to directly control production, while miners engaged in it to gain access to ore that could be smelted and used for tribute or purchases in the emergent market. This was the context in which kajcheo—both legal and illicit forms—developed, although it was not called that at the time.

The Colonial Regime

The reforms implemented by Viceroy Toledo in the 1570s established the lineaments of a colonial system that was to endure, with some changes, until independence in the early nineteenth century. In addition to his well-known policies of resettling Native populations, reorganizing the mita, and promoting the use of the patio process, Toledo also codified two customs that offset the low wages paid to mitayos: the right to mine on weekends and to high-grade ore during the work week. In 1609 Llanos (2009) noted that formally these institutions had nearly disappeared by the 1590s due to the decline in ore quality, but both practices continued, particularly because mingas, or wage laborers, demanded this subsidy. These workers, who could be the very same mitayos who labored in the mines or mills the previous week, were a key component of a mercantile system in which state control over labor as well as the sale and purchase of many products were integrated with a market economy. Large- and small-scale mining and mineral processing were thus interdependent as owners refused to pay adequate wages, and kajchas insisted on access to ore as part of their compensation.

The direct appropriation of silver ore by miners working for large-scale enterprises as mitayos or mingas as well as small-scale production by independent miners generated an "informal" or parallel economic sector (Barragán 2017a; Rodríguez Ostria 1989). Small-scale millowners advanced money and supplies to the miners and allowed them to use their facilities, in return for the amalgam that remained in the mills after the initial cleaning. The term *kajcha* was used for the first time in the eighteenth century to describe miners who directly appropriated ore on the weekends, and, not coincidentally, it was also the period during which these workers developed a rudimentary class identity, particularly in Potosí. Kajchas were reviled as a threat to social order, and local authorities considered destroying the mills that served them. However, their overall productivity as well as the fact that miners would not work without access to "ore-sharing" on weekends prevented them from implementing such drastic sanctions.

The clear bifurcation of mining and mineral processing into large- and small-scale operations occurred after the introduction of the patio process

CONCLUSION

in the late sixteenth century. The legal framework imposed by the colonial state, privileging ownership over labor in determining the legality of mineral extraction (Barragán 2017a) and requiring registration of the product and payment of taxes generated an illicit, informal sector that coexisted with large-scale, state-authorized mining. The dynamic between azogueros, large-scale employers unwilling to pay adequate wages, and miners, who refused to work without supplementary income, continued to characterize the industry. During the eighteenth century, though, kajcheo appears to have become more widespread and institutionalized with the concomitant development of a social identity associated with the direct appropriation and small-scale processing of ore.

Industrialization and the Republican State

The liberal state did not emerge immediately after Bolivian independence but developed slowly over the course of the nineteenth century as it shed colonial practices. From the perspective of mining, the two most important shifts were the abolition of forced labor a decade before independence (1812) and the end of the government's monopoly on the purchase of silver in mid-century. The first was a blow to azogueros who depended on the state for subsidized labor. The withdrawal of this labor force along with the destruction caused by the War of Independence resulted in the stagnation of mining during the first three quarters of the nineteenth century. Over one-third of the silver that was registered in the Potosí district between 1830 and 1850 was mined by kajchas who worked under contract (Rodríguez Ostria 1991, 33). The delivery of a formal proposal for regulating kajcheo to the Gremio de Azogueros in Potosí in 1837 (Platt 2000) indicates a continuing sense of collective identity on the part of these miners. The second reform resulted in the revitalization of the silver industry in southern Bolivia. Along with the modernization of the currency and consequent influx of foreign investment, allowing silver to be sold on the free market raised prices and jumpstarted the late nineteenth century boom that lasted from 1872 to 1895 (Mitre 1981). Both these phases are reflected at Porco, which was exploited by kajchas engaged in contract work during the 1840s and then by a large company in the 1880s. Robert Peele's (1893) description of huayrachinas operating in the area makes it clear that silver continued to be directly appropriated by miners and smelted in small quantities by local specialists during this time.

Large-scale industrialization arrived in southern Bolivia with the advent of tin mining, which was facilitated by the construction of railroads that made the transport of ore to Pacific ports less costly. New technologies were introduced along with modern approaches to labor discipline, including the development of company towns that offered amenities as well as greater control of workers. Porco Tin Ltd. was formed with British capital in 1912, the same year that the railway arrived, and quickly installed modern processing technology as well as an aerial ropeway to move ore from the mines to the mill. Archaeological survey revealed that roughly coeval with these developments was the establishment of rural homesteads, most likely by families attracted by the availability of wage labor. A number of these were associated with smelting and refining technology that is almost identical in form and disposition to the huayrachinas and cupellation hearths used by Carlos Cuiza in the twenty-first century and most likely employed for the same purpose—to produce silver from illicitly obtained ore that could be used to augment household incomes.

The interdigitation of mining and agriculture that characterized kajcheo—and even salaried employment in the mines—over the centuries is particularly visible at the rural homesteads surrounding Porco. However, during the first half of the twentieth century the industrialization of large mines in places like Llallagua in northern Potosí also resulted in the development of a workforce that identified as miners and unionized in the face of harsh working conditions and violent repression. These organizations formed the vanguard of a labor movement that was strongly influenced by Trotskyism. They played a key role in the Bolivian Revolution of 1952, which resulted in the nationalization of the three big tin mining companies and the formation of the Corporación Minera de Bolivia (COMIBOL) that controlled mining operations for the next thirty years. These dramatic events do not, however, seem to have affected Porco, where deposits were exploited by a small North American company and also continued to be worked by kajchas who leased mines from COMIBOL.

In addition to unions, the 1930s saw the emergence of the first mining cooperatives in Bolivia. Initially formed in Potosí by kajchas who demanded the right to sell the mineral they produced on the free market (Absi 2014), cooperatives were subsequently created by unemployed miners during the Great Depression and successive economic downturns. This was the case in Porco, where workers who had been employed by the defunct Empresa Minera Porco founded the first cooperative in 1958; two others were later formed under similar circumstances. Cooperatives absorbed miners who would have become kajchas in previous years, and they acted much like earlier associations of kajchas, with some important differences: official recognition by the Bolivian state facilitated their development as formal institutions that, in

CONCLUSION 207

turn, enhanced their status as important political actors at the local, regional, and national levels. In many cases it has also resulted in an increased scale of production and a shift in labor relations, with cooperative members hiring poorly paid wage workers to extract and transport the ore.

By the turn of the twenty-first century, small-scale mineral extraction in Porco was dominated by cooperatives, although some individuals continued to work depleted ore faces leased from the mining companies, an activity that barely provided a subsistence income. The coexistence of cooperative and company mining had real effects on the social dynamics of the village, as reflected in schools, access to healthcare, and municipal political organization.

High-grading and the theft of larger quantities of ore and equipment (jukeo) still occur in Porco and other hard-rock mines in southern Bolivia. The technology associated with small-scale extraction and processing, though, has largely disappeared as cooperatives have increased in size, and improved transportation has facilitated the sale of illegally obtained ore to rescatiris, middlemen who operate out of Potosí and other urban centers. Huayrachinas and cupellation hearths are no longer employed to smelt and refine silver, and even quimbaletes—used to crush ore—are disappearing.

Long-Term and Worldwide Perspectives on ASM

Several distinct ruptures in the way in which *kajcheo* was organized in Bolivia are apparent in this account. The most profound shift is the one about which the least information exists—the transition from small-scale mining in the context of a state-run economy under the Inkas to the direct appropriation—and sale of—ore under the Spaniards. Another important change was the introduction of mercury amalgamation along with the systematization of the mita, which generated a parallel economy of kajchas and small-scale mills. And finally, the growth and institutionalization of cooperatives during the late twentieth and early twenty-first century resulted in the formalization of kajcheo and the increasing political influence of these groups. The nature of kajcheo has thus shifted with changes in state intervention in the mining sector, the development of large-scale enterprises, and the continual struggle of small-scale miners to maintain access to productive mineral deposits.

A common thread running through the history of kajcheo is the critical role it has played in the subsistence strategies of many Indigenous households, at least since the Spanish conquest. Historically, kajcheo, even more than wage labor, has been intertwined with agricultural endeavors, as miners used mineral extraction and metal production as a source of cash to complement subsistence activities. More recently, the opposite seems to be the case, as miners use farm products to subsidize households that rely primarily on wage labor.

While the ways in which LSM has shaped kajcheo are obvious—for example, kajchas' use of existing or abandoned mines created by LSM as sources of ore, the exclusion of small-scale miners from land leased by corporations, or the dismissal of miners during economic downturns—the reverse can be difficult to detect as the lineaments of the relationship lay beneath the surface. Kajcheo allowed large commercial enterprises and the state to avoid the costs associated with the reproduction of much of the labor force; rather than receiving a wage and other benefits from formal employment, kajchas relied on their own abilities and luck to support their families. Related to this, kajcheo redirected the financial risk inherent in mining from capital to the workers. Rather than expending resources on potentially unproductive deposits, kajchas worked them and often sold what they recovered to the company at lower than market prices. Kajcheo also tempered discontent by providing unemployed miners with a means of survival, albeit often at a subsistence level or less. Under some historical conditions, however, kajcheo—and its recent incarnation in the form of cooperatives—resulted in the formation of a collective identity that led to concerted action against LSM and the state that protects it. These, in turn, were forced to make legal and economic concessions to avoid further conflict.

Viewed from a global vantage point, kajcheo is a regional expression of the much broader phenomenon of artisanal and small-scale mining that is practiced by families living in poor nations throughout the world. Most people who engage in ASM reside in formerly colonized countries where the legal exclusion of Indigenous households from direct access to extractive resources began with the imposition of foreign rule. What Barragán (2017a) notes for Bolivia is characteristic of most countries where ASM occurs; control of property through ownership or lease rather than labor became the determinant of mineral rights.

Worldwide, ASM accounts for a large percentage of the minerals produced and employs the majority of workers in the mining sector. It is also associated with a variety of social ills, with poverty, environmental degradation, health and safety issues, and conflict the most salient among them. Increasingly, governments and nongovernmental organizations have turned their attention to these problems and have implemented a variety of policies to mitigate them. Requiring large-scale enterprises to provide small-scale miners with access to mineral sources and the formalization of ASM are two common approaches. Neither is particularly effective; in the first case there is an inherent conflict between ASM and LSM over productive deposits, and in the second, governments continue to favor LSM over ASM because large enterprises produce more revenue—in the form of taxes, royalties, and bribes—than do small ones. This continues to be the case even in Bolivia, where progressive governments have recognized the economic and political importance of mining cooperatives but still favor large corporations. An examination of the long-term history of kajcheo suggests that ASM and its associated problems will continue to exist in Bolivia and elsewhere until contemporary governments shed neocolonial policies and instead prioritize household livelihoods.

References Cited

Abbott, Mark B., and Alexander P. Wolfe. 2003. "Intensive Pre-Incan Metallurgy Recorded by Lake Sediments from the Bolivian Andes." *Science* 301 (5641): 1893–95.

Abercrombie, Thomas A. 1996. "Qaqchas and La Plebe in Rebellion." *Journal of Latin American and Caribbean Anthropology* 2 (1): 62–111.

Abercrombie, Thomas A. 1998. *Pathways of Memory and Power: Ethnography and History among an Andean People.* Madison: University of Wisconsin Press.

Absi, Pascale. 2005. *Los ministros del diablo. El trabajo y sus representaciones en las minas de Potosí.* La Paz: Fundación PIEB, Instituto Francés de Estudios Andinos, and Institut de Recherche pour le Dévelopement en Bolivie.

Absi, Pascale. 2010. "La parte ideal de la crisis: Los mineros cooperativistas de Bolivia frente a la recesión." *Cuadernos de Antropología Social* 31: 33–54.

Absi, Pascale. 2014. "Q'aqchas y obreros. Apuntes sobre la organización del trabajo minero en Potosí, 1930–1940." *Anuario de Estudios Bolivianos, Archivísticos y Bibliográficos* 20: 221–46.

Absi, Pascale, and Jorge Pavez. 2015. *Imagenes de la revolución industrial: Robert Gertsmann en las minas de Bolivia (1925–1936).* La Paz: Plural Editores.

Achtenberg, Emily. 2014. "Conflict Over New Bolivian Law Highlights Mining Sector Contradictions." *Rebel Currents* (blog). May 9, 2014. https://nacla.org/blog/2014/5/9/conflict-over-new-bolivian-law-highlights-mining-sector-contradictions.

Achtenberg, Emily. 2016. "What's Behind Bolivia's Cooperative Mining Wars?" *Rebel Currents* (blog). 2016. https://nacla.org/blog/2016/11/23/what%E2%80%99s-behind-bolivia%E2%80%99s-cooperative-mining-wars.

Acosta, José de. 1954 [1590]. *Historia natural y moral de las Indias.* Biblioteca de Autores Españoles. Madrid: Ediciones Atlas.

Acuto, Félix, and Ivan Leiboweicz. 2018. "Inca Colonial Encounters and Incorporation. Northern Argentina." In *The Oxford Handbook of the Incas*, edited by Sonia Alconini and Alan Covey, 333–54. Oxford: University of Oxford Press. https://doi.org/10.1093/oxfordhb/9780190219352.013.2.

Adán, Leonor, and Mauricio Uribe. 2005. "El dominio inca en la localidad de Caspana: Un acercamiento al pensamiento político andino (Río Loa, Norte de Chile)." *Estudios Atacameños* 29: 41–66.

Adunbi, Omolade. 2017. "'We Own This Oil': Artisanal Refineries, Extractive Industries, and the Politics of Oil in Nigeria." In *Governance in the Extractive Industries: Power, Cultural Politics, and Regulation*, edited by Lori Leonard and Siba N. Grovogui, 77–94. New York: Routledge.

Agencia DPA. 2018. "Bolivia cambia una ley y autoriza trabajo infantil desde los 14 años." *El Comercio*, December 14, 2018. https://www.elcomercio.com/actualidad/bolivia-ley-autorizacion-trabajador-infantil.html.

REFERENCES CITED

Agricola, Georgius. 1950 [1556]. *De Re Metallica*. New York: Dover Publications.

Alcón, Sofía. 2004. "Informe etnográfico sobre Porco, Potosí." Manuscript on file in the Department of Anthropology and Geography, Colorado State University.

Aldenderfer, Mark, Nathan M. Craig, Robert J. Speakman, and Rachel Popelka-Filcoff. 2008. "Four-Thousand-Year-Old Gold Artifacts from the Lake Titicaca Basin, Southern Peru." *Proceedings of the National Academy of Sciences of the United States of America* 105 (13): 5002–5.

Alonso Barba, Álvaro. 1992 [1640]. *Arte de los metales, en que se enseña el verdadero beneficio de los de oro, y plata por azogue. El modo de fundirlos todos, y como se han de refinar y apartar unos de otros*. Madrid: Consejo Superior de Investigaciones Científicas.

Alonso, Ricardo N. 1995. *Diccionario minero. Glosario de voces utilizadas por los mineros de Iberoamérica*. Madrid: Consejo Superior de Investigaciones Científicas.

Álvarez Calderón, Rosabella V. 2016. Arqueología histórica en las "huacas" de la ciudad de Lima: ampliando la narrativa. *Boletín de Arqueología PUCP* 20: 83–102.

Amengual, Matthew. 2018. "Buying Stability: The Distributive Outcomes of Private Politics in the Bolivian Mining Industry." *World Development* 104: 31–45.

Andrén, Anders. 1998. *Between Artifacts and Texts: Historical Archaeology in Global Perspective*. New York: Plenum Press.

Andreucci, Diego, and Isabella M. Radhuber. 2015. "Limits to 'Counter-Neoliberal' Reform: Mining Expansion and the Marginalisation of Post-Extractivist Forces in Evo Morales's Bolivia." *Geoforum* 84: 280–91.

Angiorama, Carlos I. 2004. "Acerca de incas y metales en Humahuaca. Producción metalúrgica en los Amarillos en tiempos del Tawantinsuyu." *Relaciones de la Sociedad Argentina de Antropología* 29, 39–58.

Angiorama, Carlos I. 2005. "Nuevas evidencias de actividades metalúrgicas pre-incaicas en la quebrada de Humahuaca (Jujuy, Argentina)." *Anales del Museo de América* 13: 173–98.

Angiorama, Carlos I., and María Florencia Becerra. 2010. "Antiguas evidencias de minería y metalurgia en Pozuelos, Santo Domingo y Coyahuayma (Puna de Jujuy, Argentina)." *Boletín del Museo Chileno de Arte Precolombino* 15 (1): 81–104.

Angiorama, Carlos I., and María Florencia Becerra. 2021. "Minería y metalurgia prehispánica en el Noroeste Argentino: una puesta al día de las evidencias arqueológicas recuperadas en la actual provincia de Jujuy." *Estudios Atacameños* 67. https://doi.org/10.22199/issn.0718-1043-2021-0030.

Angiorama, Carlos I., María Florencia Becerra, and María Josefina Pérez Pieroni. 2015. "El mineral de Pan de Azúcar. Arqueología histórica de un centro minero colonial en la Puna de Jujuy (Argentina)." *Chungara* 47 (4): 1–17.

Antwi-Boateng, Osman, and Mamudu Abunga Akudugu. 2020. "Golden Migrants: The Rise and Impact of Illegal Chinese Small-Scale Mining in Ghana." *Politics & Policy* 48 (1): 135–67.

Archivo General de Indias. Charcas 55. Sevilla, Spain.

Arzáns de Orsúa y Vela, Bartolomé. 1965 [c. 1705–36]. *Historia de la Villa Imperial de Potosí*, Vol. 3. Edited by Lewis Hanke and Gunnar Mendoza. Providence, R.I.: Brown University Press.

REFERENCES CITED

Assadourian, Carlos Sempat. 1980. *Minería y espacio económico en los Andes, siglos XVI–XX*. Lima: Instituto de Estudios Peruanos.

Assadourian, Carlos Sempat. 1992. "Base técnica y relaciones de producción en la minería de Potosí." In *Ciencia colonial en América*, edited by Antonio Lafuente and José Sala Catalá, 121–42. Madrid: Alianza Editorial.

Ayala, Roberto, Rubén Taquichiri, Cristian Velásquez, and Catherine Ayllon. 2010. "Análisis técnico del área de Hundimiento. Cooperativa Minera 'Veneros Porco Ltda.' Yacimiento Minero de Porco." https://www.academia.edu/25592673/ANALISIS_TECNICO_COOP_VENEROS_PORCO.

Bakewell, Peter. 1984a. *Miners of the Red Mountain: Indian Labor in Potosí, 1545–1650*. Albuquerque: University of New Mexico Press.

Bakewell, Peter. 1984b. "Mining in Colonial Spanish America." In *The Cambridge History of Latin America*, Vol. 2, edited by Leslie Bethell, 105–51. Cambridge: Cambridge University Press.

Bakewell, Peter. 1988. *Silver and Entrepreneurship in Seventeenth-Century Potosí: The Life and Times of Antonio López de Quiroga*. Albuquerque: University of New Mexico Press.

Bakewell, Peter. 1994. "The First Refining Mills in Potosí: Design and Construction." In *In Quest of Mineral Wealth: Aboriginal and Colonial Mining and Metallurgy in Spanish America*, Vol. 287, edited by Alan K. Craig and Robert C. West. Baton Rouge, La.: Geoscience Publications, Dept. of Geography and Anthropology, Louisiana State University.

Banchirigah, Sadia Mohammed. 2008. "Challenges with Eradicating Illegal Mining in Ghana: A Perspective from the Grassroots." *Resources Policy* 33 (1): 29–38.

Banchirigah, Sadia Mohammed, and Gavin Hilson. 2010. "De-Agrarianization, Re-Agrarianization and Local Economic Development: Re-Orientating Livelihoods in African Artisanal Mining Communities." *Policy Sciences* 43 (2): 157–80. https://doi.org/10.1007/s11077-009-9091-5.

Barnett, James. 2023. "The Oil Thieves of Nigeria." *New Lines Magazine*. Accessed June 20, 2023. https://newlinesmag.com/reportage/the-oil-thieves-of-nigeria/.

Barragán, Rossana. 2015. "¿Ladrones, pequeños empresarios o trabajadores independientes? K'ajchas, trapiches y plata en el Cerro de Potosí en el siglo XVIII." *Nuevo Mundo Mundos Nuevos*. http://journals.openedition.org/nuevomundo/67938.

Barragán, Rossana. 2017a. "Working Silver for the World: Mining Labor and Popular Economy in Colonial Potosí." *Hispanic American Historical Review* 97 (2): 193–222.

Barragán, Rossana. 2017b. "Los k'ajchas y los proyectos de industria y nación en Bolivia (1935–1940)." *Revista Mundos do Trabalho* 9 (18): 25–48.

Barragán, Rossana. 2020. "Women in the Silver Mines of Potosí: Rethinking the History of 'Informality' and 'Precarity' (Sixteenth to Eighteenth Centuries)." *International Review of Social History* 65 (2): 289–314. https://doi.org/10.1017/S0020859019000555.

Bauer, Brian, and Charles Stanish. 2001. *Ritual and Pilgrimage in the Ancient Andes: The Islands of the Sun and the Moon*. Austin: University of Texas Press.

REFERENCES CITED

Beltrán, C. L. 2016. *La ruta de la plata: de Potosí al Pacífico. Caminos, comercio y caravanas en los siglos XVI y XVII*. La Paz: Plural Editores. https://books.google.com/books?id=ojFgAQAACAAJ.

Benavides del Carpio, Maya. 2004. "Informe de investigación etnográfica Proyecto Porco." Manuscript on file in the Department of Anthropology and Geography, Colorado State University.

Berthelot, Jean. 1986. "The Extraction of Precious Metals at the Time of the Inka." In *Anthropological History of Andean Polities*, edited by John Murra, Nathan Wachtel, and Jacques Revel, 69–88. Cambridge: Cambridge University Press.

Besom, Thomas. 2010. "Inka Sacrifice and the Mummy of Salinas Grandes I." *Latin American Antiquity* 21 (4): 399–422.

Besom, Thomas. 2013. *Inka Human Sacrifice and Mountain Worship: Strategies for Empire Unification*. Albuquerque: University of New Mexico Press.

Betancourt, Orlando. 2007. "La apropriación de la figura del kajcha en la historia de la Villa Imperial de Potosí de Arzáns de Orsúa y Vela." *Revista Iberoamericana* 73 (220): 437–52.

Bigelow, Allison Margaret. 2016. "Women, Men, and the Legal Languages of Mining in the Colonial Andes." *Ethnohistory* 63 (2): 351–80.

Blacut, Carlos Camargo. 1968. *Agenda minera de Bolivia*. La Paz: Editorial en Marcha.

Bocángel Jerez, Danilo, and Camilo Leyton Michovich. 2009. "Fundación MEDMIN. Apoyo real y efectivo a la gestion ambiental de las cooperativas y comunidades mineras de Bolivia." *Minería Sustentable*. La Paz: Medio Ambiente Minería e Industria. https://cebem.org/revistaredesma/vol6/pdf/instituciones/MEDMIN.pdf.

Boman, Eric. 1908. *Antiquités de la Région Andine de la République Argentine y du Désert d'Atacama*. Paris: Imprimerie Nationale Librairie H. Le Soudier.

Bouysse Cassagne, Thérèse. 1975. "Pertenencia étnica, status económico y lenguas en Charcas a fines del siglo XVI." In *Tasa de la visita general de Francisco de Toledo*, edited by David N. Cook, 312–28. Lima: Universidad Nacional Mayor de San Marcos.

Bouysse Cassagne, Thérèse. 1987. *La identidad Aymara, Aproximación histórica (Siglo XV, Siglo XVI)*. La Paz: HISBOL-IFEA.

Bouysse Cassagne, Thérèse. 2004. "El sol de adentro: Wakas y santos en las minas de Charcas y en el lago Titicaca (Siglos XV–XVII)." *Boletín de Arqueología PUCP* 8: 59–97.

Bouysse Cassagne, Thérèse. 2005. "Las minas del centro-sur andino, los cultos prehispánicos y los cultos cristianos." *Bulletin de l'Institut Français d'Études Andines* 34 (3): 443–62.

Boza Cuadros, Maria Fernanda. 2022. "Bridge and Boundary: The Maritime Connections of Colonial Arequipa, Peru." *International Journal of Historical Archaeology* 26 (2): 291–315.

Bray, Tamara L. 2015. "Andean Wak'as and Alternative Configurations of Persons, Power, and Things." In *The Archaeology of Wak'as: Explorations of the Sacred in the Pre-Columbian Andes*, edited by Tamara L. Bray, 3–19. Boulder: University Press of Colorado.

Bullock, Stanley C. 1915. "A Trip through Bolivia." *Engineering and Mining Journal* 100 (11): 421–24.

REFERENCES CITED

Burke, Melvin. 1987. *The Corporación Minera de Bolivia (Comibol) and the Triangular Plan: A Case Study in Dependency*, Vol. 4: *Latin American and Caribbean Studies*. http://sites.allegheny.edu/latinamericanstudies/latin-american-issues/volume-4/.

Calys-Tagoe, Benedict N. L., Edith Clarke, Thomas Robins, and Niladri Basu. 2017. "A Comparison of Licensed and Un-Licensed Artisanal and Small-Scale Gold Miners (ASGM) in Terms of Socio-Demographics, Work Profiles, and Injury Rates." *BMC Public Health* 17: 862–70. https://doi.org/o.1186/s12889-017-4876-5.

Capoche, Luis. 1959 [1585]. "Relación general de la Villa Imperial de Potosí." In *Biblioteca de Autores Españoles*, Vol. 122, edited by Lewis Hanke, 69–221. Madrid: Ediciones Atlas.

Capriles Villazón, Orlando. 1977. *Historia de la minería boliviana*. La Paz: Banco Minero de Bolivia.

Carrillo, Felix, Ton Salman, and Carola Soruco. 2013. "Cooperativas de minería de pequeña escala en Bolivia: De salvavidas de los pobres a maquinaria de manipulación política." *Letras Verdes. Revista Latinoamericana de Estudios Socioambientales* 14 (September): 233–54.

Cayo, Ludwing, and Delfor Ulloa. 2003. "Informe sobre el proceso de elaboración de carbón." Manuscript on file in the Department of Anthropology and Geography, Colorado State University.

Centro de Estudios de Potosí. 1892. *Monografía del departamento de Potosí*. Potosí, Bolivia: Imprenta El Tiempo.

Chase, Zachary James. 2018. "The Inca State and Local Ritual Landscapes." In *The Oxford Handbook of the Incas*, edited by Sonia Alconini and Alan Covey, 519–40. Oxford: Oxford University Press. https://doi.org/10.1093/oxfordhb/9780190219352.013.9.

Chirinos Ogata, Patricia, and Daniel Dante Saucedo Segami. 2021. "Towards an Archaeology of the Japanese Diaspora in Peru." *International Journal of Historical Archaeology* 25: 784–802. https://doi.org/10.1007/s10761-020-00562-8.

Chuhue, R., L. Ning Na, and A. Coello. 2012. *La immigración china al Peru: Arqueología, historia y sociedad*. Lima: Universidad Ricardo Palma.

Chukwu, Ogbuagu C., and Abiodun Oladejo. 2020. "The Dynamics of Corporate and Local Complicities in Environmental Pollution in the Niger Delta Region of Nigeria." *AFRIKA: Journal of Politics, Economics, & Society* 10 (1):121–41.

Cieza de León, Pedro de. 2005 [c. 1549–53]. *La crónica del Peru: El señorío de los Incas*. Caracas: Biblioteca Ayacucho.

Coben, Lawrence S. 2015. "Ushnu." In *Encyclopedia of the Inkas*, edited by Gary Urton and Adriana Von Hagen, 275–79. Lanham, Md.: Rowan & Littlefield.

Cohen, Claire R., Mary Van Buren, Barbara Mills, and Thilo Rehren. 2010. "Current Silver Smelting in the Bolivian Andes: A Review of the Technology Employed." *Historical Metallurgy* 44 (2): 153–62.

Cohen, Claire R. 2008. "The Winds of Change: An Archaeometallurgical Study of Silver Production in the Porco Potosí Region, Southern Bolivia, AD 1500–2000." PhD diss., University College London.

Cohen, Claire, Thilo Rehren, and Mary Van Buren. 2008. "La huayrachina por dentro y por fuera: Un estudio arqueo-metalúrgico de la tecnología de fundición de plomo en

Porco-Potosí, Bolivia." In *Mina y metalurgía en los Andes del sur desde la época prehispánica hasta el siglo XVII*, edited by Pablo Cruz and Jean-Joinville Vacher, 29–56. Sucre: Institut de Recherche pour le Développement and Instituto Francés de Estudios Andinos.

Cole, Jeffrey. 1985. *The Potosí Mita, 1573–1700: Compulsory Indian Labor in the Andes*. Stanford, Calif.: Stanford University Press.

Constitute. 2009. "Bolivia (Plurinational State of) 2009." Translated by Max Planck Institute. Constitute Project. https://www.constituteproject.org/constitution/Bolivia2009.

Contreras, Carlos. 1986. *Mineros y campesinos en los Andes: Mercado laboral y economía campesina en la sierra central siglo XIX*. Lima: Instituto de Estudios Peruanos.

Contreras, Manuel E., and Mario Napoleón Pacheco. 1989. *Medio siglo de minería mediana en Bolivia, 1939–1989*. La Paz: Minera Boliviana.

Cooke, Colin A., Mark B. Abbott, and Alexander P. Wolfe. 2008. "Late-Holocene Atmospheric Lead Deposition in the Peruvian and Bolivian Andes." *Holocene* 18 (2): 353–59.

Cooper, Frederick. 2005. *Colonialism in Question: Theory, Knowledge, History*. Berkeley: University of California Press.

Corcoran-Tadd, Noa, Jorge Ulloa Hung, Andrzej T. Antczak, Eduardo Herrera Malatesta, and Corinne L. Hofman. 2021. "Indigenous Routes and Resource Materialities in the Early Spanish Colonial World: Comparative Archaeological Approaches." *Latin American Antiquity* 32 (3): 468–85. https://doi.org/10.1017/laq.2021.6.

Costin, Cathy Lynne, ed. 2016. *Making Value, Making Meaning: Techné in the Pre-Columbian World*. Washington, D.C.: Dumbarton Oaks Research Library and Collection.

Craig, Alan K. 1993. "The Ingenious Ingenios: Spanish Colonial Water Mills at Potosí." In *Culture, Form, and Place: Essays in Cultural and Historical Geography*, Vol. 32, edited by K. Mathewson, 125–56. Geoscience and Man. Baton Rouge: Louisiana State University.

Cross, Harry. 1983. "South American Bullion Production and Export, 1550–1750." In *Precious Metals in the Later Medieval and Early Modern Worlds*, edited by J. F. Richards, 397–424. Durham, N.C.: Carolina Academic Press.

Cruz, Pablo. 2006. "Mundos permeables y espacios peligrosos. Consideraciones acerca de punkus y qaqas en el paisaje altoandino de Potosí, Bolivia." *Boletín del Museo Chileno de Arte Precolombino* 11 (2): 35–50.

Cruz, Pablo. 2007. "Qaraqara e Inkas: El rostro indígena de Potosí. Las estrategías de poder y supervivencia durante los siglos XV–XVI." *Chachapuma. Revista de Arqueología Boliviana* 2: 29–40.

Cruz, Pablo. 2009a. "Huacas olvidadas y cerros santos. Apuntes metodológicos sobre la cartografía sagrada en los Andes del sur de Bolivia." *Estudios Atacameños* 38: 55–74.

Cruz, Pablo. 2009b. "Tumbas, metalurgía y complejidad social en un paramo del altiplano surandino. Pulacayo, Bolivia, 1er milenio D.C." *Revista Andina* 49: 71–104.

Cruz, Pablo. 2012. "El mundo se explica al andar. Consideraciones en torno a la sacralización del paisaje en los Andes del sur de Bolivia (Potosí, Chuquisaca)." *Indiana* 29: 221–51.

Cruz, Pablo. 2022. "Metals for the Inka. Mining, Power, and Religion in Qullasuyu." In *Rethinking the Inka: Community, Landscape, and Empire in the Southern Andes*, edited by Frances M. Hayashida, Andrés Troncoso, and Diego Salazar, 35–56. Austin: University of Texas Press.

Cruz, Pablo, and Pascale Absi. 2008. "Cerros ardientes y huayras calladas. Potosí antes y durante el contacto." In *Mina y metalurgía en los Andes del sur desde la época prehispánica hasta el siglo XVII*, edited by Pablo Cruz and Jean-Joinville Vacher, 91–120. Sucre, Bolivia: Institut de Recherche pour le Développement and Instituto Francés de Estudios Andinos.

Cruz, Pablo, Eríc Crubézy, and Patrice Gérard. 2013. "Los adoratorios de altura inkaicos. Una mirada desde el cerro Cuzco, Departamento de Potosí, Bolivia." *Memoria Americana* 21 (1): 93–120.

Cruz, Pablo, Heather N. Lechtman, and Claudia Rivera Casanovas. 2022. "The Escaramayu Complex: A Prehispanic Metallurgical Establishment in the South Andean Altiplano (Escara, Potosi, Bolivia), Ninth to Fifteenth Centuries AD." *Latin American Antiquity*, 1–19. https://doi.org/10.1017/laq.2022.77.

Cruz, Pablo, and Florian Téreygeol. 2014. "Yanaconas del rayo. Reflexiones en torno a la producción de metales en el espacio surandino (Bolivia, siglos XV–XVI)." *Estudios Atacameños* 49: 19–44.

Cruz, Pablo, and Florian Téreygeol. 2020. "Los hornos de reverbero andinos. Dinámicas de transferencias e innovaciones de technologías metalúrgicas indígenas y europeas." *Estudios Atacameños* 66. http://dx.doi.org/10.22199/issn.0718-1043-2020-0039.

Cunningham, Charles G., Hugo N. Aparicio, Fernando S. Murillo, Néstor C. Jiménez, José Luis B. Lizeca, Edwin H. McKee, George E. Ericksen, and Frank V. Tavera. 1994. "The Relationship between the Porco, Bolivia, Ag-Zn-Pb-Sn Deposit and the Porco Caldera." *Economic Geology* 89: 1833–41.

Dalence, José Maria. 1851. *Bosquejo estadistico de Bolivia*. Sucre, Bolivia: Ymprenta de Sucre.

D'Altroy, Terence, and Timothy Earle. 1985. "Staple Finance, Wealth Finance, and Storage in the Inka Political Economy." *Current Anthropology* 26 (2): 187–206.

Daniel, Frank Jack, and Matthias Williams. 2013. "The 'Coal Mafia' Plunders India." *Power Grab*, May 14, 2013.

De Nigris, Mario Ricardo. 2012. "Los molinos mineros andinos." *Antropólogo*. https://www .academia.edu/2000342/De_Nigris_M._Los_Molinos_Mineros_Andinos.

Deagan, Kathleen. 1987. *Artifacts of the Spanish Colonies of Florida and the Caribbean 1500–1800*, Vol. 1: *Ceramics, Glassware, and Beads*. Washington, D.C.: Smithsonian Institution Press.

Deagan, Kathleen. 1996. "Colonial Transformation: Euro-American Cultural Genesis in the Early Spanish-American Colonies." *Journal of Anthropological Research* 52 (2): 135–60.

Deagan, Kathleen. 2002. *Artifacts of the Spanish Colonies of Florida and the Caribbean, 1500–1800*, Vol. 2: *Portable Personal Possessions*. Washington, D.C.: Smithsonian Institution Press.

Deb, Mihir, Garima Tiwari, and Kuntala Lahiri-Dutt. 2008. "Artisanal and Small Scale Mining in India: Selected Studies and an Overview of the Issue." *International Journal of Mining, Reclamation, and Environment* 22 (3): 194–209.

deFrance, Susan D. 2003. "Diet and Provisioning in the High Andes: A Spanish Colonial Settlement on the Outskirts of Potosí, Bolivia." *International Journal of Historical Archaeology* 7 (2): 99–125.

deFrance, Susan D. 2012. "Dieta y uso de animales en el Potosí colonial." *Chungara* 44 (1): 9–24.

deFrance, Susan D. 2021. "Guinea Pigs in the Spanish Colonial Andes: Culinary and Ritual Transformations." *International Journal of Historical Archaeology* 25 (1): 116–43. https://doi.org/10.1007/s10761-020-00548-6.

DeLeonardis, Lisa. 2011. "Itinerant Experts, Alternative Harvests: Kamayuq in the Service of Qhapaq and Crown." *Ethnohistory* 58 (3): 445–89.

del Río, Mercedes. 1995a. "Estrategías andinas de supervivencia. El control de recursos en Chaqui (siglos XVI–XVIII)." In *Espacios, étnias, frontera. Atenuaciones políticas en el sur del Tawantinsuyu, siglos XV–XVIII*, edited by Ana María Presta, 49–78. Sucre, Bolivia: Ediciones Antropólogos de Surandino 4.

del Río, Mercedes. 1995b. "Estructuración étnica qharaqhara y su desarticulación." In *Espacios, étnias, frontera: Atenuaciones políticas en el sur del Tawantinsuyu, siglos XV–XVIII*, edited by Ana María Presta, 3–47. Sucre, Bolivia: Ediciones Antropólogos de Surandino 4.

Díaz Cuellar, Vladimir. 2017. "Ganancia, salario y renta en el sector minero en Bolivia durante el gobierno del MAS (2006–2015)." In *Reporte Anual de Industrias Extractivas*, 39–70. La Paz: Centro de Estudios para el Desarrollo Laboral y Agraria. https://cedla .org/publicaciones/ieye/reporte-anual-de-industrias-extractivas-%E2%80%A2-2017/.

Diez de San Miguel, Garci de. 1964 [1567]. *Visita hecha en la provincia de Chucuito por Garci de San Miguel en el año 1567*. Lima: Casa de la Cultura Peruana.

Dobres, Marcia-Anne. 2000. *Technology and Social Agency: Outlining a Practice Framework for Archaeology*. Malden, Mass.: Blackwell.

Dumett, Raymond E. 1999. *El Dorado in West Africa: The Gold-Mining Frontier, African Labor, and Colonial Capitalism in the Gold Coast, 1875–1900*. Athens: Ohio University Press.

Earle, Timothy. 1994. "Wealth Finance in the Inka Empire: Evidence from the Calchaqui Valley, Argentina." *American Antiquity* 59 (3): 443–60.

Eichler, Anja, Gabriela Gramlich, Thomas Kellerhals, Leonhard Tobler, Thilo Rehren, and Margarit Schwikowski. 2018. "Ice-Core Evidence of Earliest Extensive Copper Metallurgy in the Andes 2700 Years Ago." *Chimia* 72 (3): 152.

El Potosí. 2017. "Jucus se aproprian 25% de la producción minera de Porco," 2017. https:// elpotosi.net/local/20171016_jucus-se-aropian-25--de-la-produccion-minera-de -porco.html.

Epstein, Stephen Matheson. 1993. "Cultural Choice and Technological Consequences: Constraint of Innovation in the Late Prehistoric Copper Smelting Industry of Cerro Huaringa, Peru." PhD diss., University of Pennsylvania.

Espinoza Morales, Jorge. 2010. *Minería Boliviana: Su realidad*. La Paz: Plural.

REFERENCES CITED

Espinoza Soriano, Waldemar. 1969. "El Memorial de Charcas. 'Cronica' inedita de 1582." *Revista Cantuta* 4: 117–32.

Evia, José Luís. 2008. *Conflicto social y crecimiento económico en Bolivia (1970–2005)*. Bolivia: Centro de Estudios de La Realidad Económica y Social, COSUDE, and Instituto para la Democracia.

Eylar, Christy. 2007. "Illness Vulnerability in Bolivia: A Comparative Approach to Understanding Health in a Mining Community." Master's thesis, Colorado State University.

Falcón, Francisco. 2018 [1567]. "Representación de Francisco Falcón. Nueva versión paleográfica." Transcribed by Lydia Fossa. Folio 220–237v. Biblioteca Nacional de España. https://www.academia.edu/79984753/Representaci%C3%B3n_de_Francisco_Falc%C3%B3n_Nueva_versi%C3%B3n_paleogr%C3%A1fica.

Ferring, David, Heidi Hausermann, and Emmanuel Effah. 2016. "Site specific: Heterogeneity of small-scale gold mining in Ghana." *Extractive Industries and Society* 3 (1): 171–84.

Figueroa, Valentina, Diego Salazar, Hernán Salinas, Paz Núñez-Regueiro, and German Manríquez. 2013. "Pre-Hispanic Mining Ergology of Northern Chile: An Archaeological Perspective." *Chungara* 45 (1): 61–81.

Fisher, Eleanor. 2007. "Occupying the Margins: Labour Integration and Social Exclusion in Artisanal Mining in Tanzania." *Development and Change* 38 (4): 735–60. https://doi.org/10.1111/j.1467-7660.2007.00431.x.

Flores Ochoa, Jorge A. 1974–76. "Enqa, Enqaychu, Illa y Khuya Rumi: Aspectos mágicos-religiosos entre pastores." *Journal de la Société des Américanistes* 83: 245–62.

Fortune. 2015. "Fortune Global 500." https://fortune.com/ranking/global500/2015/.

Francescone, Kirsten. 2015. "Cooperative Miners and the Politics of Abandonment in Bolivia." *Extractive Industries and Society* 2: 746–55.

Franco Berton, Eduardo. 2016. "Gold Rush in Bolivia Sparks Conflict between Miners and the Community." *Mongabay*, October 28, 2016. https://news.mongabay.com/2016/10/gold-rush-in-bolivia-sparks-conflict-between-miners-and-the-community/#:~:text=Mercury%20is%20used%20to%20increase,gold%20particles%20in%20the%20water.&text=This%20means%20that%20Bolivia%20is,environment%20due%20to%20gold%20mining.

Franco Olmedo, Luis Taski. n.d. "Fiesta andino cristiana del Pujllay Warak'aku de la natividad de Señor en Porco." Manuscript on file in the Department of Anthropology and Geography, Colorado State University.

Gade, Daniel W. 1999. *Nature and Culture in the Andes*. Madison: University of Wisconsin Press.

Gale, Valerie, and Alan Taylor. 2009. "'Daffodils Never Hear.' The Life of a Cornish Family in the 1880's, Including Working in Bolivian Silver Mines." *J B Williams' Journey: Transfer to Porco* (blog). January 15, 2009. http://at.orpheusweb.co.uk/Daffodil/.

García-Albarido, Francisco. 2022. "La ruta colonial de Potosí a Cobija y la vieja nueva praxis de modelos andinos mercantiles." *Estudios Atacameños* 68: e5008. https://doi.org/10.22199/issn.0718-1043-2022-0013.

Garcilaso de la Vega, Inca. 1941 [1609]. *Los comentarios reales de los Incas*. 2nd ed. Vols. 2–3. Colección de Historiadores Clásicos del Perú. Lima: Gil.

Garner, Richard L. 1988. "Long-Term Silver Mining Trends in Spanish America: A Comparative Analysis of Peru and Mexico." *American Historical Review* 93 (4): 898–935.

Garrido, Francisco. 2016. "Rethinking Imperial Infrastructure: A Bottom-up Perspective on the Inca Road." *Journal of Anthropological Archaeology* 43: 94–109.

Garrido, Francisco, and Tao Li. 2017. "A Handheld XRF Study of Late Horizon Metal Artifacts: Implications for Technological Choices and Political Intervention in Copiapó, Northern Chile." *Archaeological and Anthropological Sciences* 9 (5): 935–42.

Garrido, Francisco, and María Teresa Plaza. 2020. "Provincial Inca Metallurgy in Northern Chile: New Data for the Viña del Cerro Smelting Site." *Journal of Archaeological Science—Reports* 33 (October): 1–13. https://doi.org/10.1016/j.jasrep.2020.102556.

Garrido, Francisco, and Diego Salazar. 2017. "Imperial Expansion and Local Agency: A Case Study of Labor Organization Under Inca Rule." *American Anthropologist* 119 (4): 631–44.

Gavira Márquez, María Concepción. 2003. "Labor Discipline and Resistance: The Oruro Mining District in the Late Colonial Period." *Bulletin of Latin American Research* 22 (1): 1–26.

Gavira Márquez, María Concepcíon. 2006. *Historia de una crisis: La minería en Oruro a fines del período colonial*. Lima: Instituto Francés de Estudios Andinos.

Gavira Márquez, María Concepción. 2008. *Población indígena, sublevación y minería en Carangas. La Caja Real de Caranga y el mineral de Huantajaya, 1750–1804*. Chile: Instituto Francés de Estudios Andinos and Centro de Investigaciones del Hombre el Desierto.

Gavira Márquez, María Concepción. 2014. "El triunfo de la minería informal. Conflictos por el control de los recursos mineros en Carangas a fines del siglo XVIII." *Estudios Atacameños* 48: 71–84.

Gil Montero, Raquel. 2014. *Ciudades efímeras: El ciclo minero de la plata en Lípez (Bolivia), siglos XVI–XIX*. Lima: Instituto Francés de Estudios Andinos / Plural Editores.

Gil Montero, Raquel, and Florian Téreygeol. 2021. "Ore Dressing Techniques in the Andes During the Seventeenth Century: The Case of San Antonio del Nuevo Mundo, Lípez, Present-Day Bolivia." *International Journal of Historical Archaeology* 25 (1): 65–91.

Gil Montero, Raquel, and Paula Zagalsky. 2016. "Colonial Organization of Mine Labour in Charcas (Present-Day Bolivia) and Its Consequences (Sixteenth to the Seventeenth Centuries)." *International Review of Social History* 61 (24): 71–92.

Gisbert, Teresa, and Luis Prado, eds. 1990. *Potosí: Catalogación de su patrimonio urbano y arquitectónico*. Bolivia: Instituto Boliviano de Cultura.

Godoy, Ricardo A. 1990. *Mining and Agriculture in Highland Bolivia: Ecology, History, and Commerce Among the Jukumanis*. Tucson: University of Arizona Press.

Goldstein, David. 2006. "Informe paleobotánico." Manuscript on file in the Department of Anthropology and Geography, Colorado State University.

González, Luis R. 2004. *Bronces sin nombre. La metalurgia prehispánica en el noroeste argentino*. Buenos Aires: Fundación CEPPA.

González, Luis R. 2007. "Tradición tecnológica y tradición expresiva en la metalurgia prehispánica del noroeste argentino." *Boletín del Museo Chileno de Arte Precolombino* 15 (1): 33–48.

REFERENCES CITED

González, Luis R. 2010. "Fuegos sagrados. El taller metalúrgico del Sitio 15 de Rincón Chico (Catamarca, Argentina)." *Boletín del Museo Chileno de Arte Precolombino* 15 (1): 47–62.

González, Luis R. 2016. "Heredarás el bronce: Incas y metalurgia en el sur del valle de Yocavil." *Intersecciones en Antropología* 3: 55–68.

González, Luis R., and Geraldine A. Gluzman. 2007. "Innovación y continuidad en la metalurgia del noroeste argentino. El caso de bronce." *Mundo de Antes* 5: 187–210.

González-Tennant, Edward. 2009. "Using Geodatabases to Generate 'Living Documents' for Archaeology: A Case Study from the Otago Goldfields, New Zealand." *Historical Archaeology* 43 (3): 20–37.

Gudynas, Eduardo. 2009. "Diez tesis urgentes sobre el nuevo extractivismo: Contextos y demandas bajo el progresismo sudamericano actual." In *Extractivismo, Política y Sociedad*, 187–225. Quito: CAAP/CLAES.

Guerrero, Saúl. 2016. "The History of Silver Refining in New Spain, 16c to 18c: Back to the Basics." *History and Technology* 33 (1): 2–32. http://doi.org/10.1080/07341512.2016.1191864.

Gyarmati, János. 2015. "Paria La Viexa and an Expanding Empire: Provincial Centers in the Political Economy of the Inka Empire (a.d. 1440–1532)." *Journal of Field Archaeology* 40 (1): 37–54.

Hagan, Nicole A., Nicholas Robins, Heileen Hsu-Kim, Susan Halabi, Mark Morris, George M. Woodall, Tong Zhang, Allan Bacon, Daniel D. Richter, and John J. Vandenberg. 2011. "Estimating Historical Atmospheric Mercury Concentrations from Silver Mining and Their Legacies in Present-Day Surface Soil in Potosí, Bolivia." *Atmospheric Environment* 45 (40): 7619–26. http://doi.org/10.1016/j.atmosenv.2010.10.009.

Hanke, Lewis. 1959. "Luis Capoche y la historia de Potosí (1545–1585)." In *Biblioteca de Autores Españoles*, Vol. 122, 39–68. Madrid: Ediciones Atlas.

Hardesty, Donald. 1998. "Power and the Industrial Mining Community in the American West." In *Social Approaches to an Industrial Past: The Archaeology and Anthropology of Mining*, edited by A. Bernard Knapp, Vincent Pigott, and Eugenia W. Herbert, 81–96. London: Routledge.

Harvey, Charles, and Jon Press. 1989. "Overseas Investment and the Professional Advance of British Metal Mining Engineers, 1851–1914." *Economic History Review* 42 (1): 64–86.

Hayashida, Frances M. 1999. "Style, Technology, and State Production: Inka Pottery Manufacture in the Leche Valley, Peru." *Latin American Antiquity* 10 (4): 337–52.

Hayashida, Frances M., Andrés Troncoso, and Diego Salazar, editors. 2022. *Rethinking the Inka: Community, Landscape, and Empire in the Southern Andes*. Austin: University of Texas Press.

Henderson, G. M. 1916. "Preliminary Report on the Porco Tin Mines Ltd. Agua de Castilla, Bolivia." Box 87, Folder 5, Thayer Lindsley Papers, Accession Number 6034. American Heritage Center. Laramie: University of Wyoming.

Hentschel, Thomas, Felix Hruschka, and Michael Priester. 2002. *Global Report on Artisanal and Small-Scale Mining*. London: International Institute for Environment and Development and World Business Council for Sustainable Development.

Hilson, Gavin. 2002. "Harvesting Mineral Riches: 1000 Years of Gold Mining in Ghana." *Resources Policy* 28: 13–26.

Hilson, Gavin, ed. 2003. *The Socio-Economic Impacts of Artisanal and Small-Scale Mining in Developing Countries*. Lisse, Netherlands: A. A. Balkema.

Hilson, Gavin, and Chris Garforth. 2013. "'Everyone Now is Concentrating on the Mining': Drivers and Implications of Rural Economic Transition in the Eastern Region of Ghana." *Journal of Development Studies* 49 (3): 348–64.

Hilson, Gavin, Abigail Hilson, and Roy Maconachie. 2018. "Opportunity or Necessity? Conceptualizing Entrepreneurship at African Small-Scale Mines." *Technological Forecasting and Social Change* 131 (June): 286–302. https://doi.org/10.1016/j.techfore.2017.12.008.

Hilson, Gavin, and Roy Maconachie. 2017. "Formalising Artisanal and Small-Scale Mining: Insights, Contestations and Clarifications." *Area* 49 (4): 443–51.

Hilson, Gavin and Clive Potter. 2005. "Structural Adjustment and Subsistence Industry: Artisanal Gold Mining in Ghana." *Development and Change* 36: 103–31. http://doi.org/10.1111/j.0012-155X.2005.00404.x.

Hilson, Gavin, and Natalia Yakovleva. 2007. "Strained Relations: A Critical Analysis of the Mining Conflict in Prestea, Ghana." *Political Geography* 26: 98–119.

Hoerlein, Sara. 2006. "Informal Economic Strategies Practiced by Women in Porco, Bolivia: Persistent and Dynamic Socio-Economic Models." Manuscript on file in the Department of Anthropology and Geography, Colorado State University.

Hosler, Dorothy. 1994. *The Sounds and Colors of Power: The Sacred Metallurgical Technology of Ancient West Mexico*. Cambridge, Mass.: MIT Press.

Howard, April, and Benjamin Dangl. 2006. "Tin War in Bolivia: Conflict Between Miners Leaves 17 Dead." *Upside Down World* (blog). https://upsidedownworld.org/archives/bolivia/tin-war-in-bolivia-conflict-between-miners-leaves-17-dead/.

Hu, Di. 2022. *The Fabric of Resistance: Textile Workshops and the Rise of Rebellious Landscapes in Colonial Peru*. Tuscaloosa: University of Alabama Press.

Hudson-Edwards, Karen A., Mark G. Macklin, Jerry R. Miller, and Paul J. Lechler. 2001. "Sources, Distribution and Storage of Heavy Metals in the Río Pilcomayo, Bolivia." *Journal of Geochemical Exploration* 72 (3): 229–50. https://doi.org/10.1016/S0375-6742(01)00164-9.

Ibaba, Ibaba S. 2008. "Alienation and Militancy in the Niger Delta: Hostage Taking and the Dilemma of the Nigerian State." *African Journal on Conflict Resolution* 8 (2): 11–34. https://www.accord.org.za/ajcr-issues/alienation-and-militancy-in-the-niger-delta/.

Intergovernmental Forum on Mining, Minerals, Metals and Sustainable Development (IGF). 2017. *Global Trends in Artisanal and Small-Scale Mining (ASM): A Review of Key Numbers and Issues*. Winnipeg: IISD.

International Co-operative Alliance. 2021. "Cooperative Identity, Values, and Principles." International Co-operative Alliance. https://www.ica.coop/en/cooperatives/cooperative-identity?_ga=2.234900739.328945284.1616261811-323476792.1616261811#member-economic-participation.

REFERENCES CITED

International Institute for Environment and Development. 2002. *Breaking New Ground: Mining, Minerals and Sustainable Development*. London: International Institute for Environment and Development. https://www.iied.org/9084iied.

Isayev, Elena. 2006. "Archaeology ≠ Object as History ≠ Text: Nudging the Special Relationship into the Post-Ironic 1." *World Archaeology* 38 (4): 599–610.

Izagirre, Ander. 2010. "Mineritos. Niños trabajadores en las entrañas de Bolivia." *Nuestro Tiempo*. https://nuestrotiempo.unav.edu/es/grandes-temas/mineritos-ninos-trabajadores-en-las-entranas-de-bolivia.

Jacka, Jerry K. 2018. "The Anthropology of Mining: The Social and Environmental Impacts of Resource Extraction in the Mineral Age." *Annual Review of Anthropology* 47: 61–77.

Jackson, Richard. 1992. "New Mines for Old Gold: Ghana's Changing Mining Industry." *Geography* 77 (2): 175–78.

Jamieson, Ross. 2005. "Colonialism, Social Archaeology and lo Andino: Historical Archaeology in the Andes." *World Archaeology* 37 (3): 352–72.

Jiménez de la Espada, Marcos, ed. 1965 [1836]. "Descripción de la villa y minas de Potosí. Año de 1603." In *Relaciones Geográficas de Indias: Peru*. Vol. 2372–85. Biblioteca de Autores Españoles. Madrid: Ediciones Atlas.

Julien, Catherine. n.d. "How to Study Inca Labor Organization at Porco." Manuscript on file in the Department of Anthropology and Geography, Colorado State University.

Kemp, Deanna, and John R. Owen. 2019. "Characterising the Interface between Large and Small-Scale Mining." *Extractive Industries and Society* 6 (4): 1091–100. https://doi.org/10.1016/j.exis.2019.07.002.

Kennedy, Sarah A. 2021. "Marginalized Labor in Colonial Silver Refining: Reconstructing Power and Identity in Colonial Peru (1600–1800 AD)" PhD diss., University of Pittsburgh.

Kennedy, Sarah A., and Sarah J. Kelloway. 2020. "Identifying Metallurgical Practices at a Colonial Silver Refinery in Puno, Peru, Using Portable X-Ray Fluorescence Spectroscopy (pXRF)." *Journal of Archaeological Science Reports* 33 (4). http://www.doi.org/10.1016/j.jasrep.2020.102568.

Kennedy, Sarah A., and Sarah J. Kelloway. 2021. "Heavy Metals in Archaeological Soils: The Application of Portable X-Ray Fluorescence (PXRF) Spectroscopy for Assessing Risk to Human Health at Industrial Sites." *Advances in Archaeological Practice* 9 (2): 145–59.

Kessler, Michael. 2002. "The 'Polylepis Problem': Where Do We Stand?" *Ecotropica* 8: 97–110.

Klein, Herbert S. 1971. "Prelude to the Revolution." In *Beyond the Revolution: Bolivia since 1952*, edited by James M. Malloy and Richard S. Thorn, 25–52. Pittsburgh, Pa.: University of Pittsburgh Press.

Knapp, Bernard A., Vincent Pigott, and Eugenia W. Herbert, eds. 1998. *Social Approaches to an Industrial Past: The Archaeology and Anthropology of Mining*. London: Routledge.

La Razón. 2018. "Mineros piden militarización de Huanuni y declaran duelo por 30 días," *La Razón*. http://www.la-razon.com/economia/Mineros-militarizacion-Huanuni-fallecidos-explosion_0_2908509167.html.

Lahiri-Dutt, Kuntala. 2007. "Illegal Coal Mining in Eastern India: Rethinking Legitimacy and Limits of Justice." *Economic and Political Weekly* 42 (49): 57–66.

Lahiri-Dutt, Kuntala. 2016. "The Diverse Worlds of Coal in India: Energising the Nation, Energising Livelihoods." *Energy Policy* 99: 203–13.

Lahiri-Dutt, Kuntala, ed. 2018a. *Between the Plough and the Pick: Informal, Artisanal, and Small-Scale Mining in the Contemporary World.* Canberra: Australian National University Press.

Lahiri-Dutt, Kuntala. 2018b. "Extractive Peasants: Reframing Informal Artisanal and Small-Scale Mining Debates." *Third World Quarterly* 39 (8): 1561–82.

Lahiri-Dutt, Kuntala, and David J. Williams. 2005. "The Coal Cycle: Small Scale Illegal Coal Supply in Eastern India." *Resources, Energy, and Development* 2: 93–105.

Lane, Kris. 2017. "From Corrupt to Criminal: Reflection on the Great Potosí Mint Fraud of 1649." In *Corruption in the Iberian Empires: Greed, Custom, and Colonial Networks*, edited by Christoph Rosenmüller, 33–62. Albuquerque: University of New Mexico Press.

Lane, Kris. 2019. *Potosí: The Silver City That Changed the World.* Oakland: University of California Press.

Langer, Erick D. 1989. *Economic Change and Rural Resistance in Southern Bolivia, 1880–1930.* Stanford, Calif.: Stanford University Press.

Langer, Erick D. 1996. "The Barriers to Proletarianization: Bolivian Mine Labour, 1826–1918." *International Review of Social History* 41: 27–51.

Langer, Erick D. 2021. "Desarrollo económico y contrabando de plata en el siglo XIX (Andes centromeridionales)." *Diálogo Andino* 66: 313–24.

Lapham, Heather A. 2001. "More Than 'A Few Blew Beads': The Glass and Stone Beads from Jamestown Rediscovery's 1994–1997 Excavations." *Journal of the Jamestown Rediscovery Center* 1.

Larson, Brooke. 2004. *Trials of Nation Making: Liberalism, Race and Ethnicity in the Andes, 1810–1910.* Cambridge: Cambridge University Press.

Latasa Vasallo, Pilar. 1998. "El transporte de plata en el atlántico: Conflicto entre los intereses peruanos y metropolitanos." In *Economía maritima del Atlántico: Pesca, navegación y comercio*, edited by José A. Armillas Vicente, 1567–82. Spain: Gobierno de Aragón, Departamento de Educación y Cultura.

Lawson, L. 2018. "Rice, Sapphires and Cattle: Work Lives of Women Artisanal and Small-scale Miners in Madagascar." In *Between the Plough and the Pick: Informal, Artisanal, and Small-Scale Mining in the Contemporary World*, edited by Kuntala Lahiri-Dutt, 171–92. Canberra: Australian National University Press.

Lechtman, Heather. 1976. "A Metallurgical Site Survey in the Peruvian Andes." *Journal of Field Archaeology* 3: 1–42.

Lechtman, Heather. 1988. "Traditions and Styles in Central Andean Metalworking." In *The Beginning of the Use of Metals and Alloys*, edited by Robert Maddin, 344–78. Cambridge, Mass.: MIT Press.

Lechtman, Heather. 1993. "Technologies of Power: The Andean Case." In *Configurations of Power: Holistic Anthropology in Theory and Practice*, edited by John S. Henderson and Patricia Netherly, 244–80. Ithaca, N.Y.: Cornell University Press.

REFERENCES CITED

Lechtman, Heather. 1996. "Arsenic Bronze: Dirty Copper or Chosen Alloy? A View from the Americas." *Journal of Field Archaeology* 23 (4): 477–514. https://doi.org/10.2307 /530550.

Lechtman, Heather, Pablo Cruz, Andrew P. Macfarlane, and Sidney Carter. 2010. "Procesamiento de metales durante el Horizonte Medio en el altiplano surandino (Escaramayu), Pulacayo, Potosi, Bolivia." *Boletín del Museo Chileno de Arte Precolombino* 15 (2): 9–27.

Lechtman, Heather, and Andrew W. Macfarlane. 2005. "La metalurgia del bronce en los Andes sur centrales: Tiwanaku y San Pedro de Atacama." *Estudios Atacameños* 30: 7–27.

Lecoq, Patrice. 2003. "La ocupación en los valles de Yura y los alrededores de Potosí durante los períodos Intermedio Tardío e Inka, a la luz de nuevos descubrimientos arqueológicos." *Textos Antropológicos* 14 (2): 105–32.

Lecoq, Patrice, and Ricardo Cespedes. 1996. "Nuevas investigaciones arqueológicas en los Andes meridionales de Bolivia: Una visión prehispánica de Potosí." *Revista de Investigaciones Históricas*, 183–267.

Lecoq, Patrice, and Ricardo Cespedes. 1997. "Nuevos datos sobre la ocupación prehistórica en los Andes meridionales de Bolivia." *Cuadernos*, Revista de la Facultad de Humanidades y Ciencias Sociales, Universidad Nacional de Jujuy, 9: 111–52.

Lemonnier, Pierre. 1986. "The Study of Material Culture Today: Toward an Anthropology of Technical Systems." *Journal of Anthropological Archaeology* 5: 147–86.

Lengyel, Stacey N., Jeffrey L. Eighmy, and Mary Van Buren. 2011. "Archaeomagnetic Research in the Andean Highlands." *Journal of Archaeological Science* 38 (1): 147–55.

Leone, Mark, Parker B. Potter Jr., and Paul A. Shackel. 1987. "Toward a Critical Archaeology." *Current Anthropology* 28 (3): 283–92.

Lightfoot, Kent G. 1995. "Culture Contact Studies: Redefining the Relationship between Prehistoric and Historical Archaeology." *American Antiquity* 60 (2): 199–217.

Lightfoot, Kent G. 2005. *Indians, Missionaries, and Merchants: The Legacy of ColoniaEncounters on the California Frontiers.* Berkeley: University of California Press.

Little, Barbara J. 1991. *Text-Aided Archaeology.* 1st ed. Boca Raton, Fla.: CRC Press.

Llanos, García de. 2009 [1609]. *Diccionario y maneras de hablar que se usan en las minas y sus labores en los ingenios y beneficios de los metales.* Madrid: Consejo Superior de Colegios de Ingenieros de Minas.

Lofstrom, William Lee. 1973. *Dámaso de Uriburu, a Mining Entrepreneur in Early Nineteenth-Century Bolivia.* Buffalo: State University of New York at Buffalo, Council on International Studies, Special Studies No. 35.

Lora, Guillermo. 1977. *A History of the Bolivian Labour Movement 1848–1911.* Edited by Laurence Whitehead. Translated by Christine Whitehead. New York: Cambridge University Press.

Lowe, Peter. 2005. *Fuego en el hielo: Mujeres mineras de Chorolque.* Bolivia: Corporación Minera de Bolivia.

Macfarlane, Andrew P., and Heather Lechtman. 2016. "Andean Ores, Bronze Artifacts, and Lead Isotopes: Constraints on Metal Sources in Their Geological Context." *Journal of Archaeological Method and Theory* 23 (1): 1–72.

MacQuarrie, Kim. 2007. *The Last Days of the Incas*. New York: Simon & Schuster.

Mamani, Lidia. 2018. "El número de cooperativas mineras se duplicó en 12 años." *Página Siete*, 2018. https://www.paginasiete.bo/economia/2018/1/26/nmero-cooperativas-mineras-duplic-aos-167799.html.

Mangan, Jane E. 2005. *Trading Roles: Gender, Ethnicity, and the Urban Economy in Colonial Potosí*. Durham, N.C.: Duke University Press.

Marston, Andrea, and Amy Kennemore. 2018. "Extraction, Revolution, Plurinationalism: Rethinking Extractivism from Bolivia." *Latin American Perspectives* 20: 1–20.

Marston, Andrea, and Tom Perreault. 2017. "Consent, Coercion, and Cooperativismo: Mining Cooperatives and Resource Regimes in Bolivia." *Environment and Planning A* 49 (2): 252–72.

Martire, Eduardo. 1977. "Tolerancias, prevenciones y regulación participadora de los indios 'Capchas' de Potosí, en la explotación del Cerro." *Estudios Sobre Política Indigenista Española en América* 3.

Marx, Karl, and Friedrick Engels. 1947. *The German Ideology*. New York: International Publishers.

McMahon, Gary, José Luis Evia, Alberto Pascó-Font, and José Miguel Sánchez. 1999. "An Environmental Study of Artisanal, Small, and Medium Mining in Bolivia, Chile, and Peru." World Bank Technical Paper 429. Washington, D.C.: The World Bank.

Meadow, M. A. 2002. "Merchants and Marvels: Hans Fugger and the Origins of the Wunderkammer." In *Merchants and Marvels: Commerce, Science, and Art in Early Modern Europe*, edited by Pamela H. Smith and Paula Findlen, 182–200. New York: Routledge.

Meddens, Frank M. 2015. "The Importance of Being Inka: Ushnu Platforms and Their Place in the Andean Landscape." In *The Archaeology of Wak'as: Explorations of the Sacred in the Pre-Columbian Andes*, edited by Tamara L. Bray, 239–63. Boulder: University Press of Colorado.

Medinacelli González, Ximena. 2013. "De Sariris, Marcanis e Inkas: Contrapunto desde Carangas al 'Ensayo de Interpretación' del libro Qaraqara-Charka." In *Aportes multidisciplinarios al estudio de los colectivos étnicos surandinos. Reflexiones sobre Qaraqara-Charka tres años después*, edited by Ana María Presta, 245–64. Lima: Instituto Francés de Estudios Andinos.

Menzel, Sewall. 2004. *Cobs, Pieces of Eight, and Treasure Coins*. New York: The American Numismatic Society.

Michard, Jocelyn. 2008. "Cooperativas mineras en Bolivia. Formas de organización, producción y comercialización." Cochabamba, Bolivia: Centro de Documentación e Información.

Michel, Marcos. 2000. "El señorío prehispánico de Carangas." Master's thesis, Universidad de la Cordillera. https://www.academia.edu/3196783/El_Se%C3%B1orio_Prehispanico_de_Carangas.

Mining and Scientific Press. 1912. "London. Progress at the Geevor.—Tin Mining Booming.— Development in Bolivia." *Mining and Scientific Press*, October 26, 1912, 538.

Miller, Rory. 2000. "British Business in Peru from the Pacific War to the Great Depression." In *Dinero y negocios en la historia de América Latina: veinte ensayos dedicados a*

REFERENCES CITED

Reinhard Liehr / *Geld und Geschäft in der Geschichte Lateinamerikas: zwanzig Aufsätze, gewidmet Reinhard Liehr*, edited by Nikolaus Böttcher and Bernd Hausberger, 379–411. Madrid / Frankfurt am Main: Iberoamericana / Vervuert.

Mira, Guillermo. 2000. "Panorama de la organización y las bases de la producción de plata en Potosí durante el Período Colonial (1545–1825)." In *Potosí: Plata para Europa*, edited by Juan Marchena Fernández, 105–24. Seville: Fundación El Monte.

Miranda Díaz, Bartolomé. 2014. "Las minas y asiento del Porco: Nuevos datos sobre la hacienda rica de Hernando Pizarro en Indias." *Temas Americanistas* 33: 149–70.

Mitchem, Jeffrey M., and Bonnie G. McEwan. 1988. "New Data on Early Bells from Florida." *Southwestern Archaeology* 7 (1): 39–49.

Mitre, Antonio. 1981. *Los patriarcas de la plata: Estructura socioeconómica de la minería boliviana en el siglo XIX*. Lima: Instituto de Estudios Peruanos.

Montes de Oca, Ismael. 1989. *Geografía y recursos naturales de Bolivia*. 2nd ed. La Paz: Academia Nacional de Ciencias de Bolivia.

Moreland, John. 2001. *Archaeology and Text*. London: Duckworth.

Moore, Jason. 2010. "'This lofty mountain of silver could conquer the whole world': Potosí and the Political Ecology of Underdevelopment, 1545–1800." *Journal of Philosophical Economics* 4 (1): 58–103.

Moyano, Ricardo. 2009. "El adoratorio del cerro El Potro: Arqueología de alta montaña en la Cordillera de Copiapó, Norte de Chile." *Estudios Atacameños* 38: 39–54.

Mumford, Jeremy Ravi. 2012. *Vertical Empire: The General Resettlement of Indians in the Colonial Andes*. Durham, N.C.: Duke University Press.

Muñoz Rojas, Lizette Alda. 2019. "Cuisine and the Conquest: Contrasting Two Sixteenth Century Native Populations of the Viceroyalty of Peru." PhD diss., University of Pittsburgh.

Murra, John. 1964. "Una apreciación etnológica de la visita." In *Visita hecha a la provincia de Chucuito por Garci Diez de San Miguel*, 419–42. Lima: Casa de Cultura.

Murra, John. 1967. "La visita de los Chupachos como fuente etnológica." In *Visita de la provincia de León de Huánuco en 1562*, Vol. 1, by Iñigo Ortiz de Zúñiga, 81–406. Huánuco, Peru: Universidad Nacional Hermilio Valdizan.

Murra, John. 1972. "El 'control vertical' de un máximo de pisos ecológicos en la economía de las sociedades andinas." In *Visita de la provincia de León de Huánuco en 1562*, Vol. 2, 427–76. Huánuco, Peru: Universidad Nacional Hermilio Valdizan.

Murra, John. 1975. *Formaciones económicas y políticas del mundo andino*. Lima: Instituto de Estudios Peruanos.

Murra, John. 1978. *La organización económica del estado inca*. Mexico: Siglo XXI.

Muysken, Pieter. 2017. "Multilingüismo y lenguaje mezclado en las minas de Potosí (Bolivia)." *Lingüística* 33 (2): 97–124.

Naanen, Ben. 2019. "When Extractive Governance Fails: Oil Theft as Resistance in Nigeria." *The Extractive Industries and Society* 6 (3): 702–10. https://doi.org/10.1016/j.exis.2019.03.019.

Nash, June. 1979. *We Eat the Mines and the Mines Eat Us: Dependency and Exploitation in Bolivian Tin Mines*. New York: Columbia University Press.

Nash, June. 1984. "Religion, Rebellion, and Working Class Consciousness in Bolivian Tin Mining Communities." In *Religion and Rural Revolt*, edited by János M. Bak and Gerhard Benecke, 453–68. Manchester, UK: Manchester University Press.

Nicolas, Vincent. 2018. *Mita y mitayos en la villa de Potosí (siglos XVI–XVIII)*. La Paz: Casa Nacional de Moneda.

Nielsen, Axel. 2006. "Pobres jefes: Aspectos corporativos en las formaciones sociales pre-inkaicas de los Andes circumpuneños." In *Contra la tiranía tipológico en arqueología: Una vision desde Suramérica*, edited by Cristóbal Gnecco and Carl Henrik Langebaek, 121–50. Bogota: Universidad de los Andes.

Niemeyer, Hans, Miguel Cervellino G., and Eduardo Muñoz. 1983. "Viña del Cerro, expresión metalúrgica inca en el valle de Copiapó." *Creces* 4 (4): 32–35.

Norman, Scotti M. 2021. "Catholicism and Taki Onqoy in the Early Colonial Period: Colonial Entanglements of Church Interments at Iglesiachayoq (Chicha-Soras Valley, Ayacucho, Peru)" *American Anthropologist* 123 (3): 490–508. https://doi.org/10.1111/aman.13591.

Nugent, David. 1996. "From Devil Pacts to Drug Deals: Commerce, Unnatural Accumulation, and Moral Community in 'Modern' Peru." *American Ethnologist* 23 (2): 258–90.

Núñez, Lautaro. 1999. "Valoración minero-metalúrgica circumpuneña: Menas y mineros para el Inka Rey." *Estudios Atacameños* 18: 177–221.

Núñez, Lautaro, Carolina Agüero, Bárbara Cases, and Patricio de Souza. 2003. "El campamento minero Chuquicamata-2 y la explotación cuprífera prehispánica en el Desierto de Atacama." *Estudios Atacameños* 25: 7–34.

Ocaña, Diego de. 1969 [c.1599–1608]. *Un viaje fascinante por la América hispana del siglo XVI*. Edited by Arturo Alvarez. Madrid: STVDIVM ediciones.

Oehm, V. P. 1984. *Investigaciones sobre minería y metalurgía en el Perú hispánico*. Bonner Amerikanistische Studien 12. Bonn, Germany.

Ofosu-Mensah, Emmanuel Abibio. 2017. "Historical and Modern Artisanal Small-Scale Mining in Akyem Abuakwa, Ghana." *Africa Today* 64 (2): 68–91.

Oil Spill Intelligence Report. 2011. "UN Reports on Oil Pollution in Nigeria." *Oil Spill Intelligence Report* 34 (46): 2–4.

Ollman, Bertell. 2003. *Dance of the Dialectic: Steps in Marx's Method*. Urbana: University of Illinois Press.

Orche, Enrique, and María Pilar Amaré. 2011. "El mito del Tío de las minas bolivianas, ¿Fenómeno colonial o republicano?" XII Congreso Internacional Sobre Patrimonio Geológico y Minero, Boltaña (Huesca), 29 de Septiembre al 2 de Octubre. 507–38. Sociedad Española para la Defensa del Patrimonio Geológico y Minero.

Oropeza, Daniel. 2013. *La falsificación de la moneda en la Villa Imperial de Potosí, siglo XVII*. Potosí, Bolivia: Casa Nacional de Moneda.

Orser, Charles E. Jr. 2001. "The Anthropology in American Historical Archaeology." *American Anthropologist* 103 (3): 621–32.

Oskarsson, Patrik, Kuntala Lahiri-Dutt, and Patrick Wennstrom. 2019. "From Incremental Dispossession to a Cumulative Land Grab: Understanding Territorial Transformation in India's North Karanpura Coalfield." *Development and Change* 50 (6): 1485–1508. http://doi.org/10.1111/dech.12513.

Otero, Clarisa, and Maria Beatriz Cremonte. 2014. "Local Ceramic Technology of the Pucara of Tilcara during the Inka Period (Quebrada of Humahuaca, Argentina)." *Journal of Anthropological Archaeology* 33: 108–88.

Ovando-Sanz, Guillermo. 1965. "British Interests in Potosi, 1825–1828; Unpublished Documents from the Archivo de Potosi." *Hispanic American Historical Review* 45 (1): 64–87.

Pai, Sandeep, and Savannah Carr-Wilson. 2018. *Total Transition: The Human Side of the Renewable Energy Revolution.* Victoria, Canada: Rocky Mountain Books.

Panich, Lee M. 2020. *Narratives of Persistence: Indigenous Negotiations of Colonialism in Alta and Baja California.* Archaeology of Indigenous-Colonial Interactions in the Americas. Tucson: University of Arizona Press.

Patel, Kayla, John Rogan, Nicholas Cuba, and Anthony Bebbington. 2016. "Evaluating Conflict Surrounding Mineral Extraction in Ghana: Assessing the Spatial Interactions of Large and Small-Scale Mining." *The Extractive Industries and Society* 3: 450–63.

Pease, Franklin. 1973. *El dios creador andino.* Lima: Mosca Azul Editores.

Pease, Franklin. 1976. "Etnohistoria andina: Un estado de la cuestión." *Historia y Cultura* 10: 207–28.

Pease, Franklin. 1978. *Del Tawantinsuyu a la historia del Perú.* Lima: Instituto de Estudios Peruanos.

Pentland, Joseph Barclay. 1975 [1827]. *Informe sobre Bolivia.* Colección de la Cultura Boliviana, Vol. 13. Translated by Jack Aitken Soux. Potosí, Bolivia: Casa de la Moneda.

Peele, Robert Jr. 1893. "A Primitive Smelting Furnace." *School of Mines Quarterly* 15: 8–10.

Pérez Bocanegra, Juan. 1631. *Ritual formulario.* Lima: Geronymo de Contreras, iunto al Conuento de santo Domingo. http://archive.org/details/ritualformulariooopr.

Perreault, Tom. 2017. "Tendencies in Tension: Resource Governance and Social Contradictions in Contemporary Bolivia." In *Governance in the Extractive Industries: Power, Cultural Politics and Regulation,* 17–38. New York: Routledge.

Pfaffenberger, Bryan. 1992. "The Social Anthropology of Technology." *Annual Review of Anthropology* 21: 491–516.

Pinsky, Valerie, and Alison Wylie, eds. 1989. *Critical Traditions in Contemporary Archaeology.* Cambridge, UK: Cambridge University Press.

Platt, Tristan. 1982. *Estado boliviano y ayllu andino. Tierra y tributo en el Norte de Potosí.* Lima: Instituto de Estudios Peruanos.

Platt, Tristan. 1983. "Conciencia andina y conciencia proletaria. Qhuyaruna y ayllu en el norte de Potosí." *Revista Latinoamericana de Historia Económica y Social,* HISLA, 2: 47–73.

Platt, Tristan. 2000. "Señorío aymara y trabajo minero: De la mita al k'ajcheo en Potosí (1545–1837)." In *Potosí: Plata para Europa,* edited by Juan Marchena Fernández and José Villa Rodríguez, 189–211. Seville: Universidad de Sevilla and Fundación el Monte.

Platt, Tristan. 2014. "Caccheo y minería mediana en las provincias de Potosí." *Estudios Atacameños* 48: 85–118.

REFERENCES CITED

Platt, Tristan, Thérèse Bouysse Cassagne, and Olivia Harris. 2006. *Qaraqara-Charka: Mallku, inka y rey en la provincia de Charcas (siglos XV–XVII): Historia antropológica de una confederación aymara*. La Paz: Instituto Francés de Estudios Andinos.

Platt, Tristan, and Pablo Quisbert. 2007. "Knowing Silence and Merging Horizons: The Case of the Great Potosí Cover-Up." In *Ways of Knowing: New Approaches in the Anthropology of Experience and Learning*, edited by Mark Harris, 113–38. New York: Berghahn Books.

Platt, Tristan, and Pablo Quisbert. 2010. "Tras las huellas del silencio: Potosí, los Incas, y Toledo." *Runa* 31 (2): 115–52.

Plaza, María Teresa, and Marcos Martinón-Torres. 2015. "Metallurgical Traditions under Inka Rule: A Technological Study of Metals and Technical Ceramics from the Aconcagua Valley, Central Chile." *Journal of Archaeological Science* 54: 86–98.

Povea Moreno, Isabel María. 2012. "Los buscones de metal. El sistema de pallaqueo en Huancavelica (1793–1820)." *Anuario de Estudios Americanos* 69 (1):109–38.

Presta, Ana María. 2000. *Encomienda, familia y negocios en Charcas colonial (Bolivia): los encomenderos de La Plata, 1550–1600*. Lima: Instituto de Estudios Peruanos.

Presta, Ana María. 2008. "La primera joya en la corona en el altiplano surandino. Descubrimiento y explotación de un yacimiento minero inicial: Porco, 1538–1576." In *Mina y metalurgía en los Andes del sur desde la época prehispánica hasta el siglo XVII*, edited by Pablo José Cruz and Jean-Joinville Vacher, 201–29. Sucre, Bolivia: Instituto Francés de Estudios Andinos and Institut de Recherche pour le Développement.

Priester, Michael, Thomas Hentschel, and Bernd Benthin. 1993. *Tools for Mining: Techniques and Processes for Small Scale Mining*. Wiesbaden, Germany: Vieweg.

Probert, Alan. 1997. "Bartolomé de Medina: The Patio Process and the Sixteenth Century Silver Crisis." In *Mines of Silver and Gold in the Americas*, edited by Peter Bakewell, 96–130. United Kingdom: Variorum.

Quispe Condori, Jorge H. 2021. "'Niños topos,' eslabón oculto de minería cooperativizada en Porco." *Página Siete* (January). https://www.paginasiete.bo/sociedad/2021/1/4/ninos-topos-eslabon-oculto-de-mineria-cooperativizada-en-porco-279978.html.

Raffino, Rodolfo. 1983. *Los Inkas del Kollasuyu*. 2nd ed. La Plata, Argentina: Ramos Americana Editora.

Raffino, Rodolfo, J. Diego Gobbo, Anahí Iácoba, and Reinaldo A. Morelejo. 2013. "La minería y metalurgia de los Inkas del Kollasuyu." *Actas del V Congreso de la Arqueología Histórico*, Vol. 1, 187–216. Frankfurt am Main, Germany: Verlag.

Raffino, Rodolfo, Rubén Iturriza, Anahí Iácona, Aylen Capparelli, Diego Gobbo, Victoria G. Montes, and Rolando Vázquez. 1996. "Quillay. Centro metalúrgico inka en el noroeste argentino." *Tawantinsuyu* 2: 59–69.

Ramírez, Baltasar. 1965 [1836]. "Descripción del reyno del Perú." In *Relaciones geográficas de Indias: Perú*, Vol. 2, edited by Marcos Jiménez de la Espada, 119. Biblioteca de Autores Españoles. Madrid: Ediciones Atlas.

Ramón, Gabriel. 2016. "Producción y distribución alfarera colonial temprana en los Andes centrales: modelos y casos." *Boletín de Arqueología PUCP* 20: 25–48. https://doi.org/10.18800/boletindearqueologiapucp.201601.002.

REFERENCES CITED

Rasnake, Roger Neil. 1988. *Domination and Cultural Resistance: Authority and Power among an Andean People*. Durham, N.C.: Duke University Press.

Redacción BBC Mundo. 2016. "Bolivia: Por qué los mineros 'consentidos' de Evo Morales llegaron al extremo de matar a uno de sus viceministros." *BBC News*, August 26, 2016. https://www.bbc.com/mundo/noticias-america-latina-37199462.

Redacción Central. 2010. "Unos 600 mineros de Porco toman rehenes." *Los Tiempos*, December 5, 2010. https://www.lostiempos.com/actualidad/economia/20100512/600-mineros-porco-toman-rehenes.

Rice, Prudence. 2013. *Space-Time Perspectives on Early Colonial Moquegua*. Boulder: University Press of Colorado.

Robins, Nicholas A. 2011. *Mercury, Mining, and Empire: The Human and Ecological Cost of Colonial Silver Mining in the Andes*. Bloomington: University of Indiana Press.

Robins, Nicholas A., and Nicole A. Hagan. 2012. "Mercury Production and Use in Colonial Andean Silver Production: Emissions and Health Implications." *Environmental Health Perspectives* 120 (5): 627–31.

Rodríguez Ostria, Gustavo. 1989. "Kajchas, trapicheros, y ladrones de mineral en Bolivia (1824–1900)." *Siglo XIX* 4 (8): 125–39.

Rodríguez Ostria, Gustavo. 1991. *El socavón y el sindicato: ensayos históricos sobre los trabajadores mineros, siglos XIX–XX*. La Paz: ILDIS.

Rodríguez Ostria, Gustavo. 2014. *Capitalismo, modernización y resistencia popular, 1825–1952*. La Paz: Centro de Investigaciones Sociales.

Rostworowski de Diez Canseco, María. 1977. *Etnía y sociedad: costa peruana prehispánica*. Historia Andina 4. Lima: Instituto de Estudios Peruanos.

Rostworowski de Diez Canseco, María. 1978. *Señoríos indígenas de Lima y Canta*. Lima: Instituto de Estudios Peruanos.

Rostworowski de Diez Canseco, María. 1983. *Estructuras andinas del poder: Ideología religiosa y política*. Historia Andina 10. Lima: Instituto de Estudios Peruanos.

Sagárnaga Meneses, Jedú Antonio. 2021. "Revisiones en torno al laurake." In *Los metales en nuestra historia*, edited by Roberto Lleras Pérez and Luisa Vetter Parodi, 85–115. Lima: Instituto Francés de Estudios Andinos and Academia Colombiana de Historia.

Saignes, Thierry. 1985a. *Caciques, Tribute and Migration in the Southern Andes. Indian Society and the 17th Century Colonial Order (Audiencia de Charcas)*. Occasional Papers 15. London: University of London, Institute of Latin American Studies.

Saignes, Thierry. 1985b. "Notes on the Regional Contribution to the Mita in Potosí in the Early Seventeenth Century." *Bulletin of Latin American Research* 4 (1): 65–76.

Saito, Akira, and Claudia Rosas Lauro. 2017. *Reducciones: La concentración forzada de las poblaciones indígenas en el Virreinato del Perú*. Lima: PUCP.

Saitta, Dean J. 2007. *The Archaeology of Collective Action*. The American Experience in Archaeological Perspective. Gainesville: University Press of Florida.

Salazar, Diego. 2008. "La producción minera en San José del Abra durante el Período Tardío atacameño." *Estudios Atacameños* 36: 43–72.

Salazar, Diego, José Berenguer R., Victoria Castro, Frances M. Hayashida, César Parcero-Oubiña, and Andrés Troncoso. 2022. "Copper Rich, Water Poor: Atacama during Inka Rule." In *Rethinking the Inka: Community, Landscape, and Empire in the Southern*

Andes, edited by Frances M. Hayashida, Andrés Troncoso and Diego Salazar, 57–81. Austin: University of Texas Press.

Salazar, Diego, José Berenguer, and Gabriela Vega. 2013. "Paisajes minero-metalúrgicos incaicos en Atacama y el altiplano sur de Tarapacá (norte de Chile)." *Chungara* 45 (1): 83–103.

Salazar, Diego, Valentina Figueroa, Diego Morata, Benoit Milleiv, Germán Manríquez, and Ariadna Cifuentes. 2011. "Metalurgia en San Pedro de Atacama durante el Período Medio: Nuevos datos, nuevas preguntas." *Revista de Antropología* 23: 123–48.

Salazar-Soler, Carmen. 1987. "El Tayta Muki y el Ukupacha. Prácticas y creencias religiosas de los mineros de Julkani, Huancavelica, Perú." *Journal de la Société des Américanistes* 73: 193–217.

Salazar-Soler, Carmen. 1997a. "Las huacas y el conocimiento científico en el siglo XVI: A propósito del descubrimiento de las minas de Potosí." In *Saberas y memorias en los Andes: In Memoriam Thierry Saignes*, 237–57. Paris: Institut Français des Hautes d'Études de l'Amérique Latine.

Salazar-Soler, Carmen. 1997b. "Socavones de mestizaje: Saberes, técnicas y trabajo en la Villa Imperial de Potosí (siglos XVI–XVIII)." In *Ciudades mestizas: Intercambios y continuidades en la expansión occidental siglos XVI a XIX. Actas del 3er. Congreso Internacional Mediadores Culturales*, edited by Clara Garcia Ayluardo and Manuel Ramos Medina, 271–301. Mexico City: Centro de Estudios de Historia de México.

Salazar-Soler, Carmen. 2002. "La Villa Imperial de Potosí: Cuna del mestizaje (siglos XVI–XVII)." In *Colonzación, resistencia, y mestizaje en las Américas (siglos XVI–XX)*, edited by Guillaume Bocarra, 139–60. Lima: Instituto Francés de Estudios Andinos; Quito: Abya-Yala.

Salazar-Soler, Carmen, and Frédérique Langue. 1997. "De huaira a malacate: una historia cultural a partir del vocabulario minero en América española (siglos XVI–XIX)." In *El Siglo XIX: Bolivia y América Latina*, edited by Rossana Barragán, Dora Cajías, and Seemin Qayum, 373–93. La Paz: Muela del Diablo Editores.

Sanborn, Margaret D., Alan Abelsohn, Monica Campbell, and Erica Weir. 2002. "Identifying and Managing Adverse Environmental Health Effects: 3. Lead Exposure." *Canadian Medical Association Journal* 166 (10): 1287–92.

Scattolin, M. Cristina, M. Fabiana Bugliani, Leticia I. Cortés, Lucas Pereyra Domingorena, and Marilin Calo. 2010. "Una mascara de cobre de tres mil años. Estudios arqueometalúrgicos y comparaciones regionales." *Boletín del Museo Chileno de Arte Precolombino* 15 (1): 25–46.

Schiffer, Michael Brian. 2002. "Studying Technology Differentiation: The Case of 18th-Century Electrical Technology." *American Anthropologist* 104 (4): 1148–61.

Schultze, Carol A., Jennifer A. Huff, Thilo Rehren, and Abigail R. Levine. 2016. "The Emergence of Complex Silver Metallurgy in the Americas: A Case Study from the Lake Titicaca Basin of Southern Peru." *Cambridge Archaeological Journal* 26 (1): 53–64.

Schultze, Carol A., Charles Stanish, David A. Scott, Thilo Rehren, Scott Kuehner, and James K. Feathers. 2009. "Direct Evidence of 1,900 Years of Indigenous Silver Production in the Lake Titicaca Basin of Southern Peru." *Proceedings of the National Academy of Sciences of the United States of America* 106 (41): 17280–83.

REFERENCES CITED

Shackel, Paul A. 2009. *Archaeology of American Labor and Working-Class Life*. American Experience in Archaeological Perspective. Gainesville: University Press of Florida.

Shimada, Izumi, and Alan K. Craig. 2013. "The Style, Technology and Organization of Sicán Mining and Metallurgy, Northern Peru: Insights from Holistic Study." *Chungara* 45 (1): 3–31.

Shimada, Izumi, and Ursel Wagner. 2007. "A Holistic Approach to Pre-Hispanic Craft Production." In *Archaeological Anthropology: Perspectives on Method and Theory*, edited by James Skibo, Michael Graves, and Miriam Stark, 163–97. Tucson: University of Arizona Press.

Shutzer, Matthew. 2021. "Subterranean Properties: India's Political Ecology of Coal, 1870–1975." *Comparative Studies in Society and History* 63 (2): 400–432. https://doi.org/10.1017/S0010417521000098.

Sillar, Bill. 2009. "The Social Agency of Things? Animism and Materiality in the Andes." *Cambridge Archaeological Journal* 19 (3): 369–79.

Sillar, Bill. 2017. "Animating Relationships: Inca *Conopa* and Modern *Illa* as Mediating Objects." In *The Inbetweeness of Things: Materializing Mediation and Movement between Worlds*, edited by Paul Basu, 130–47. London: Bloomsbury.

Silliman, Stephen. 2006. "Struggling with Labor, Working with Identities." In *Historical Archaeology*, edited by Martin Hall and Stephen W. Silliman, 147–66. Oxford: Blackwell.

"Silver Prices—100 Year Historical Chart." n.d. *Macrotrends* (blog). Accessed June 11, 2022. https://www.macrotrends.net/1470/historical-silver-prices-100-year-chart.

Singewald, Joseph T., and Benjamin L. Miller. 1917. "New Developments in the Porco District, Bolivia." *Engineering and Mining Journal* 103: 329–33.

Singh, Nigel. 2013. "India's Coal Cycle Wallahs: 'People have no alternative but to steal from mines.'" *Guardian*, September 6, 2013. https://www.theguardian.com/global-development/2013/sep/06/india-coal-cycle-wallahs.

Sippl, Kristin, and Henrik Selin. 2012. "Global Policy for Local Livelihoods: Phasing Out Mercury in Artisanal and Small-Scale Gold Mining." *Environment* 54 (3): 18–29. https://doi.org/10.1080/00139157.2012.673452.

Smale, Robert L. 2010. *'I Sweat the Flavour of Tin': Labor Activism in Early Twentieth-Century Bolivia*. Pittsburgh: University of Pittsburgh Press.

Smit, Douglas. 2018. "Mercury and the Making of the Andean Market: An Archaeological Study of Indigenous Labor in Colonial Peru." PhD diss., University of Illinois at Chicago.

Smit, Douglas K., and Parker VanValkenburgh. 2023. "Indigenous Labor and the Circulation of Majolica in the Colonial Andes." *Journal of Archaeological Science: Reports* 49: 1–10.

Smith, James H. 2021. *The Eyes of the World: Mining the Digital Age in the Eastern D.R. Congo*. Chicago: University of Chicago Press.

Smith, Marvin T., and Mary Elizabeth Good. 1982. *Early Sixteenth Century Glass Beads in the Spanish Colonial Trade*. Greenwood, Miss.: Cottonlandia Museum Publications.

Soto Rodriguez, Catalina, and Diego Salazar. 2016. "Mullu (Spondylus Sp.) en el complejo minero San José del Abra (Alto Loa, Norte de Chile)." *Intersecciones en Antropología* 17: 129–35.

Sovacool, Benjamin K. 2021. "When Subterranean Slavery Supports Sustainability Transitions? Power, Patriarchy, and Child Labor in Artisanal Congolese Cobalt Mining." *The Extractive Industries and Society* 8 (1): 271–93.

Spalding, Karen. 1984. *Huarochirí: An Andean Society Under Inca and Spanish Rule.* Stanford, Calif.: Stanford University Press.

Spina, Josefina, and Marco Giovannetti. 2014. "Metalurgia prehispánica en el valle de Hualfín. Nuevos datos sobre Quillay." *Intersecciones e Antropología* 15: 473–77.

Stahl, Ann B. 1993. "Concepts of Time and Approaches to Analogical Reasoning in Historical Perspective." *American Antiquity* 58 (2): 235–60.

Stahl, Ann B. 1994. "Change and Continuity in the Banda Area, Ghana: The Direct Historical Approach." *Journal of Field Archaeology* 21 (2): 181–203.

Stakeholder Democracy Network. 2018. "'More Money, More Problems': Economic Dynamics of the Artisanal Oil Industry in the Niger Delta over Five Years." https://www .stakeholderdemocracy.org/wp-content/uploads/2019/06/AOR-digital-layout-28.05 .19-JB-24.06.19-DT.pdf.

Starn, Orin. 1991. "Missing the Revolution: Anthropologists and the War in Peru." *Cultural Anthropology* 6 (1): 63–91.

Stavig, Ward. 2000. "Continuing the Bleeding of These Pueblos will Shortly Make them Cadavers: The Potosi Mita, Cultural Identity, and Communal Survival in Colonial Peru." *The Americas* 56 (4): 529–62.

Stubbe, Carlos F. 1945. *Vocabulario minero antiguo.* Buenos Aires: El Ateneo.

Suttill, Keith. 1993. "Modernizing Porco." *Engineering and Mining Journal* 194 (1): 32–35.

Swenson, Edward, and Andrew P. Roddick. 2018. "Rethinking Temporality and Historicity from the Perspective of Andean Archaeology." In *Constructions of Time and History in the Pre-Columbian Andes,* edited by Edward Swenson and Andrew P. Roddick, 3–43. Boulder: University Press of Colorado.

Swenson, Edward Reuben, and John P. Warner. 2012. "Crucibles of Power: Forging Copper and Forging Subjects at the Moche Ceremonial Center of Huaca Colorada, Peru." *Journal of Anthropological Archaeology* 31 (3): 314–33.

Swenson, Jennifer J., Catherine E. Carter, Jean-Christophe Domec, and Cesar I. Delgado. 2011. "Gold Mining in the Peruvian Amazon: Global Prices, Deforestation, and Mercury Imports." *PLoS ONE* 6 (4): 1–7.

Tándeter, Enrique. 1981a. "La producción como actividad popular: 'Ladrones de minas' en Potosí." *Nova Americana* 4: 43–65.

Tándeter, Enrique. 1981b. "Mineros de 'Week-End.' Los ladrones de minas de Potosí." *Todo Es Historia* 15: 32–46.

Tándeter, Enrique. 1991. *Trabajo forzado y trabajo libre en el Potosí colonial tardío.* Cochabamba, Bolivia: Centro de Estudios de la Realidad Económica y Social.

Tándeter, Enrique. 1993. *Coercion and Market: Silver Mining in Colonial Potos, 1692–1826.* Albuquerque: University of New Mexico Press.

Tarragó, Myriam N., and Luis R. González. 1996. "Producción especializada y diferención social en el sur del valle de Yocavil." *Anales de Arqueología y Etnología* 50–51: 85–108.

REFERENCES CITED

Taussig, Michael T. 1980. *The Devil and Commodity Fetishism in South America*. Chapel Hill: University of North Carolina Press.

Taylor, Gerald. 1980. "Supay." *Amérindia* 5: 47–63.

Téreygeol, Florian, and Pablo Cruz. 2014. "Metal del viento: Aproximación experimental para la comprensión del funcionamiento de las wayras andinas." *Estudios Atacameños* 48: 39–54.

The Times. 1912. "Bolivia Soon to be the Chief Tin-Producing Country in the World." September 30, 1912, 15. Accessed June 15, 2023. https://www.newspapers.com/image /33262061/?terms=Porco%20Bolivia&match=1.

Toro Montoya, Juan José. 2017. "Desarrollan complejo turístico minero en Porco." *Correo del Sur*, June 18, 2017. https://correodelsur.com/ecos/20170618_desarrollan -complejo-turistico-minero-en-porco.html.

Traslaviña, Abel, Zachary Chase, Parker VanValkenburgh, and Brendan J. M. Weaver, eds. 2016b. *Historical Archaeology in Peru. Part I and II, Boletín de Arqueología PUCP 21.* Lima: Pontificia Universidad Católica del Perú.

Tschakert, Petra. 2016. "Shifting Discourses of Vilification and the Taming of Unruly Mining Landscapes in Ghana." *World Development* 86: 123–32.

USGS. n.d. "Porco Mine." Accessed June 11, 2022. https://mrdata.usgs.gov/mrds/show -mrds.php?dep_id=10068799.

Umejesi, Ikechukwu, and Wilson Akpan. 2013. "Oil exploration and local opposition in colonial Nigeria: understanding the roots of contemporary state-community conflict in the Niger Delta." *South African Review of Sociology* 44 (1): 111–30.

Van Bueren, Thad. 2004. "The Poor Man's Mill: A Rich Vernacular Legacy." *Journal of the Society for Industrial Archaeology* 30 (2): 5–23.

Van Buren, Mary. 1996. "Rethinking the Vertical Archipelago: Ethnicity, Exchange, and History in the South Central Andes." *American Anthropologist* 98 (2): 338–51.

Van Buren, Mary. 2003. "Un estudio etnoarqueológico de la tecnología de fundición en el sur de Potosí, Bolivia." *Textos Antropológicos* 14 (2): 133–48.

Van Buren, Mary. 2016. "Conectando el pasado con el presente: La antropología histórica de la producción de metal de pequeña escala en Porco, Bolivia." *Boletín de Arqueología PUCP* 20: 63–82.

Van Buren, Mary, and Claire Rebekah Cohen. 2010. "Technological Changes in Silver Production after the Spanish Conquest in Porco, Bolivia." *Boletín del Museo Chileno de Arte Precolombino* 15 (2): 29–46.

Van Buren, Mary, and Barbara H. Mills. 2005. "Huayrachinas and Tocochimbos: Traditional Smelting Technology of the Southern Andes." *Latin American Antiquity* 16 (1): 3–25. https://doi.org/10.2307/30042484.

Van Buren, Mary, and Brendan J. M. Weaver. 2012. "Contours of Labor and History: A Diachronic Perspective on Andean Mineral Production and the Making of Landscapes in Porco, Bolivia." *Historical Archaeology* 46 (3): 79–101.

Van Buren, Mary, and Brendan J. M. Weaver. 2014. "Exigir una diferencia: El uso estratégico de la cerámica inka provincial en el Período Colonial Temprano." In

Ocupación inka y dinámicas regionales en los Andes (siglos XV–XVII), edited by Claudia Rivera Casanova, 247–68. La Paz: Instituto Francés de Estudios Andinos / Plural.

Van Valkenburgh, Parker. 2021. *Alluvium and Empire: The Archaeology of Colonial Resettlement and Indigenous Persistence on Peru's North Coast*. Archaeology of Indigenous-Colonial Interactions in the Americas. Tucson: University of Arizona Press.

Van Vleet, Krista E. 2011. "On Devils and the Dissolution of Sociality: Andean Catholics Voicing Ambivalence in Neoliberal Bolivia." *Anthropological Quarterly* 84 (4): 835–64.

Varón Gabai, Rafael. 1996. *La ilusión del poder: Apogee y decadencia de los Pizarro en la conquista del Perú*. Lima: Instituto de Estudios Peruanos.

Verbrugge, Boris. 2015. "The Economic Logic of Persistent Informality: Artisanal and Small-Scale Mining in the Southern Philippines." *Development and Change* 46 (5): 1023–46. https://doi.org/10.1111/dech.12189.

Vetter Parodi, Luisa, Susana Petrick Casagrande, Yezeña Huaypar Vásquez, and Martín MacKay Fulle. 2008. "Los hornos metalúrgicos del sitio inca de Curamba (Perú): Estudio por DRX, espectroscopia mössbauer y datación por métodos de luminiscencia." *Bulletin de l'Institut Français d'Études Andines* 37 (3): 451–75.

Villanueva Criales, Juan. 2015. "Evaluando la frontera Pacajes-Carangas para el período Intermedio Tardío (1100–1450 D.C.) en el altiplano boliviano central a partir de análisis de pastas cerámicas." *Chungara* 47: 1–8.

Voss, Barbara L. 2008. "Gender, Race, and Labor in the Archaeology of the Spanish Colonial Americas." *Current Anthropology* 49 (5): 861–93. https://doi.org/10.1086/591275.

Watts, Michael J. 2004. "Antinomies of Community: Some Thoughts on Geography, Resources and Empire." *Transactions of the Institute of British Geographers* 29 (2): 195–216.

Weaver, Brendan. 2008. "Ferro Ingenio: An Archaeological and Ethnohistorical View of Labor and Empire in Colonial Porco and Potosí." Master's thesis, Western Michigan State University.

Weaver, Brendan. 2021. "'The Grace of God and Virtue of Obedience': The Archaeology of Slavery and the Jesuit Hacienda Systems of Nasca, Peru, 1619–1767." *Journal of Jesuit Studies* 8 (3): 430–53. https://doi.org/10.1163/22141332-0803P005.

Weekly Sun. 1912. "Bolivia's Tin Resources. A Promising Flotation." *Weekly Sun*, November 3, 1912.

Wernke, Steven A. 2007. "Negotiating Community and Landscape in the Peruvian Andes: A Transconquest View." *American Anthropologist* 109 (1): 130–52.

Wernke, Steven A. 2013. *Negotiated Settlements: Andean Communities and Landscapes under Inka and Spanish Colonialism*. Gainesville: University Press of Florida.

Wolf, Eric R. 1982. *Europe and the People without History*. Berkeley: University of California Press.

Wright, Marie Robinson. 1907. *Bolivia: The Central Highway of South America, a Land of Rich Resources and Varied Interest*. Philadelphia: George Barrie & Sons.

Wurst, LouAnn, and Stephen A. Mrozowski. 2014. "Toward an Archaeology of the Future." *International Journal of Historical Archaeology* 18 (2): 210–23.

REFERENCES CITED

Yankson, Paul W. K., and Katherine V. Gough. 2019. "Gold in Ghana: The Effects of Changes in Large-Scale Mining on Artisanal and Small-Scale Mining (ASM)." *Extractive Industries and Society* 6 (1): 120–28.

Zagalsky, Paula. 2014. "Trabajadores indígenas mineros en el Cerro Rico de Potosí: Tras los rastros de sus prácticas laborales (siglos XVI y XVII)." *Revista Mundos do Trabalho* 6 (12): 55–82.

Zagorodny, Nora, Carlos Angiorama, M. Florencia Becerra, and M. Josefina Pérez Pieroni. 2015. "Evidencias de actividades metalúrgicas en el sitio Campo de Carrizal (Belén, Catamarca)." *Intersecciones en Antropología* 16: 439–50.

Zárate, Agustín. 1965 [1555]. *Historia del descubrimiento y conquista del Perú.* Buenos Aires: Universidad de Buenos Aires, Facultad de Filosofía y Letras.

Zori, Colleen. 2016. "Valuing the Local: Inka Metal Production in the Tarapacá Valley of Northern Chile." In *Making Value, Making Meaning: Techné in the Pre-Columbian World,* edited by Cathy Costin, 167–92. Washington, D.C.: Dumbarton Oaks.

Zori, Colleen. 2019. "Extracting Insights from Prehistoric Andean Metallurgy: Political Organization, Interregional Connections, and Ritual Meanings." *Journal of Archaeological Research* 27 (4): 501–56.

Zori, Colleen, and Peter Tropper. 2013. "Silver Lining: Evidence for Inka Silver Refining in Northern Chile." *Journal of Archaeological Science* 40 (8): 3282–92.

Zori, Colleen, Peter Tropper, and David Scott. 2013. "Copper Production in Late Prehispanic Northern Chile." *Journal of Archaeological Science* 40: 1166–75.

Zulawski, Ann. 1987. "Wages, Ore Sharing, and Peasant Agriculture: Labor in Oruro's Silver Mines, 1607–1720." *Hispanic American Historical Review* 67 (3): 405–30. https://doi.org/10.2307/2515579.

Index

Note: figures and maps are indicated by page numbers followed by *f* and *m* respectively.

Abercrombie, Thomas A., 11, 115

Absi, Pascale, 25, 34–36, 75, 83, 133

abstractions (*sensu* Ollman), 7–10, 22, 200–201

Acuto, Félix, 178

agriculture: government policies and, 188; *kajcheo* mining and, 56, 207–8; maize cultivation, 170; mining connections, 26, 33, 36, 44, 56, 65, 70, 206; pre-Hispanic, 163; ritual and belief systems in, 35–36, 38, 73; rural households and, 17, 35, 56, 69–70, 77, 188; *yanaconas*, 97–98

Agua de Castilla: mining cooperatives in, 42; sandstone outcrops, 138; stamp mills in, 93; tin mining in, 40, 67–68, 68*f*; veneration of Apu Porco, 42; village of, 28–29

Alcón, Sofía, 24, 42

Almagro, Diego de, 126–28, 130

Alonso Barba, Álvaro, 116, 119, 122–23, 134

Álvarez, Antonio, 128

Álvarez, Bartolomé, 149

Álvarez, Cristóbal, 128, 130–31

Álvarez, Diego, 92

Amaré, María Pilar, 75

Andes: animistic worldviews, 147, 149; ASM in, 14–15, 180; British investment in, 57, 67; copper objects, 153–54; Indigenous mining techniques, 18, 21, 116, 121; Inka expansion in, 151–52, 160, 162, 171–78; *kajcheo* in, 12–13, 58, 180; labor struggles in, 95, 147; metallurgy in, 152–58, 171, 173,

202; mineral production in, 18, 21, 121, 123–24, 130, 151–53; *originarios* in, 30–31; political economy of, 87; Spanish conquest of, 3, 9, 16

Angiorama, Carlos I., 119, 155

Anglogold Ashanti, 197

antimony, 100–101

Antofagasta, Chile, 61, 67

Apu Porco, 27*f*, 97*m*; *adoratorios* near, 42; ceramics from, 160–61; COMSUR and, 52; contemporary mining at, 164; hard-rock deposits, 85; industrial mining in, 10, 28, 52; male gender of, 35; rural homesteads around, 69; sacred spaces on, 10, 36, 161–62, 165, 178; veneration of, 42, 152, 161

Aramayo, Carlos Victor, 66–67

Aramayo, Félix, 62

Aramayo, Isidoro, 62

Aramayo, José Avelina, 62

Aramayo Francke Company, 67

Arana, Arturo, 67

Arce, Aniceto, 62

Argentina, 153*m*; copper smelting, 173–74; *huayrachinas* in, 78; metallurgy technologies in, 116, 119, 154, 171, 176; mineral deposits in, 151; transport of silver to, 59

Arica, 95–96, 108

artisanal and small-scale mining (ASM): defining, 14–15; environmental impacts of, 14, 193, 197–98, 208; formalization initiatives, 199–200, 208; global processes, 14, 22, 187–88, 208; growth in, 187–88; illegality of,

239

240

INDEX

artisanal and small-scale mining (ASM)
(*continued*)
58, 190–93, 196–97, 199; Indigenous
technologies in, 18–20, 44–45, 50–
53, 55; *kajcheo* and, 180, 201, 208–9;
mining cooperatives and, 13, 22; poor
countries and, 10, 13–14, 187–88,
198–99; relation to LSM, 15–16, 18,
21–22, 187–89, 197–200, 208–9;
secrecy in, 24, 51–52; silver production, 44–51; women in, 191, 194. *See
also kajcheo*
Arzáns de Orsúa y Vela, Bartolomé, 114
ASM. *See* artisanal and small-scale mining
(ASM)
Assadourian, Carlos Sempat, 24, 88
azogueros: industrial mining and, 21, 88;
kajcheo miners and, 114–15, 205; *mingas* and, 113; *mitayos* and, 21, 90, 104,
112, 124, 205; payment of the royal
fifth, 90, 108

Bakewell, Peter, 24, 133, 135, 150
Bargas, Teodora de, 96
Barragán, Rossana, 11, 24, 83, 112–13,
115–16, 136, 208
Belasco, Bartolome de, 93
Belen, 173
Beltrán, Diego, 92–93, 98
Benavides del Carpio, Maya, 24, 38, 42
Berthelot, Jean, 21, 164–65
Besom, Thomas, 161
Blacut, Carlos Camargo, 11
Bolívar, Simón, 57
Bolivia, *94m*, *153m*; Constituent Assem-
bly of 1938, 83; Constitution of, 183;
contemporary small-scale mining in,
181–87; cooperative and company
miner tensions, 41, 43–44; Decree of
Pukara, 57; environmental impacts of
hard-rock mining, 185–86; indepen-
dence from Spain, 9, 57, 205; *kajcheo*,
10–13, 15, 24, 65, 180, 202–7; labor

movement in, 56, 79–83; liberal
reforms in, 62, 83, 85; military juntas
and, 81, 85; mineral production in,
3–5, 10, 56, 65, 70, 199; mining
cooperatives and, 13, 19; pre-Hispanic
cultures in, 5–6; public art in, 82–83;
tin barons in, 4, 56, 66–67, 81, 83. *See
also* Bolivian Revolution of 1952
Bolivian Mining Company (COMIBOL),
39, 81, 181, 206
Bolivian Revolution of 1952: decline of
rural populations after, 54; mining
unions and, 16, 56–57, 81, 83, 85,
206; political economy and, 9
Bouysse Cassagne, Thérèse, 24, 147, 160,
162
British Gold Coast Colony, 195
bronze, 143–44, 156–57, 172, 174, 176
bunkering, 192–93

Caltama, 147–48, 160
Campo, Juan del, 92
Cañete, Pedro Vicente, 114
Capoche, Luis, 91–92, 95, 98, 104, 113
Carangas, 94–95, 104, 108, 112
Catamarca, Argentina, 154, 173, 176
Catholicism, 32, 74, 147–48
ceramics: Belen, 173; Chillpe-Carangas,
145, *146f*, 164; colonial, 77, 118, 136;
found at Ferro Ingenio, *139f*; found at
Porco, 61, 70, 77, 109, 134, 136, 138,
145; found at Uruquilla, 142; Indigenous wares, 136, 138, *138f*, 145, 169;
Late Horizon, 167, 176; Panamanian
blue-on-white, 138, *139f*; Polychrome
A majolica, 138, *139f*; provincial Inka
vessels, 109, 142, 145, *146f*, 166–67
Cerro Rico of Potosí: cooperative mining
and, 25; crosses in, 36; El Tío in,
34–36; as feminine, 34–35; *huacas*
and, 133, 147–48; *kajcheo*, 84; silver
mining in, 3, 35; Spanish exploitation
of, 10; as wife of Apu Porco, 35

INDEX 241

Chaquí, 94, *94m*, 96, 104, 160

charcoal: *adoratorios* and, 42; *churqui*, 45, 48; *huayrachinas* and, 45–48, 51, 134, 136; Indigenous sales of, 97; *queñua*, 46; smelting and, 51, 109, 119, 123, 170; windbreaks for, 47–48

Charka federation, 96, 127, *159m*, 160, 162–63, 170

Charkas: encomienda system, 128; *mita*yos (forced labor), 96; pilgrimages to Porco *huaca*, 147, 170; silver production and, 165; soldiers for the Inkas, 160

Chase, Zachary James, 162

Chile, *153m*, 156, 171, 173–75, 178

Chiriguanos, 160, 162

Chuquicamata, 156, 174

Cieza de Léon, Pedro de, 164

coal, 188–91, 197

Coal India Limited, 190

Cochabamba, 94, 127, 170

Cohen, Claire, 120

Cole, Jeffrey, 11, 24, 106

colonialism: hybrid economic systems, 127; ideological violence and, 147–49; Indian *zamindari* system, 189–90; mining fraud and, 108; *mita* (forced labor) and, 16–17, 21, 88–90, 92–98; patio process and, 87–88, 204; silver production and, 20–21, 90–97, 124–32, 204; small-scale mineral production, 108–12; Toledan reforms and, 20–21, 96, 104, 115, 124, 132, 204

COMIBOL. *See* Bolivian Mining Company (COMIBOL)

Compañía Minera del Sur (COMSUR), 20, 37–39, 52, 186

Compañia Minera Unificada de Potosí, 83

Compañía Tornohuaico, 62

company miners: *corregidor* recommendations, 30; differences with mining cooperatives, 41–44; family health and

wellness, 43; higher incomes in, 38; illness vulnerability in, 24; mobility of workers, 33; treatment and behavior of children, 42–43; unionized, 25

COMSUR. *See* Compañía Minera del Sur (COMSUR)

Condoriri, 29, 45, 61, 95, 163–64

conquistadors: assignments of silver veins, 21, 128, 131; destruction of *huacas*, 147–49; encomienda system, 126, 131, 203; mine ownership, 90, 203. *See also* Spanish conquest

Contreras, Carlos, 64

Cooperativa Minera Huayna Porco, 40, *41f*, 85, 183

Cooperativa Minera Porco, 40, 85

Cooperativa Minera Veneros, 40, 84–85

cooperative mining. *See* mining cooperatives

copper: altiplano polity and, 157–58; at Chuquicamata, 156, 174; at El Abra, 174–75; gifted to elites, 152, 155; Inka workshops and, 171–75, 178; Late Intermediate Period (Late Period), 154–58, 172; Potosí mint fraud, 108; pre-Hispanic mining, 156–57; at Pulaco50, 157–58; at Quillay, 173; at Rincón Chico 15, 154–55, 171–72; ritual practices and, 152–53, 175; smelting and refining, 172–74; at Tarapacá Viejo, 171–73; Tiwanaku and, 154, 156–58; as tribute, 173; at Viñas del Cerro, 173–74

Corporación Minera de Bolivia (COMIBOL). *See* Bolivian Mining Company (COMIBOL)

Cruz, Pablo, 24, 53, 121, 133–34, 144–45, 157, 161

Cruz Pampa: ceramics found at, *146f*; Inka occupation, 167; material culture at, 137, 142, 144–45; mineral production in, 137–38; silver production at, 142–43

Cuiza, Carlos: charcoal production, 45–46, 51; cupellation furnace, 49, 49f, 50, 53, 121; homestead of, 45; household economics and, 51–52; *huayrachina* use, 44–47, 47f, 48–50, 53, 78–79; rituals and beliefs, 48, 50–51, 149; smelting of argentiferous lead ore, 46–48, 51, 78–79; social marginalization of, 50–51; traditional silver production, 20, 26, 45–53, 77

cupellation hearths: cultural origins and history of, 121, 123; Indigenous use of, 123–24; rural households and, 52–53, 77, 78f; silver ore refining, 49–50, 110, 110f, 111, 123

Cusco, 152, 162, 165, 167, 171, 175, 177

Dalence, José María, 61
D'Altroy, Terence, 151
Deagan, Kathleen, 132
dialectical approach, 7–8, 15, 19, 55, 189, 195, 199–200, 208
Díaz, Miranda, 128
Dumett, Raymond E., 193–94

Earle, Timothy, 151
Ecos, Bautista, 35–36, 91
Ecos, Dionisio, 44
El Abra, 121, 174–75, 177–78
El Tío: as Christian devil, 74–76; cult of, 34–36, 38, 70–76; *k'araku* ritual, 71–72; Marxist analysis of, 73–74; private bargains with, 71, 75; representations of, 71, 74–75
Empresa Minera Porco Ltda, 39–40, 206
encomienda system: conquistadors and, 126, 131, 203; *hatunruna*, 133; Indigenous people and, 126–28; *indios de vara*, 135, 203; tribute and, 131; *yanaconas* and, 127, 131, 133, 135, 203
environment: damage to, 13–14, 22, 85, 185, 191–93, 198, 208; effects on

enslaved Africans, 131; in Porco, 27, 45, 170, 177; regulation of, 183–87
Equise, Juan, 44, 77, 78f
Estrada, Jhoan de, 93, 98, 103–4
Eylar, Christy, 24, 42–43

Federación Obrera Central de Uncía (FOCU), 80
FENCOMIN. *See* National Federation of Mining Cooperatives (FENCOMIN)
Ferro Ingenio, 97m; artifacts found at, 103–4; ceramics from, 140f; colonial stamp mill, 23, 93, 101, 102f, 103; early colonial, 139, 139f, 140; material culture at, 99, 144–45; mineral production in, 98, 103–5, 108, 137–38, 140; *mita* (forced labor) at, 104–5; theft of silver in, 108
Fiesta of Santa Rosa, 31–32, 38
Fiesta of Señor Ckaccha, 36–37, 37f, 38
Fiesta of the Virgin of Candelaria, 32–33

galamsey, 196–98
Garrido, Francisco, 173–75
Ghana: artisanal gold mining in, 22, 188–89, 193–98; Chinese miners in, 197–98; colonial regime in, 195, 198; large-scale mining, 195, 197–99; nationalization of gold mines, 195–96; precolonial mining, 194–95; Small-Scale Gold Mining Act, 197; Wassa economy, 194–95
Gil Montero, Raquel, 65, 88
Gironás, Ciriaco, 62
Glencore, 20, 39
gold mining: *abusa* system, 195; alluvial, 181, 185; artisanal, 177, 187–89, 193–98; colonial regime and, 21, 170; environmental impacts, 186, 196–98; Inkas and, 164–65; large-scale, 195; mining cooperatives and, 185; open-pit, 196; ore theft and, 52; ritual use, 147, 153

INDEX   243

Gómez de la Rocha, Francisco, 108
González, Luis R., 154
González de la Casa, Hernán, 147–49, 160, 165, 179
Gremio de Azogueros, 58, 205
Guallpa, Diego, 90, 132–33, 145
Guaman Poma de Ayala, Felipe, 11

Hagan, Nicole A., 107
Harris, Olivia, 24, 147, 160
hatunruna, 133, 136, 150
Henderson, G. M., 68, 81
Hilson, Gavin, 194
Hochschild, Mauricio, 66
Hoerlein, Sara, 24, 33–34, 38, 43
huacas, 147–49, 151, 160–62
Huajje, 156–57
Huancavelica, 58, 107, 186
Huanchaca Mining Company, 62
Huanuni, 13, 35, 57, 183
Huayna Porco, 27f; chapels on, 36; *huaca* and, 160; location of, 10, *137m*; mineral production, 168–69; reverberatory furnaces, 119, 141; rural homesteads around, 69, 167; silver production in, 28, 35, 67, 136, 146, 163, 166; Spanish settlement at foot of, 128
huayrachinas, *138f*; *acendrada* (litharge) in, 48; contemporary use of, 44–45; design of, 134; Indigenous use of, *79f*, 117, 124, 134, *135f*, 201; Inka occupation and, 169; metallurgy workshops and, 172; patterned workspaces for, 47–48; silver production and, 4–5, 20, 44–50, 53, 77, 205; smelting in, 45–48, 78–79, 120, 134, 136; *yanaconas* and, 133, 135
Huayrachinas, 137–38, 140, 143–44, *144f*, *146f*, 166
Hundimiento, 91–92, 129

Illanes, Rodolfo, 184
Illapa, 39, 160–62, 165

illas, 35–36, 76, 148, 162
independent miners: economic crisis and, 83; foreign investment and, 58–59; *indios de vara*, 104, 135; middlemen and, 58–59; ore-sharing arrangements, 135–36; *pailliris* (ore-pickers), 105; *pallaqueo* system, 58; silver production and, 3, 58. *See also kajcheo*
India, 22, 188–91
Indigenous miners: *forasteros* (outsiders), 113–14; *huayrachina* use, 23, 117, 124, 134–35, *135f*; illicit ore appropriation, 59, 136; *pallaqueo* system, 58; rituals and beliefs, 71–74; silver production, 9, 18, 21, 45, 53, 90, 131–32; small-scale mining, 15, 18, 21; technologies, 18, 20–21, 44–45, 50–52, 55, 74, 124–25, 127, 203; *trapicheros* and, 59–61; tribute and, 65, 89, 124; wage labor and, 90. *See also kajcheo*; *mitayos* (forced laborers); Native population
indios de plata (silver Indians), 96
indios de vara, 104, 135, 203
industrial mining: control of productive deposits, 39, 52, 54, 84, 183, 187, 207, 209; cult of El Tío in, 70–72, 75–76; dispossession of farmers, 196; early 20th century, 20, 56; environmental contamination by, 186–87; hazardous conditions in, 106–7; labor mobilization, 79–80, 85; *mita* (forced labor) and, 89–90, 92–98, 104–5; stamp mills and, 21, 101, 106–7; theft of silver ore, 107–8; tin production, 20, 57, 66–68, 85; wage labor and, 57, 206
ingenios. *See* stamp mills (*ingenios*)
Inkas: asymmetrical reciprocity, 151, 174–75; *capacocha* ceremonies, 161; financing of government, 151–52; gold mining, 164; *huacas* and, 148, 151; *kancha* buildings, 166; large-scale

244 INDEX

Inkas (*continued*)

mining, 165, 171–75, 202; legal monopoly on mining, 164, 202–3; local expertise and, 171–72; metallurgy and, 14, 21, 151–52, 158, 169, 171, 202–3; mineral production and, 130, 137, 171–78; *mit'a* (rotating labor), 74, 168–70, 173–74; *mitmaqkuna* (resettled communities), 168, 170; occupation of Porco, 9, 152, 158, 162–67, 202; political economy of, 9, 14, 151–52; pre-Hispanic mines, 3–4, 14–15; ritual items, 165, 167, 171–72, 202; sacred landscapes and, 161–62, 178; silver mining and, 3–4, 127, 165–67, 173; small-scale mining, 165, 175–77, 179, 202; socio-spatial order, 178; wealth finance and, 151–52; *yanakuna*, 168–69

International Institute for Environment and Development (IIED), 14–15

Jalantaña, 166

juku (ore thief). *See* ore theft (*jukeo*)

kajcheo: agro-pastoral activities and, 56, 207–8; ASM and, 180, 201, 208–9; collective identity and, 114–15, 205; defining, 10–12; history of Bolivian, 202–7; illicit appropriation and, 11–13, 58–59, 77, 90, 112, 125, 150, 181; Indigenous technologies and, 10, 180; informal economy and, 58–59, 112–13, 124, 204–5; large-scale mining and, 180, 201–4, 208; mercury production and, 58; middlemen and, 58–59, 85; mining cooperatives and, 83–84, 181, 206; political economy and, 201, 207–8; rights to ore, 11–13, 58, 89–90, 113–15, 205; silver production and, 58, 66, 135–36, 205; small-scale mineral production, 10–13, 15, 20, 56, 58–59, 66, 83–85;

subsidizing of low wages, 112–13, 207–8; *trapiches* and, 113, 115, 124; *yanaconas* and, 135, 149

kamayoc, 169–70

Kemp, Deanna, 188

Khelkhata Valley, 93, 98, 104

labor: child workers, 185–87, 197; gendered, 33–34; industrial mining and, 57, 206; Marxist analysis of, 80, 82; mobilization of, 79–80; *peones* (day laborers), 39–40, 182; seasonal workforce, 63–65; shortages, 62–65, 95; social relations in, 16–17, 22; tasks assigned, 104–5; tin production, 68–69; Uncía massacre, 80; understandings of time, 63–64, 64f; unionization and, 16, 25, 56, 79–81, 85, 206; wage laborers, 16, 21, 56; women sorters (*pailliris*), 68, 105, 186. *See also mingas* (free laborers); *mitayos* (forced laborers)

Lahiri-Dutt, Kuntala, 187, 190–91

Lake Poopó, 94, 94m, 145

Lake Titicaca, 94, 104, 145, 156, 169

Langer, Erick D., 59, 70

large-scale mining (LSM): conflict with cooperatives, 185; Inka occupation and, 165, 171–75; *kajcheo* and, 180, 201–4, 208; labor organization, 17, 86; relationship with ASM, 15–16, 18, 21–22, 187–89, 197–200, 208–9; tin production, 83, 205–6

La Salvadora Mining Company, 80

Late Horizon, 163, 166–67, 174–76, 178

Late Intermediate Period: *ayllus* (kin groups) in, 160; chiefdoms (*señoríos*), 159; metal production, 121, 157–58, 172; Porco during, 69, 148, 162–64; silver artifacts, 177–78

Lechtman, Heather, 116, 156, 177

Lecoq, Patrice, 23, 163, 165–66

Leiboweicz, Ivan, 178

Llallagua, 35, 57, 206

INDEX 245

Llanos, García de, 90, 106, 204
lo andino, 6, 8, 201
López de Quiroga, Antonio, 90–91
Los Amarillos, 155, 171–72, 178
LSM. *See* large-scale mining (LSM)

Macfarlane, Andrew P., 156, 177
Mamani, Eloy, 35, 45, 47, 61, 123
Martinón-Torres, Marcos, 176
Marxism, 7, 73, 80, 82
MAS (Movement Towards Socialism), 183
Medina, Bartolomé de la, 122
Mendieta, Lope de, 131
Mendoza, Gunnar, 12
mercury: amalgamation technique, 4, 44, 59, 88, 103, 105, 107, 122, 134, 207; environmental contamination, 107, 186, 196, 198; pricing of, 91, 113; production, 58; transportation of, 95
Mercury Ordinance (Ghana), 196
metallurgy: colonial regime and, 124–25; copper, 152–54; cupellation hearths, 20, 48–49, 49f, 50, 52–53, 71m, 77–78, 78f, 110, 110f, 111, 121–24, 140, 157, 167, 169, 203, 206–7; domestic activities and, 109, 142–43, 150, 155, 172; elite involvement in, 202; European techniques in, 122, 127–28; *huayrachinas* and, 23, 78, 169, 172; Indigenous, 3, 14–15, 18, 23, 123, 152–58; Inkas and, 14, 21, 151–52, 158, 169, 171–72, 202–3; lost wax process, 172; pre-Hispanic, 116; *quimbaletes* and, 116; recycling of materials, 48; reverberatory furnaces, 110, 122; rituals and beliefs, 149, 178; small-scale, 20–21, 23, 44, 54, 115, 150, 175–76; social differentiation and, 156–58; southern Andes and, 152–58, 202; Tiwanaku, 154, 156–58; *tocochimbos*, 110, 117, 123, 134. *See also* mineral production
Michel, Garci, 128

Miller, Benjamin L., 69
mineral deposits: ASM exclusion, 15, 21, 86, 207; cooperatives and, 181–84, 187; Inkas and, 151, 164; private subleases and, 40–41; tensions over access, 17, 21, 41, 183–84, 187
mineral production: archaeological research and, 19, 21, 44–45, 48; decentralized, 137–46, 150, 167; gendered nature of, 34–35, 38; *huacas* and, 147–49; labor shortages and, 62–64; medium-scale, 14, 199; mine locations, 63m; *mit'a* (forced labor under Inkas), 168–69; *mita* (forced labor under Spaniards), 16, 21, 88–89; nationalization of, 81, 206; patio process, 87–88; pre-Inka, 23, 152; rituals and beliefs, 42; seasonal workforce, 63–65; social relations in, 22; Toledan reforms, 9, 20–21, 87–88; traditional techniques for, 9–10, 127, 156, 203. *See also* artisanal and small-scale mining (ASM); *kajcheo*; large-scale mining (LSM); ore theft (*jukeo*); silver production; small-scale mineral production
miners: average life expectancy, 182; conflicts between, 41, 183–84, 187; conflict with the state, 5, 19, 22; creation of mining cooperatives, 40, 84, 181; organized labor, 25, 80–81, 206; protests against maltreatment, 79–80; rights to ore, 11–13; rituals and beliefs, 70–74, 92; on *sacrificado* (sacrifice), 38; surveillance of, 136–37; unemployed, 40, 59, 80, 84–86, 113, 181. *See also* company miners; independent miners; Indigenous miners; *kajcheo*
mingas (free laborers): cutting ore, 104–5; earnings of, 89, 105; ethnicity of, 105; Indigenous miners, 89, 96, 127; ore-sharing arrangements, 113, 204; silver tribute and, 124

246 INDEX

mining cooperatives: ASM and, 13, 22; conflict with LSM, 36–37, 41–44, 183–85; conflict with the state, 183–84, 187; development of, 84–86; family wellness, 43; FENCOMIN and, 40, 181, 185; gendered labor in, 34, 181; harsh labor conditions, 182, 185; *illas* of the mines, 35–36; income inequality in, 185; *kajcheo* and, 83–84, 181, 206; leased rights, 26, 39, 52, 54, 182–83, 187; negative characterization of, 184–85, 187; *peones* (day laborers), 39–40, 182, 185; political mobilization, 183–87, 207; rituals and beliefs of, 34–38, 41–42; *socios* (official members), 39–40, 181–83, 185; treatment of children of, 42–43; unemployed miner creation of, 40, 84, 181

mining unions: Bolivian Revolution and, 16, 56–57, 81, 83, 85, 206; company resistance to, 66–67; organization of, 79–81; state violence against, 80

mit'a (forced labor under Inkas), 168–70, 173–74

mita (forced labor under Spaniards): abolishment of, 16, 58, 62, 64; avoidance of, 96–98, 114; in Porco, 91–95; in Potosí, 91; Toledan reforms and, 88, 124, 204, 207

mitayos (forced laborers): *azogueros* and, 21, 104, 124, 205; colonial regime and, 16, 21, 88–90, 92–98; earnings of, 105; elimination of, 58, 62, 64, 205; ethnicity of, 93–94, 104–6; harsh conditions of, 106; impact on Native communities, 3, 89, 124, 147; *indios de plata* (silver Indians), 96–97; *kajcheo* and, 89–90; llama herding and transport, 95–96; redistribution of, 93–96, 104; silver production and, 58, 88–90, 92–95; tasks of, 104–5; Toledan reforms, 88–90, 124, 204

mitmaqkuna (communities resettled by the Inkas), 168, 170

Monje, Martín, 129

Montesclaros, Viceroy, 92–93, 95, 101, 103

Morales, Evo, 9, 22, 183–87

Mrozowski, Stephen A., 7–8

Murra, John, 6

Muysken, Pieter, 106

Nash, June, 25, 72–74

National Federation of Mining Cooperatives (FENCOMIN), 40, 181, 185

Nationalist Revolutionary Movement (MNR), 81

Native population: animistic worldviews, 147, 149; *ayllus* (kin groups), 89, 96–97; Catholic practices, 147–48; encomienda system, 126–28; *forasteros* (outsiders), 97, 113; llama herding and transport, 95–96; mercantilist economy, 74–75, 96–97; rituals and beliefs, 71–74, 147–49; Spanish campaign against religious practices, 147–49; threat of mining sector, 184; tribute and, 65, 75, 89, 115, 126; *yanaconas*, 97–98. *See also* Indigenous miners; *mitayos* (forced laborers)

Nicolas, Vincent, 104–5

Nielsen, Axel, 159

Nigeria, 22, 189, 191–93

Nigerian Bitumen Corporation, 191

Nugent, David, 75

Núñez, Lautaro, 156, 174–75

Núñez Vela, Blasco, 127

Ocaña, Diego de, 136

oil production, 189, 191–93, 197

Ollman, Bertell, 7–8

ore theft (*jukeo*): colonial, 113, 130, 150, 203; common practice of, 21, 51–52, 107–8; contested nature of, 112, 135–36; high-grade silver and, 54;

INDEX   247

illicit *kajcheo* and, 58, 83, 125, 181; Inka mining and, 202–3; in Porco, 13, 52, 207; subsistence mining and, 191; unemployed and, 83

Oruro: *forasteros* (outsiders) in, 97, 113; harsh conditions in, 106; mining cooperatives in, 41; ore theft, 13, 112–13; rituals and beliefs in, 35; tin miners in, 72; unionized miners in, 25

Owen, John R., 188

Pachamama, 34, 72–73, 75

Pachatata, 73–75

Pacheco, Gregorio, 62

pailliris (ore-pickers), 18, 34, 54, 68, 84, 105, 186

PAPP. *See* Proyecto Arqueológico Porco-Potosí (PAPP)

Paria, 106, 170, 177

Patiño, Simón, 66–67, 80

patio process, 87–88, 124, 204

Paz Estenssoro, Victor, 81

Peele, Robert, 77–79, 205

Pentland, John, 57

peones (day laborers), 39–40, 182, 185

Pérez Bocanegra, Juan, 107

Peru: Indigenous metallurgy in, 152–53; Inka mining centers in, 165, 171; ore-sharing, 64–65; silver artifacts, 177–78; Spanish conquest of, 3, 9, 87, 126–27; tribute in, 64–65

Pizarro, Francisca, 92, 128

Pizarro, Francisco, 126–27

Pizarro, Gonzalo, 127–28, 130–33

Pizarro, Hernando, 127–33

Platt, Tristan, 24, 36, 58, 72–74, 76, 133, 147, 160, 162

Plaza, María Teresa, 173–74, 176

political economy: ASM and, 14; gifting of silver, 172, 177–78, 202; Inkas and, 9, 14, 151–52; *kajcheo* and, 201, 207–8; mineral production and, 9, 50–51, 196; Spanish conquest and, 87, 127

Porco, *30f*; agro-pastoral community in, 20, 69–70; archaeological research in, 61, 69–70, 168; *ayllus* (kin groups) in, 5, 30–32, 70; ceramics at, 48, 61, 70, 77, 109, 118, 134, 136, 138–39, 145; cupellation hearths, 121, 123; ethnicity of workers, 169; ethnographic work in, 24, 168; European material culture, 144–46; gendered labor in, 33–34; household demographics, 33; *huaca* of, 147–48, 160–62; *huayrachina* use in, 134–35; Inka occupation at, 9, 152, 158, 162–67, 177, 202; labor organization at, 168–71; Late Horizon, 163, 166; Late Intermediate Period, 69, 148, 162–64; location of, *4m*, 27–28, *28m*, 29, *94m*, *97m*, *137m*; mountaintop shrines, 161–62; pilgrimages to, 147–48, 160, 170; political organization in, 29–30; pre-Inka occupation, 163–64; public art in, 82, *82f*, 83; reverberatory furnaces at, 117–19, 121–22; ritual significance of, 165; rural homesteads around, 69–70, *71m*; rural *trapiche* in, 59–60; social differences in, 38; Spanish control of, 21, 127–32; *vecinos* (Spanish residents), 91–93, 95–96; veneration of *illas*, 76. *See also* Porco mines

Porco Ltd., 35, 37, 40

Porco mines: agricultural connections, 44, 56, 65, 70; colonial regime and, 9, 87–98; COMSUR and, 38–39; conflicts in, 5, 183; divisions in, *129f*; flooding in, 61, 90–91; Indigenous technologies in, 21, 23, 127; industrial mining in, 20, 26, 52, 56–57, 60, 70, 81, 206; informal miners and, 58–61; labor and, 16, 18–19, 81–82, *82f*; mining as *sacrificado* (sacrifice), 38; mining cooperatives in, 20, 26, 40, 54, 84–85, 181, 207; *mitayos* (forced labor), 104; ore theft, 13, 21, 52, 59,

Porco mines (*continued*)

112, 150, 207; silver production in, 3–6, 57–58, 90–96, 98, 127–33, 137–39, 162, 165–67, 171, 179; small-scale production in, 5, 9–10, 19, 21, 26, 39, 50–52, 54–55, 81, 108–12, 115–24, 127, 177, 179, 207; state control of, 165–66; tin production, 20, 69

Porco Tin Ltd., 67, 69, 206

Porco Viejo. *See* Uruquilla (Porco Viejo)

Potosí: El Tío cult in, 34–35; ethnic groups in, 106, 145; *huayrachina* use in, 44, 133–34; illicit ore appropriation, 108, 112–13; independent miners in, 10–11, 58–59; Indigenous mineral market in, 75, 136, 203; Indigenous miners and, 3–4, 94, 127, 132; industrial mining in, 57, 80, 206; *kajcheo*, 10–13, 59, 83, 90, 114–15, 205; mercury contamination in, 107, 186; mining cooperatives in, 25, 34–35, 41, 83; *mitayos* (forced laborers), 16, 104, 106; silver production in, 87–91, 95, 97, 128, 132–36, 150, 205; Spanish miners and, 3–4; tin mining in, 66; transport of goods through, 61, 95–96

Potrero de Payogasta, 171–72, 178

Presta, Ana María, 24, 93, 127, 131

Proyecto Arqueológico Porco-Potosí (PAPP), 4, 20, 22–24, 29, 42, 44, 52, 117, 163

Pucapujra, 45, 77

Pucará de Tilcara, 155, 171–72

Pulacayo, 70, *94m*, 121, 157

Qaraqara: Charka alliance, 96, 127, 159, *159m*, 160; ethnic groups of, 158–59; *mitayos* (forced laborers), 96; pilgrimages, 147; silver payments for labor, 96–97; social formations of, 159–60; soldiers for the Inkas, 160; in southern

Bolivia, 145, 158–59; submission to Spanish, 127

Quespi, Augustín, 114

Quillay, 173–74

quimbaletes, 59–60, 60*f*, 115–16, 123

Raffino, Rodolfo, 173

Ramírez de Arellano, Felipe, 108

Rasnake, Roger Neil, 31

reverberatory furnaces, *118f*, *120f*; construction of, 119; cultural origins and history of, 121–23; ore processing and, 117–18, 123; silver refining, 120–23. *See also* cupellation hearths

Rincón Chico, 154, 171–72

rituals and beliefs: *adoratorios*, 42; agricultural productivity, 36, 38; *capacocha* ceremonies, 161; gendered mining, 34–35; *huacas* and, 147–49; inebriation in, 36, 38; metal objects, 153–54; miners and, 34–38, 41–42; offerings and, 31, 36, 37*f*, 42, 50, 71, 147, 149; sacred landscapes and, 161–62, 178; smelting and, 48, 50–51, 149; Spanish and, 147–49

Robins, Nicholas A., 107

Rodríguez Ostria, Gustavo, 24, 59, 62, 64, 76

Ruis Cavello, Francisco, 93

rural populations: agro-pastoral activities and, 77, 187–88; ASM and, 187–88; *ayllus* (kin groups) in, 30–31; impact of *mita* on, 89; income diversification, 33, 53, 77, 187–88; migration to towns, 44, 54; poverty and, 51, 188; small-scale mining, 14, 20, 24, 44, 53–54, 77, 206

Saignes, Thierry, 96–97

Salazar, Diego, 174–75

Salazar-Soler, Carmen, 75, 106

San Antonio del Nuevo Mundo, 65

Sánchez de Lozada, Gonzalo, 20, 38–39

San Pedro de Atacama, 156–57
Saro-Wiwa, Ken, 193
Silliman, Stephen, 16–17
silver production: *acendrada* (litharge) in, 48; artisanal methods for, 5, 44–53; charcoal production for, 45–46, 51; colonial regime and, 3–4, 20–21, 90–98, 124–25, 127–32, 204, 207; cupellation hearths, 49, *49f*, 50, 110–11, 121, 123; European techniques in, 127–28, 130, 132, 152; export of raw silver, 65, 167, 171, 177; foreign investment in, 57–59, 62; free market and, 65, 205–6; *huayrachinas* and, 4–5, 20, 44–50, 53, 77, 133–34; Indigenous technologies in, 18, 44–45, 50–52, 55, 131–32; Inka occupation and, 4, 165–67, 173, 177–78; Inka ritual items, 165, 167, 171–72, 202; *kajcheo*, 58, 66, 135–36, 205; mercury amalgamation, 4, 44, 59, 134, 207; *mitayos* and, 58, 88–90, 92–98, 205, 207; 19th century, 57–66; ore theft, 51–52, 54, 58–59, 77, 85, 90, 107–8, 112, 124, 127, 136–37, 204–6; patio process, 87–88, 124; political economy and, 172, 177–78, 202; pre-Hispanic, 152, 156–57; residential spaces and, 136–37, 139–40, 146, 150; reverberatory furnaces, 117–23; rural households and, 26, 53–54, 76–77; silver oligarchy, 62, 65; small-scale processing, 76–77, 85, 123, 150; smelting and refining, 46–49, *49f*, 50–51; status and, 74–75; technologies for, 120–21, 124
Sinchi Wayra, 39–40, 183
Sindicato Minero Choque Carmona, 40
Sindicato Minero Veneros Porco, 40
Singewald, Joseph T., 69
small-scale mineral production: agro-pastoral connections, 26, 33, 36,

44, 56, 65, 70, 206; child labor in, 185–86; colonial regime and, 108–12; contemporary, 181–87; cupellation hearths, 110, *110f*, 111, *111f*; environmental impacts of, 185–86; illicit processing, 85, 90, 203; Inka occupation and, 165, 175–77, 179; *kajcheo* and, 9–12, 15, 20, 56, 58, 66, 85; late 19th century, 62, 65, 69, 76–79, 85; social contexts and, 23–24; technologies for, 109–10, 115–24. *See also* artisanal and small-scale mining (ASM)
smelting and refining: archaeological research and, 21, 26; argentiferous lead ore, 46–48, 78–79, 120; copper and, 173–74; cupellation hearths, 49–50, 110, *110f*, 111, 121; enslaved Africans and, 130–31; illicit silver ore in, 51–52; offerings and, 48, 50–51; perforated crucibles, 173; protection rituals, 48, 50; reverberatory furnaces, 117–18, *118f*, 119–20, *120f*, 121–23; rural households and, 77–78, 206; skilled workers and, 169–70; techniques for, 20–21, 26, 44–46, 48, 50–53, 115, 117; *yanaconas* and, 144. *See also huayrachinas*
socios (official cooperative members), 39–40, 182–83, 185
Sora Sora, *97m*, *137m*; industrial mining in, 98, 100–101, 104, 106, 108; *kajcheo* miners, 61; mining features at, 98–99, *99m*, 100; *mita* (forced labor) at, 104, 106; silver production and, 92
Spanish conquest: ASM and, 15–16; conflict between Pizarro and Almagro, 126–27; destruction of *huacas*, 147–49; mercantile system and, 152; Native Andean resistance, 87; New Laws, 127; plunder economy, 16, 126, 147, 203; political economy of, 87, 127. *See also* conquistadors

Stahl, Ann B., 6, 19
stamp mills (*ingenios*): *cabezas* and *mazos*, 101; cost of mill complexes, 88, 90; Ferro Ingenio, 23, 101; industrial mining and, 21, 101, 106–7; silver production and, 88; *trapicheros* and, 60
Sucre, Antonio José de, 57
Supay, 74–75

Tándeter, Enrique, 12, 24, 113–14
Tarapacá Viejo, 121, 167, 171–73, 177
Tata Apu, 36, *37f*
Tata Ckaccha, 36–37
Taussig, Michael, 73–76
Taylor, Gerald, 74
technology: European techniques, 127–28, 130, 132; Indigenous, 20, 44–45, 52–53, 123, 127; labor and, 18–19; small-scale mining, 115–24; social contexts and, 17–18
Téreygeol, Florian, 53, 88, 145
tin barons, 4, 56, 66–67, 81, 83
Tin Company of Llallagua, 80
tin production: alluvial ore, 84, *84f*, 85; Bolivian exports, 56, 206; contamination by, 84–85; foreign investment in, 67–69; increase in, 65–66; industrial, 20, 57, 66–68, 83, 205–6; laborers in, 68–69, 181, 206; Late Horizon, 174; nationalization of, 81, 206; political consciousness and, 66, 72; price collapse, 181; rituals and beliefs, 72; small-scale, 84–85
Titicaca region, 144–45, 154, 156
Tiwanaku, 154, 156–58
Toledo, Francisco de: labor and technology reforms, 9, 20–21, 87–89, 96, 104, 124, 132, 168, 204; *mita* (forced labor) and, 88–89, 95; patio process and, 87–88
Torres y Portugal, Hernando de, 91
trapicheros, 59, 113

trapiches, 59–60, *60f*, 113, 115–16, 124
tribute: *abusa* system, 195; colonial regime and, 126–27; copper objects as, 173; encomienda workers and, 131; *kajcheo* payments, 59, 204; *mingas* (free laborers) and, 124; Native payments, 64–65, 75, 89, 96, 115, 126; silver payments, 89, 96, 115

Union Federation of Bolivian Mine Workers (FSTMB), 81
Uriburu, Dámaso de, 57
Uruquilla (Porco Viejo): Inka regime in, 166; location of, 140; material culture at, 142, 167; mineral production in, 119, 137, 140, 142; reuse of site as corrals, 141, *141f*; reverberatory furnaces in, 117, *118f*, 119–20, *120f*, 141

vantage point (*sensu* Ollman), 8–9, 26, 41, 200, 202, 208
Van Vleet, Krista E., 75
Vejel, Juan, 92
Velázquez, Gabriel, 128–31
Vendrel, Juan, 128
Viña del Cerro, 173–74, 178
Visijsa, 94, *94m*, 96, 170
Voss, Barbara L., 16–17

Watts, Michael J., 193
Weaver, Brendan, 23, 101, 103, 139
Wernke, Steven A., 4
Williams, J. B., 62–63, 76
women: ASM and, 191, 194; domestic tasks and, 33–34; domestic violence and, 38; exclusion from mining, 33–34, 38, 181; mine ownership, 136; mineral processing, 143–44; *pailliris* (ore-pickers), 68, 105, 186; smelting of illicit silver, 136; subsistence coal mining and, 191
Wurst, LouAnn, 7–8

yanaconas (personal retainers under Spaniards): agricultural labor and, 97, 113, 133; encomienda system, 127, 131, 133, 135, 203; freedom from labor tax, 97, 133; *huayrachina* use, 133, 135; Indigenous, 127; ore-sharing, 135, 149; Porco site and, 129; smelting and, 144; sorting ore, 131–32

yanakuna (personal retainers under Inkas), 168–69, 177

Yquisi, Diego, 147–48, 160
Yuncaviri, 17, 33, 67, 93
Yura, 31, 61, 94, 94*m*, 163

Zárate, Juan Ortiz de, 131
zinc production, 5, 20, 85
Zora, Alonso, 92
Zori, Colleen, 172, 177
Zulawski, Ann, 112–13

About the Author

Mary Van Buren is a professor in the Department of Anthropology and Geography at Colorado State University. Much of her research focuses on the historical archaeology of mining, particularly in southern Bolivia and the red-light district of Ouray, a mining town in Colorado. She has published in *American Anthropologist, International Journal of Historical Archaeology*, and *Latin American Antiquity*, among other fora.